What people

T0302964

Degrowth i

Moving beyond the growth economy needs a movement of movements. This is an excellent anthology, establishing a much needed dialogue between the different groups struggling for a good life for all within planetary limits.
Giorgos Kallis, author of *Degrowth* (2018) and co-editor of *Degrowth: A Vocabulary for a New Era* (2014)

How to get beyond the Green Economy? This rich account of the global degrowth alliance, in all its socio-ecological dimensions - horizontal and prefigurative - shows us how.
Give this book to your neighbours and friends - and let degrowth grow!
Ariel Salleh, author of *From Eco-Sufficiency to Global Justice* (2009)

Everyone knows the years ahead will be challenging, but they can also be filled with the praxis of hope. In writing a rich guide for how to change the world these chapters have, for some of their authors, been a process of metamorphosis. The same can be true for you. Think of this book as a flint. Find some friends, read it, and use it to spark your own transformations.
Raj Patel, co-author of *A History of the World in Seven Cheap Things* (2017)

As many struggle to imagine worlds shaped by desires other than economic growth, this collection shows that multiform pathways are possible, and already in practice. The pluriversal approach supports readers to learn with wildly diverse initiatives and ideas.
Susan Paulson, editor of *Degrowth: Culture, Power and Change* (2017).

This is a powerfully important topic to engage. Physics and chemistry are indicating that we're going to have to inhabit this planet differently - here are some ideas on how we might do that.
Bill McKibben, author and activist with *350.org*

Degrowth in Movement(s)

Exploring pathways for transformation

Degrowth in Movement(s)

Exploring pathways for transformation

Edited by Corinna Burkhart,
Matthias Schmelzer and Nina Treu

zer0 books

Winchester, UK
Washington, USA

JOHN HUNT PUBLISHING

First published by Zero Books, 2020
Zero Books is an imprint of John Hunt Publishing Ltd., No. 3 East St., Alresford,
Hampshire SO24 9EE, UK
office@jhpbooks.com
www.johnhuntpublishing.com
www.zero-books.net

For distributor details and how to order please visit the 'Ordering' section on our website.

ISBN: 978 1 78904 186 6
978 1 78904 187 3 (ebook)
Library of Congress Control Number: 2019903217

A CIP catalogue record for this book is available from the British Library.

Design: Stuart Davies

UK: Printed and bound by CPI Group (UK) Ltd, Croydon, CR0 4YY
US: Printed and bound by Thomson-Shore, 7300 West Joy Road, Dexter, MI 48130

Contents

Preface

Donatella della Porta (Scuola Normale Superiore)

Neoliberalism and its crises (especially visible after the financial turmoil which started in 2008) have deeply affected social movements, challenging citizens' rights, in their civic, political and social forms. As market liberalization has been accompanied by illiberal political tendencies, traditional forms of associations have been weakened and channels for protests restricted, while societal ties and values of solidarity have been disrupted.

However, we find ourselves in what the Italian political thinker Antonio Gramsci called an Interregnum, as the old is dying and the new is not born yet, various forms of resistance have developed, being at times successful in contrasting neoliberal tendencies. Progressive social movements have adapted to new challenges but also actively defied them, transforming their structures, practices and cultural message along the way.

The Great Recession has indeed prompted defensive counter-movements, oriented to re-instating old rights, but also anti-systemic movements, challenging capitalism altogether. New protest waves have adopted fluid organizational structures, invented new repertoires of contention and invested in identity work, trying to connect various struggles and their main actors. Claims for social justice have been bridged with claims for recognition in the re-emergence of broad visions of problems and solutions.

Degrowth in movement(s) contributes to the resistance against neoliberalism in different ways.

First, *Degrowth in movement(s)* recognizes that the degrowth world is in transformation. De-growth is defined as an emerging movement that brings together alternative economies, building a society that aims at the well-being for all and ecological sustainability. The economic and then political and social crises have made thinking about economic alternatives as well as experimenting with these alternatives all the more relevant. At the same time, as the anti-austerity protest spread, involving a broad social coalition of the affected, this has brought about a need for different forms of organization, repertoires of actions and frames. Reacting to the consequences of the economic crisis on the everyday life of the citizens, specific social practices (such as squats, housing occupations, self-managed schools and solidarity clinics) have been oriented to directly produce effects through activities like fair trade shops, anti-sweatshop campaigns, eco-villages and transition towns, slow food initiatives and community sustained agricultural practices, solidarity. Purchasing groups have all spread during the crisis as grassroots practices of resilience and resistance to it. So, degrowth is in movements as it is changing forms, involving individual and collective actors well beyond its initial basis.

Second, *Degrowth in movement(s)* shows that degrowth is composed of different streams but also connected to different movements. Some of the ideas developed within the degrowth perspective have been inspiring for the various forms of innovations in the movements resisting the crisis through the construction of alternatives in the health system, housing, food-production and distribution, cooperatives for production and services. Forms of direct social action based on solidarity and cooperation have been re-invented in the struggles of the unemployed, homeless and migrants. In this process, the debate on degrowth has moved attention from "what" is consumed to "how and how much" is both produced and consumed, aiming at changing the dominant economic paradigm. Sustainable community movement organizations have mobilized citizens not only through individual actions but also through local grassroots organizations. Cooperatives, voluntary associations, informal community groups, social enterprises have functioned as "niches of innovation." So, the cultural critique of the mainstream food industry and the need to tackle urban poverty and social exclusion are bridged in these grassroots innovations.

Third, *Degrowth in movement(s)* points at the importance of movement, in terms of action, for the development of connections among different innovative practices. As neoliberalism fragments identities, free spaces are needed in which, without denying differences, common visions can be built. Degrowth is in movement, as all the aforementioned crises make an urgent case for a convergence of struggles linking the thousands of emancipatory and solidarity oriented innovations. The mosaic of existing initiatives on the left—from unions to social movements, from self-help groups to NGOs—nurtures a networking in action. A deep paradigmatic change can develop only from the creation of public spaces for communicating and exchanging practices. Common action is required for better understanding each other.

In these ways, *Degrowth in movement(s)* challenges the current hegemonic economic system. The many inspiring existing alternatives show what people can do and encourage everyone to join and act. Enjoy exploring.

Foreword

Barbara Muraca (University of Oregon)

Degrowth in Movement(s) represents an original, indispensable, and long-overdue volume in the crisis-ridden and frustrated socio-political landscape of the early twenty-first century. Wherever we turn our attention, two themes resound in the same unimaginative and worrisome way. On the one hand, we hear the tired mantra that growth is the solution for all problems, promoting more deregulation, globalization, free trade, competition, and open markets. On the other, we (yet again) hear the drone of right-wing populists who translate the wholly legitimate insecurity that many people feel into fables of culturally monochromatic, insular communities, channeling their frustration against those who look, love, or live differently.

Degrowth in Movement(s) offers, by contrast, a real alternative for the good life under completely different conditions. *Degrowth in Movement(s)* brazenly takes the liberty of not only forging completely different visions of the future. The volume also shows that such visions are already being put to the test in many different, colorful, and courageous ways through workshops of liberation in Germany and around the world.

As the editors argue in the introduction, degrowth is an emerging social movement. This state of becoming is not temporary. Degrowth is and will hopefully remain a project in the process of becoming. In this respect, degrowth is in movement rather than a movement with clearly defined characteristics and an established structure. It serves as a space of connection and amplification for several different groups that are fighting collectively against the uniformity of neoliberalism and for alternative forms of co-existence. Degrowth is therefore much more of a platform, something like an archipelago where different kinds of social movements, initiatives, and currents come together and compare notes but also build alliances.

Degrowth comes into being not only as a radical critique of material oversizing in the national economies of industrialized countries, which is sustained by destroying the planet and making the lives of other human and non-human beings increasingly impossible. The primary goal of a degrowth perspective is thus not just to shrink the economy in its current state. Rather, degrowth is much more about completely reconfiguring the economy, society, and social relations. Above all, degrowth demands a reappropriation of the right and the power to determine collectively, democratically, and in solidarity how we co-exist instead of surrendering institutions and social relationships to the default model under the neoliberal mantra, for which there is purportedly no alternative.

Since the constraints of neoliberal growth logic are deeply inscribed in our conceptual world as well as in our bodies, desires, and emotions, we need workshops of liberation where radical alternatives can be thought through and tried out, wild and free from dominant narratives. Social experiments, initiatives, and movements, such as the ones presented in this volume, operate as laboratories of the future where social innovations can be developed and practical experiments with new forms of coexistence emerge under different conditions of recognition. Beyond that, these laboratories are places where participants draw motivation and strength for resistance in order to bring this goal of transformation into other areas of life.

Laboratories of the future such as these embody what Ernst Bloch once called concrete utopia. While abstract utopias act in a compensatory way, comforting us like mere daydreams, the strength of concrete utopia resides in searching out, through touch and experimentation, transformative possibilities and latent tendencies that lie dormant in the present. This calls for what Bloch terms "militant optimism." Distinct from mere naïve optimism, which is blind to power and awaits with hope some kind of automatic transformation, militant optimism identifies hidden possibilities and acts like a kind of amplifier, making those possibilities visible, engaging them actively, and weaving them into new configurations. Concrete utopias also have a prefigurative and performative power: they open up space for imagining alternatives and in doing so they act against the effectiveness of TINA-narratives (TINA: there is no alternative). They also embody such alternatives here and now in the numerous projects, social experiments and initiatives where participants don't just talk about plans for different futures but also try out and experience other ways of living.

In these protected spaces we can question critically how conceptions of the good life and perceptions of needs came about. Moreover, we can uncover the extent to which they are merely an immediate expression of established values that have been imposed on individuals in the interest of preserving and reproducing prevailing social relations. After all, an important function of concrete utopias is the "education of desire," as it is termed in utopian studies, or learning collectively about our desires and needs. In the alternative spaces of experience established through social experiments, one can learn to desire differently, better, and even more. Instead of repressing desire through a one-sided notion of voluntary simplicity, the point is rather to free oneself from the forces that limit the autonomy to demand more (in political terms). Social experiments teach us autonomy as a collective project. Autonomy also implies self-restraint, i.e., envisioning oneself as embedded in social and ecological structures that must be designed collectively. Autonomy in this sense is only possible in a society in which economic activity is oriented towards perceived and publicly articulated needs through processes of democratic decision-making and modes of production and not the other way around, i.e., a society where new needs are constantly being generated.

Degrowth in Movement(s) is an invitation to hope. Not a merely abstract hope in the sense of the naïve optimism mentioned above. This hope is rather that of concrete utopia, nourished and strengthened through militant optimism. The conversations gathered here constitute an invaluable source of social alternatives, expressed in their specificity and their own unique language.

The editors of this project at Konzeptwerk Neue Ökonomie saw this process through in the same spirit as the Leipzig Degrowth Conference in 2014, also co-organized by Konzeptwerk. Inspiring, supportive, self-critical, and open while never faltering in their unmistakable recognition of the core values of emancipation and solidarity. Numerous social movements, initiatives, and currents were invited to a common dialogue that not only foregrounds differences and commonalities, but also sketches learning processes and blueprints for future networks, collaboration, and alliances. The result is a tremendous collection of practical pathways for radical socio-ecological transformation.

Translation: Bradley Boovy

Acknowledgements

We would like to thank everyone who contributed to the making of this book. First of all, we would like to thank all the authors for having joined this extraordinary writing experiment. Thank you for having participated in this process of two years with its meetings and several rounds of editing and for sharing such inspiring stories.

We also wish to thank those who helped with editing the texts: Dennis Eversberg, Max Frauenlob, Hanna Ketterer, Kai Kuhnhenn, Christopher Laumanns, Steffen Liebig, Anne Pinnow, Christoph Sanders, Christin Schmidt und Felix Wittmann; as well as the co-editor for the German book, the DFG Research Group "Post-Growth Societies" at the University of Jena. For financial support, we thank the Friedrich Ebert Foundation and the German League for Nature Conservation (DNR).

We would like to especially thank both our German and English proof-readers, Julia Roßhart and John Ebert, and to Zer0 books more generally. Also, we thank Marc Menningmann, Caro Hempe and Christoph Hoeland, who produced the videos and podcasts available at degrowth.info/en/dim. Thanks for the translations to Bradley Boovy, Laura Broo, Mercè Ardiaca Jové, Isabel Frey, Christiane Kliemann, Gill Laumanns and Santiago Killing-Stringer.

Introduction

Degrowth and the Emerging Mosaic of Alternatives

In the face of unfettered globalization, the rise of right-wing movements around the globe and the dangers of climate catastrophe, it seems easier to imagine the end of the world than an end to capitalism, growth and domination. However, in recent years something new has emerged to counter what Mark Fisher called "capitalist realism": After decades on the defensive against neoliberalism, the left has once again started to embrace positive visions of the future. This can be seen in the movements behind the rise of Jeremy Corbyn and Bernie Sanders, for example, but also in a new wave of prefigurative social movements, ranging from community gardens or worker-owned co-ops, to the Women's Protection Units (YPJ) in Rojava —movements that "embody their ultimate goals and their vision of a future society through their ongoing social practices, social relations, decision-making philosophy and culture."[1] And it can be seen in the emergence of what have been called "transformative economies" by the 2019-20 World Social Forum in Barcelona – new economic models and practices around commons, agroecology and cooperativism aiming at transforming the existing economic system.

These progressive visions fall into two broad camps, most clearly symbolized by the eco-modernist notion of "fully automated luxury communism" on the one hand, and the provocative slogan "degrowth," on the other. While sharing an understanding of the need for systemic alternatives and a critique of domination, the split between these perspectives and the social movements associated with them runs deep. As argued by world system theorist Immanuel Wallerstein, not only are the world's economic and political elites divided between globalists and authoritarians, there is also a split within the left, between the progressive productivists who —in the tradition of the socialist and social democratic labor movement— focus on growth, productivity gains and redistribution and tend to prefer vertical forms of organization, and those movements that, closer to the tradition of anarchism, rely on self-organization from the bottom up and fundamentally question economic growth.[2]

The key point of contention is the following: The new narratives of progressive productivism —best represented by Paul Mason's "Postcapitalism" or the concept of "fully automated luxury communism" – embrace modernity, globalization and technological progress, since, so they argue, these create the conditions for liberation.[3] This strand of socialist futurism tends to ignore ecological questions and issues of global social justice (including climate justice) and flatly dismisses movements that promote localism, luddism or sufficiency as "primitivist romanticism." Leigh Phillips, for example, condemned degrowth as "austerity ecology" and criticized the movements promoting it as "collapse-porn addicts."[4]

For their part, the growth-critical, bottom-up prefigurative movements seeking social-ecological transformation argue that relying on technological innovation and global markets to solve humanity's challenges —in particular, climate change and the loss of biodiversity, with their concomitant social problems— is a dangerous illusion. Proponents of degrowth claim that the eco-modernist position cannot provide an answer to the most important challenge of the twenty-first century, i.e. how can we live well without externalizing the costs of our way of living onto others, the planet and future generations? Adequate answers to these questions, they claim, can only be found if early industrialized countries find ways to transcend the expansionary modernity. Rather than relying on techno-fixes, the expansion of the productive forces and economic growth, we need to find pathways towards post-growth societies.[5]

This volume brings together social movements and future visions of the second group —those fighting for a good life for all beyond eco-modernism and growth, from a social-ecological and global justice perspective. The vantage point is degrowth. Not because degrowth is the main or even a key term for all these movements, but because degrowth symbolizes the most radical rejection of the eco-modernist and mainstream focus on growth, extractivism and industrialism. And because degrowth has, in recent years, developed into a framework for many social-ecological movements, initiatives and projects, providing a set of theories, arguments and visions that give meaning to prefigurative "nowtopias."[6]

Degrowth, we argue, is not just a new term for an ongoing discussion on alternatives or a thriving academic research paradigm.[7] Degrowth is also an emerging social movement that overlaps considerably with other social movements, ranging from the anti-globalization or climate justice movements to movements and alternatives such as commons, Buen Vivir, food sovereignty, non-profit cooperatives, the care revolution, free software, DIY repair workshops, basic income or transition towns. This book brings individuals involved in these visions together to collectively reflect on the current state of social movements aiming at overcoming capitalism, industrialism and domination. What does a good life for all look like? How can we live well without externalizing the costs of our way of living? What is the role of social movements in bringing about this change?

What is degrowth?

Degrowth is the most radical strand of a new wave of debates regarding the need for a social-ecological transformation of high-income societies, which resurfaced after the capitalist crisis of 2007/8. The term is derived from the French word "décroissance," which was coined in the early 1970s (despite only becoming widespread in recent years). Over the past decade, the slogan "degrowth" has brought together a predominantly European movement of activists and scientists who criticize the prevailing development model of continuous capitalist growth and are searching for alternatives.

Above all, degrowth is a provocative political slogan that questions the hegemony of the growth paradigm, bringing together quite diverse and sometimes contradictory currents and positions. What they all have in common, however, is that they criticize the technological optimism of the sustainability discourse that has prevailed since the 1990s, with its promise of decoupling growth and environmental consumption. A key argument of this fundamental critique of "green growth" is that growth is not sustainable and cannot be made sustainable. Because it is impossible to completely decouple environmental consumption and economic growth, degrowth seeks an end to the global growth paradigm and a reduction in the biophysical size of the economy. In addition, based on a critical analysis of the challenges of ecological global justice, the material dimension of growth economies and the "imperial mode of living" in the capitalist centers, degrowth states that a good life for all is not possible if the rich countries do not drastically reduce their material throughput.[8] The essence of degrowth is therefore the "depriviligization" of those who currently live at the expenses of others and externalize these costs in space and time.

The second major commonality is the attempt to develop "concrete utopias" as alternatives to the growth imperative.[9] The main goal here is to conceive growth-independent institutions and infrastructures, and to combine these with antagonistic practices and alternative ways of living in the here and now. These efforts to develop pathways for different forms of social-ecological transformation tackle the fundamental growth dependency of capitalist economies and modern state institutions. Degrowth thus proposes various radical reforms —ranging from the expansion of commons and the solidarity economy, to caps on total resource use, a basic and a maximum income, a radical redistribution of income and wealth, and a work-time reduction for all. These elements of a degrowth society are not isolated or detached from prior theory and practice, but are based on a variety of traditions of thought and build upon concrete social struggles. Many important impulses, for example, come from the fields of political ecology and bioeconomics, feminist economics and eco-feminism, post-colonial and post-development studies and long-standing critiques of capitalism and industrialism. In all cases, the fundamental idea is that the economy as a sphere of independent rationality and economic calculus cannot be the sole basis of all decision-making, and that we thus require a repoliticization and democratization of social institutions, as well as a struggle for collective autonomy. It is important to note that degrowth expressly aims its proposals at the early industrialized or "overdeveloped" countries of the Global North, and not at the Global South. Social movements from the Global South such as Buen Vivir are nevertheless important allies. (A more detailed discussion of degrowth ideas as well as a brief overview of the who and how of degrowth is provided in Chapter 9.)

Degrowth in Movement(s) – the origins of the project

In recent years, degrowth has emerged both as a widely debated political project and a new academic research paradigm. And while there are many publications on the ideas of degrowth, there is insufficient knowledge on how these ideas are actually applied in various social movements and practical alternative projects. This is strange, because degrowth scholars repeatedly stress how intimately degrowth as a concept or research paradigm is linked to alternative practices and social movements.[10]

Degrowth in Movement(s) is thus the first account of the practices that underlie the degrowth discourse. It is based on a two-year interactive networking process between social movements, mainly from Germany but with strong transnational and global links. The idea for the project emerged after the International Degrowth Conference for Ecological Sustainability and Social Equity in Leipzig in 2014, which drew over 3,000 participants. The five-day activist and academic conference brought together people from a diverse range of social movements and projects and led to discussions regarding a possible confluence of alternatives.[11] However, it was clear from the beginning that there were deep misunderstandings and misconceptions regarding each other's approaches, proposals and strategies. Often, the activists and academics from one movement did not really know what other movements were actually about. Frequent questions were: "What are the proposals of degrowth?" or "How do commons actually work?" and "What is political about urban gardening?" There was also a great degree of skepticism regarding the different political focuses of each group, preferred language or strategic approach.

This networking project was launched in order to deal with these misunderstandings, strengthen existing ties and work towards collaborative strategies. To do this, we brought together individuals closely involved in or familiar with over 30 social movements or alternatives that had in recent years been connected with the degrowth debate. After two workshops and an intensive writing process, the results were published in German both online and in print, together with a collection of pictures, videos and podcasts, all available at degrowth.info (unfortunately mostly only in German). Now, after a reading and networking tour, a larger conference with many activists from the social movements involved, and presentations at several international conferences, the texts have been updated and published in book form in English.[12]

The name of the project, "Degrowth in Movement(s)", reflects its nature. First of all, degrowth is itself *in movement,* as an emerging social movement, political spectrum and "framework" for various alternative practices and struggles seeking alliances in order to achieve social-ecological change.[13] Degrowth is not a fixed concept, but one that should build on and learn from the long-standing experiences of these other movements and struggles. Thus the project asked other social movements for their views, proposals, and critiques regarding degrowth. In the second place, degrowth is *in movements*, in that its ideas and practices enter into dialogue with, are reflected in, adapted by or taken up within other social movements. The project therefore asked activists whether, how and why degrowth is discussed and possibly integrated into other perspectives. It is important to note that we do not think the degrowth perspective is more important than any other, or that degrowth should be a banner for other social movements to assemble under. Rather, we aim at amplifying the collaborative dynamics initiated by the degrowth debate to bring various protagonists together and provide opportunities for mutual learning from each other.

Five questions to advance a mosaic of alternatives

Almost a decade ago, German trade unionist Hans-Jürgen Urban stated that a "mosaic of left-wing groups" would be the "beacon of hope of the post-neoliberal era." In his view, this mosaic would be an anti-hegemonic bloc ranging from trade unions to movements critical of globalization, NGOs, social self-help organizations and critical segments of the cultural left. Urban stated: "Just as a mosaic can unfold its beauty as a complete work even though every individual piece is still recognizable as such, a newly founded left could be seen and valued as a heterogeneous collective actor."[14]

The project *Degrowth in Movement(s)* is a sample of this dynamic and constantly changing left-wing mosaic. The project brings together those pieces of the mosaic that are working to develop and test alternatives from a social-ecological perspective and which are open to questioning capitalism and industrialism.

That is the segment of the mosaic that is interested in a mutual exchange and cooperation with – as well as a critical examination of – degrowth.

The project seeks to be a gateway to understanding the different movements, creating a mutual space for learning, dialogue and opportunities to develop political strategies for diverse and common alternatives. All authors are involved in a specific social movement, thus providing a first-hand account of the activities, ideas, social composition and future perspectives of each one. Their texts are written in accessible language and in them the authors had to answer the same five questions for their respective movement. This structure makes it easy to read the book in a non-linear way and find mutual connecting points between the texts, and the questions provide inspiration for critical self-reflection and a starting point to engage with other movements. The five main headlines in each chapter correspond to the following five questions:

1. What is the key idea of your social movement (most important points of criticism of the prevailing system, central arguments, visions for alternatives)? How did it develop historically and what theory of change is used?

2. Who is part of the social movement? What do they do (social stratification, how and where are they organized, who are its protagonists, which groups, alliances, etc. exist)?

3. How do you see the relationship between your social movement and degrowth and how can or should this relationship develop in the next few years? How is the relationship with other social movements (e.g. similarities, differences, conflicts, alliances, etc.)?

4. Which proposals does your movement have for the degrowth perspective? (What is missing, which areas are not taken into account adequately, what is underestimated, which themes, questions, problems are discussed one-sidedly, insufficiently or not at all?) Which proposals can the degrowth

perspective offer your movement?

5. Space for visions, suggestions or wishes, e.g.: From the perspective of your social movement and in relation to degrowth, which opportunities do you see for the development of a strong common emancipatory social movement in the current political context (ongoing crises, emergence of right-wing parties, post-democracy, etc.?) What should a larger social movement look like for you to want to join?

The explicit goal of the project is *not* to be an exercise in purely intellectual self-reflection or a detached academic critique. Rather, its purpose is to enter into a constructive dialogue with existing social movements and projects for an alternative economy. With this dialogue, we want to actively look for common perspectives, strategies and concrete courses of action. This volume and the interactive networking process from which it emerged aim at advancing the discussions about the confluence of a mosaic of alternatives as a heterogeneous collective actor.

Differences, commonalities and confluences within the pluriverse

The notion of a "mosaic" highlights the vision of building a plural world, based in multiple struggles and with many different strategies; composed of different forms of economies, lifeworlds, and cultures, pollinating, interacting and collaborating with each other. To differentiate it from the one-way future of capitalism and economic growth, the various alternatives to economic growth have recently been termed the "pluriverse" by a group of scholar-activists from various continents.[15]

What are the differences, commonalities and confluences of the groups that make up this "mosaic of alternatives"? Inspired by and based on our dialogue with the authors, the rest of this introduction summarizes some of the key conclusions that we as editors have drawn from the project. We make no claims as to the comprehensiveness or exclusivity of these conclusions, but see them as an intermediate assessment of a continuous process.

Movements in plural – overlaps and differences

Each movement has its own particular orientation, motivations and strategies —its own specific way of analyzing society and crisis processes. And yet there are many fundamental overlaps between them, and a collective reading of the texts shows that some of the movements already integrate each other to a degree. For example: The urban gardening movement sees itself as part of the commons movement, and many of the garden projects are themselves key points of reference for the degrowth and commons movements; degrowth sees commoning as one of the main pillars of an alternative society, and the commons movement integrates degrowth ideas. In order to better understand this complexity, the following sections sketch out key similarities and differences.

Overlaps

Some of the shared aspects are especially clear. They are manifested mainly in certain fundamental world-views and values, and do not necessarily represent the specific ideas of all those involved.

- *Orientation towards needs*: The main commonality of all movements lies in their focus on concrete needs and a good life for all, replacing economic concepts, abstract production figures or the rules of market exchange.
- *Humans as complex, relational beings:* Many share a holistic image of human beings, which they express either explicitly or implicitly. People are not seen as rational utility maximizers à la *homo oeconomicus,* but rather as social and emotional beings living in relationships with and depending on each other.
- *A comprehensive analysis:* Most movements acknowledge

a comprehensive understanding of society, power and politics, taking into account the many different facets of existing inequalities and crises and not reducing their focus to individual aspects.

- *Global justice:* Instead of only discussing political questions in a national context, most groups derive their social and ecological demands for justice from a global perspective.
- *Rejection of the green economy*: Hardly any movement believes that the multiple crises of the world can be solved through a "greening" of growth and capitalism, and many criticize the (side) effects of large-scale technological solutions.
- *Democratization:* Instead of delegating the power to shape society to a selected few, most movements strive for an all-encompassing democratization that ensures the participation of all people. This includes the expansion of democratic decision-making processes into currently non-democratic areas such as the economy. In addition, this principle is reflected in the way the different networks and organizations work.
- *Social-ecological transformation:* Instead of playing off social and ecological problems against each other, all movements recognize —to varying degrees— that the two aspects are intertwined; even if one of them may be more important for a particular movement.
- *Systemic change and paradigm shift*: Instead of hoping that small changes or political reforms will solve society's problems, many movements seek to bring about comprehensive, fundamental, and systemic changes.
- *Working in the here and now:* Instead of simply making demands, most movements try to start effecting change in the here and now, either in small alternative projects in which utopias are tested out, or in social struggles with concrete goals.

Differences

Regardless of these overlaps, the various movements and perspectives in this volume still have diverging analyses, strategies, narratives and supporters. The key differences lie in the following areas:

- *Moral frame of reference*: All movements seek justice. The main difference lies in *for whom* they want to achieve this justice. Although all movements fundamentally and at least implicitly include *all* human beings in their concept of justice, the focus of their work is often reduced to their particular region and, in many cases, to the Global North. In addition to non-human animals (a key concern for the animal rights movement[16]), some movements such as Buen Vivir, urban gardening and segments of degrowth also include the rights of nature in their visions.
- *Relationship with capitalism*: Some movements place capitalism at the heart of their analysis and criticism — they are decidedly anti-capitalist or critical of capitalism (e.g. degrowth, climate justice, Peoples Global Action). Others barely refer to capitalism or do not refer to it at all. Still others are critical of capitalism in their analysis, but it is unclear what this means for their vision of an alternative society (e.g. the ecovillages movement).
- *Transformation strategies*: There are also different views on *how* society can be changed. Some are engaged in concrete struggles and social conflicts (e.g. care revolution, climate justice) or seek to spread resistance (e.g. artivism), whereas others create change at the smallest level first and build concrete alternatives (e.g. the ecovillages movement, solidarity economy, urban gardening). Still others focus on disseminating information on or promoting fundamental transformations and alternatives (e.g. commons movement).

- *Criticism of power and domination:* Criticism of power and domination is central to the work of some currents (e.g. Buen Vivir, care revolution, food sovereignty, refugee and migration movement), whereas for others it is not relevant or has a subordinate role (e.g. open workshops, urban gardening). Correspondingly, the movements vary in their degree of self-reflection regarding their own power structures, internal hierarchies or privileges.
- *Capacity to form alliances*: In all movements, there is a general openness towards other movements. However, the demands placed on potential allies vary greatly: Some groups have very strict criteria, e.g. an anti-capitalist consensus, whereas others make the case for broad alliances and seek to highlight the similarities instead of the differences.
- *Organizational structure*: The movements differ greatly in terms of their organization. This applies to their reach (local, national, regional, global) and internal democracy (grassroots vs hierarchical), as well as their degree of organization (highly organized vs flexible structures; formal vs informal networks).

Instead of pretending that they do not exist, we suggest taking advantage of these differences – and the overlaps — in order to better understand the mosaic of alternatives to which they confom. Otherwise we risk portraying ourselves as a homogeneous movement, or else exaggerating the differences and causing conflicts and division. The texts themselves provide some key suggestions for promoting this confluence of alternatives and increasing collaboration. These ideas are not only relevant for degrowth, but also provide constructive feedback to many other movements.

Relationship with the Global South

Many authors are highly critical of the relationship between the Global South and the Global North and demand that all groups and actors address this subject. Without strong South-North cooperation, we risk re-enacting climate colonialism and environmental racism. In Friederike Habermann's (Peoples Global Action) view, this means that we must seek a true and broad alliance between countries from the South and the North, instead of a mere exchange of individual intellectuals. Other texts highlight how this international perspective is essential to prevent our alternative visions from becoming too provincial and overseeing their own destructive potential and unintended side-effects. Ashish Kothari (Radical Ecological Democracy) and Alberto Acosta (Buen Vivir) stress the fact that alternatives are always rooted in their context and cannot be applied in the same way everywhere. At the same time, they call for all actors to acknowledge the alternatives and struggles in other parts of the world and respect them in their approaches.

Resistance and criticism of domination

One demand that is repeated very clearly throughout the texts is for people to be or become aware and critical of (hidden) power structures and to actively work against them. Friederike Habermann reminds us that in the course of our struggles, we must not forget other existing discriminating power structures and fight against them as well. Along the same lines, John Jordan (artivism) calls for a general culture of resistance.

Creating a material space

Another aspect highlighted is the need for permanent physical spaces. On the one hand, this means creating nowtopias (such as open workshops or climate camps), where the abstract is translated into the concrete and people "walk the talk." On the other hand, it also involves different actors coming together in concrete places to make alternatives more visible and build local relationships beyond specific events (e.g. 15-M, ecovillages movement, transition towns, urban gardening).

Overcoming the barriers of our own milieus
In order to turn a social-ecological transformation into reality, it is indispensable that we set in motion a truly broad movement. The self-critical reflection process involved in writing these texts revealed that most of those active in many of the movements are – at least in Germany – well-educated, middle-class and *white.* Many of the authors therefore appeal to themselves and to degrowth to leave their own milieu. In general, this question of who is active in the movements is perceived as important and productive, although some see it as stressful and unpleasant. In this regard, some movements are better at mobilizing diverse groups of people and can thus open up new perspectives for some of the other groups. For example, the trade unions and the Care Revolution network can teach others how to approach social-ecological questions with working class people, and Buen Vivir, climate justice, post-extractivism and Radical Ecological Democracy open up perspectives from the Global South. Many of those active in the food sovereignty or refugee and migration movements have experience with transnational organizing and the common struggles of diverse groups of people, e.g. where some have experiences of escape and migration and others do not.

Preguntando caminamos – In walking, we ask

One of the aims of *Degrowth in Movement(s)* is to encourage the different alternatives to see themselves as part of a mosaic of alternatives for social-ecological transformation and thus become jointly active. The goal for the movements involved was to better understand each other and to learn from different perspectives, strategies and experiences, thereby creating a better basis for their projects, activism and organizational processes. In terms of their vision for the future, many authors expressed the desire to work together, to achieve greater synergies and effectiveness in a context of escalating ecological and social problems. So what is the future of the mosaic? For Ashish Kothari, who is involved in similar alliance-forging processes in India, the main key achievement of *Degrowth in Movement(s)* has been to identify "the essence of these initiatives, and to see if the values and principles emerging from them can suggest a cohesive framework for challenging the currently dominant mindset and practice of growth-centred 'developmentality'."[17]

We believe that this framework is already in the making. The shape we wish to give it, however, is still being debated, negotiated and contested. What's important is that these movements actively put into practice and experiment with key principles of degrowth: They largely reject an orientation towards profit and productivity; they seek to reduce wage labor; they emphasize direct forms of democracy, relationships, sharing, and a mentality of giving, which focuses on needs, care, and reproduction; and they tend to use technologies and tools that increase autonomy, sharing and sustainability (which Ivan Illich refers to as "convivial tools"), involving lower consumption and shorter production-consumption circuits.[18] There is thus a multiplicity of prefigurative social movements that already exist which integrate degrowth ideas: what degrowth refers to as "nowtopias." We do not think degrowth itself will develop into *the* social movement bringing about the urgently needed social-ecological transformations. But we argue that the next cycle of a larger counter-hegemonic bloc of social movements and political forces opposing both neoliberal globalism and authoritarian nationalism should integrate key critiques, perspectives and proposals from the degrowth discussion.[19]

The movements discussed in this book as the mosaic of alternatives for social-ecological transformation are a fertile ground for the emergence of ideas, practices and actions leading to a good life for all. Rather than hoping that technological advances in the age of platform capitalism or the political economy of information technologies will bring about socialist liberation —as argued by progressive productivists— the movements assembled here criticize not only capitalism and capitalist forms of ownership, but also other forms of domination, they criticize industrialism and the domination embedded in technologies, they take seriously global injustices that stand in the way of a good life for all, and they focus on strategies and actions that start building alternatives in the here and now, within the cracks of capitalism and power.

There is no lack of suggestions for steps towards a common movement, or at least common action. Some wish to conceive and carry out coordinated protests. Others propose developing a common basis of understanding or at least a series of common goals in order to move on to more practical matters. Yet another possibility would be to build up concrete alternatives and then create networks between them. All of this needs to happen on a local, regional, national and transnational level, each with its own possibilities and challenges. While looking for ways to work together we should, however, not forget that cooperation is not an end in itself. The fact that different groups focus on different issues, projects and struggles is unavoidable and justified. The question is therefore: What are the conditions, goals and strategies for us to work together, to build the mosaic of alternatives to advance social-ecological transformation?

As the Zapatistas famously stated, "In walking, we ask." Whatever happens, we believe that it is important to conduct a (self-)critical examination of our own and other movements, to show solidarity with others in general, and to consider – and forge – alliances. Common perspectives are the product of an exchange, of working together, and of joining common struggles. Can the resulting alliances contribute to a social-ecological transformation, and to opposing right-wing tendencies? We don't know, but we hope so. What we do know is that none of us can do it alone. Whether or not the future enables a good life for all will depend more than anything on whether more people start recognizing the signs of the times and begin to actively work for social and ecological justice. There are more than enough places to start.

Endnotes

1 Monticelli, 2018, p. 508.

2 Wallerstein, 2013, pp. 9-36.

3 Mason, 2016; Bastani, 2019.

4 Phillips, 2015.

5 D'Alisa et al., 2014; Kallis, 2018.

6 Demaria et al., 2013; Eversberg and Schmelzer, 2018.

7 D'Alisa et al., 2014; Kallis et al., 2018.

8 Brand and Wissen, 2018; D'Alisa et al., 2014.

9 Muraca, 2014.

10 One key publication is, of course, the edited volume *Degrowth: A Vocabulary for a New Era* (D'Alisa et al., 2014), which has been translated into ten languages. For further introductions, see Muraca, 2014; Kallis, 2018; Schmelzer and Vetter, 2019. For an overview of the academic literature, see Kallis et al., 2018.

11 Eversberg and Schmelzer, 2018.

12 While the German book and online publication contains texts from 32 social movements, this English version is shorter, as some of the texts and movements had a stronger focus on the German context and were therefore not included. All German texts are available at degrowth.info.

13 Eversberg and Schmelzer, 2018.

14 Urban, 2009, p. 77; authors' translation.

15 Kothari et al., 2018.

16 See the respective chapter (only in German) at: degrowth.

info/de/dib/degrowth-in-bewegungen/tierrechtsbewegung.
17 Kothari in this volume, p. 258
18 See also Kallis, 2018.
19 See also Schmelzer and Vetter, 2019.

Literature

Bastani, A. (2019) *Fully Automated Luxury Communism. A Manifesto*, London: Verso.

D'Alisa, G., Demaria, G., and Kallis, G. (eds.) (2014) *Degrowth: A Vocabulary for a New Era*, London and New York, Routledge.

Demaria, F., Schneider, F., Sekulova, F., and Martínez-Alier, J. (2013) "What Is Degrowth? From an Activist Slogan to a Social Movement," *Environmental Values*, vol. 22, no. 2, pp. 191–215.

Eversberg, D., and Schmelzer, M. (2018) "The Degrowth Spectrum: Convergence and Divergence within a Diverse and Conflictual Alliance," *Environmental Values*, vol. 27, no. 3., pp. 245–267.

Monticelli, L. (2018) "Embodying Alternatives to Capitalism in the 21st Century," *TripleC: Communication, Capitalism & Critique*, vol. 16, no. 2, pp. 501–17.

Kallis, G. (2018) *Degrowth*, Newcastle upon Tyne, Agenda.

Kallis, G., Kostakis, V., Lange, S., Muraca, B., Paulson, S., and Schmelzer, M. (2018) "Research on Degrowth," *Annual Review of Environment and Resources*, vol. 43, pp. 291–316.

Kothari, A., Salleh, A., Escobar, A., Demaria, F., and Acosta, A. (eds.) (2019) *Pluriverse: A Post-Development Dictionary*, Delhi, Tulika and Authors Up Front.

Muraca, B. (2014) *Gut leben: Eine Gesellschaft jenseits des Wachstums*, Berlin: Wagenbach.

Phillips, L. (2015) *Austerity Ecology & the Collapse-Porn Addicts: A Defence Of Growth, Progress, Industry and Stuff*, Washington, Zero Books.

Schmelzer, M., and Vetter, A. (2019) *Degrowth/Postwachstum zur*

Einführung, Hamburg: Junius.
Urban, H.-J. (2009) "Die Mosaik-Linke: Vom Aufbruch der Gewerkschaften zur Erneuerung der Bewegung," *Blätter für deutsche und internationale Politik*, vol. 5, pp. 71–78.
Wallerstein, I., Collins, R., Mann, M., Derluguian, G., and Calhoun, C. (2013) *Does Capitalism Have a Future?* Oxford, Oxford University Press.

Chapter 1

Global Trade: Containerships in the Port of Rotterdam (Image: CC BY-ND 2.0, Frans Berkelaar)

The Growth Imperative of Capitalist Society

Eric Pineault (Université du Québec à Montréal)

Why are capitalist societies compelled to grow? What are the socio-ecological consequences of this relentless growth? Why should a postcapitalist society be a postgrowth society? These are the sorts of questions that emerge from degrowth's critique of capitalism, a critique that brings to the forefront the socio-ecological contradictions of economic growth. Of course, not all of degrowth - both as a movement and as a theory - is anti-capitalist. And obviously most critical theories of capitalism do not focus on the problem of economic growth. But as the degrowth movement matures, the intersection between these critical perspectives on contemporary society becomes ever more important.[1] Degrowth is but one of many currents challenging the modern left's "labor centric" critique of capitalist society: alongside feminism, postcolonialism and anti-racism (among others). Degrowth is part of a contemporary renewal of anti-capitalist critique and post-capitalist politics, practice and thought. A defining feature of the degrowth movement, as argued in the introduction, is that it is very self-consciously aware of being part of a wider whole. As a movement of thought and practice, degrowth offers a particular perspective alongside and to be completed by others. In doing so it differs from many more traditional critiques of capitalism which are totalizing in their claims and outlook. What then is the specific contribution of degrowth as a critical theory of capitalism?

1. The critique of growth and capitalism

Let's start with the critique of growth itself. Economic growth in modern societies of the capitalist core has come under attack primarily because, as argued by Naomi Klein, it is seen as the cause of an ecological crisis of "existential" proportions.[2] Meaning that the ecological contradictions of our mode of production have unleashed biogeophysical processes that are undermining the material basis of contemporary societies. Be it climate change, with its droughts, extreme storms and rising sea levels, biodiversity loss (bug Armageddon and the collapse of pollinator insects) or the accumulation of plastic wastes in oceans – global and systemic socio-ecological contradictions are no longer merely scientific observations, the stuff of models, experiments and scholarly debates and speculation, they are common lived experiences. The solutions put forward to limit these impacts all the while trying to preserve economic growth and growth based lifestyles, of somehow growing out of our ecological contradictions by adopting "sustainable development mechanisms" or counting on technological breakthroughs, are an utter failure. This is also a recent feature of lived experience and common sense. It is this common sense that has fostered the emergence of the degrowth movement. Economic growth and its material consequences has given rise to an accelerating ecological crisis. Furthermore, this growth is subject to diminishing social returns, as ever higher levels of economic activity in terms of output, employment or productivity in the capitalist core fail to translate into a proportional rise in happiness, security or well-being. Finally, contemporary economic growth – with the exception of some parts of Asia – has not resulted in less inequality. On the contrary, it would seem that the fruits of economic growth have been captured by an elite minority. Growth is not a tide that raises all ships, it is the tidewater that will flood all sewers, it is the treadmill that spins the gears of rising inequality at an ever faster pace.

It is this lived experience and common sense uneasiness with "really existing" economic growth and its dire socio-ecological consequences, that has sparked the emergence of degrowth both as a theory and practice. As this movement has developed, it has moved beyond the critique of the socio-ecological consequences of economic growth, progressively focusing on the nature and sources of economic growth, uncovering the social structures that drive and sustain the growth treadmill. It is in the context of this development that degrowth has engaged with capitalism, both as the predominant form of the economic process today and as a society. The results of this encounter are diverse, precisely because degrowth is a pluralistic endeavor, but a few dominant ideas have arisen. These can be found, among other places, in the recent book *Degrowth: A Vocabulary for a New Era* as well as in recent debates among degrowth scholars concerning capitalism. The following five theoretical propositions summarize some of these ideas. The rest of the chapter will develop them more fully.

1. If a capitalist economy can be defined by the drive towards accumulation, then growth is the materialization of this process and capitalism appears as growth. This appearance, capital's

materialization, is biophysical and ecological as much as it is social. A conceptual apparatus must be developed to understand critically both dimensions of growth.

2. Growth is also a powerful idea, a central ideology of capitalist society. More precisely, growth is also a system of meaning through which capitalist society understands its historical trajectory, makes sense of its past, understands its present and imagines its future. This ideology is powerful enough that most critical theories and movements trying to overcome capitalism as an economy and society have remained imprisoned in the imaginary of growth. This is especially true of modern socialism and more widely of the progressive left.

3. Economic growth is more than an imaginary, a concept degrowth draws from the critical sociology of Cornelius Castoriadis.[3] As growth of the "monetary production economy" - that which GDP measures – it is a powerful and central stabilizing mechanism in a capitalist society. Growth can mitigate some of capitalism's core class contradictions, more particularly the conflict between capital, labor and the state concerning the partition of the economic surplus. This was the defining aspect of the fordist accumulation regime known as a so-called "capitalist golden-age," and it remains today the central justification for strong economic growth: it fosters stability.

4. But, because growth is material, and not only monetary, this mitigation of the contradictions of exploitation comes with a price. Growth rests on the displacement of these contradictions towards other spheres, a process analyzed early on by Rosa Luxemburg as *Landnahme*, today known as externalization.[4] The capitalist economy does not grow in a vacuum, its growth is confronted with a "full world" which can be both a source of resistance or of opportunity for capital.

5. Following work by Marxist and feminist scholars, these appear as the boundary struggles of capitalist society which are quite different from the struggles internal to the relation of class

exploitation that have been mitigated and managed more or less successfully through growth.[5] The boundary that has been at the forefront of degrowth's critique of growth divides nature from capitalist society as much as it binds them into a whole.

2. Growth as the materialization of capitalist accumulation

That "the economy has grown" is an almost daily news item, subject of debate between experts and the stuff of promises by politicians of almost all allegiances. It can even be said that it is this discourse on growth that gives the "economy" its semblance of organic unity and objectivity as an independent being. Like trees, animals and people, the economy grows, and this growth is governed by laws seemingly as natural as those that govern living beings and their bodies. If these laws are not respected, growth falters, we have recession, stagnation or worse, economic depression. But unlike trees, animals and people, the economy is not growing to become something, it has no finality, it will never be mature and grown up, it is compelled to grow *ad infinitum*, and any slowdown is understood as pathological. A slowdown is all the more problematic since economic growth is not only a "fact," it is also a normative ideal of modernity, tightly linked to ideas of progress and emancipation both in liberal and socialist thought and ideology. But growth is also material reality. More provocatively, degrowth argues that growth is the materiality of capitalism.

In which way does growth materialize capitalism as an economy and society?

Growth appears both as a socio-economic materiality and as a biophysical materiality. When we measure an economy's size through such metrics as GDP, we are capturing growth of what we can call a class based monetary production economy. Capitalism appears as a flow of monetary income setting into motion machines, commodities and labor. Producing and distributing on the one hand commodified social wealth (output) and on the other, expanding this capacity to produce and circulate the output through investment in "inputs." This expansion of "inputs" as investment appears in two interlinked guises: Expansion can be the simple production of more machines, materials and labor power or this expansion can be the production of new forms of machines, materials and labor power, and the design of new, hitherto non-existent commodity forms. At any given moment in a capitalist monetary production economy, both these intensive and extensive forms of investment are driving its growth. But it is the intensive form which actually gives a historical direction to this growth. Most critiques of capitalism closely study this process through the lens of the relationship between "fixed capital" and labor. They study how investment changes the structural relations between machines and workers and through the category of productivity impact on the nature, size and distribution of the output.

Is capitalist growth progressive?

Looking at capitalism with these categories, growth is progressive in two combined ways. First the total social output grows, there is more commodified wealth that can potentially be spread around. Depending on the historical context, this has been interpreted either as clawing our way out of scarcity and mere subsistence or continuing our stroll through the shopping mall of abundance, bewildered by the new objects, wants and desires of the "affluent society." Of course, many of these new wants and desires are molded by a specifically capitalist logic, but we are told that these can be contested and even redefined by practices of cultural resistance. Stripped of their logos, commodities will reveal pristine underlying use-values. And states can also decommodify parts of the output through social and public forms of ownership. Either way, growth of the economic output is inherently seen as good and progressive. Postscarcity is the precondition to emancipation, we have been told.

The other progressive dimension of growth is said to lie in the development of the productive capacities of labor. Productivity implies that each unit of labor time can potentially - if it encounters the appropriate fixed capital - produce more material abundance. Of course, it is highly possible that these new forms of labor are more alienating under capitalist conditions of production. Under future socialized and more democratic conditions of production or from the result of class struggle today, however, one could imagine a number of socially progressive solutions to this problem. From full automation to a maximized reduction of shared alienating labor, to the redesign of the labor process, all of this becomes more fulfilling.

Because of this two-sided progressive nature of economic growth under capitalism, it is often argued that accumulation potentially - unbeknownst to each and every capitalist - prepares the transition to postscarcity socialism, communism or anarchism. Furthermore, in this framework the transition from capitalism to communism or socialism, though it implies a deep and clear break with existing social relations of production and distribution, does not imply a fundamental break in the economy's material base. Of course, production will be re-organized, some wasteful sectors winded down, others expanded and new ones brought into existence. But the transition is based on the material continuity from one model of society to another. Socialism needs the technologies and material artifacts created by capitalism, but will harness their potential in a more rational, emancipatory and just manner. It is this progressive nature of economic growth - and thus of capitalism - that degrowth contests on socio-ecological and cultural grounds.

The critique of the progressive nature of growth has been

developed most forcefully by the feminist movement and research.[6] In a nutshell, one can show that a growing output is a dual process of internalization and externalization, or *Landnahme*. Growth is a relentless process of colonization and recolonization of the life world and the reproductive sphere, of care and community, by commodities and commodified social relations. Growth of the productivity of labor has gone hand in hand with the growth of exploitative commodified forms of care work and the intensification of unpaid care / reproductive labor.[7] Increased mediation of reproductive activity by machines has not so much reduced as transformed the drudgery of household tasks. When growth implied the elimination of daily trips to the water fountain through the installation of running water systems, or the wiring of homes to electrical networks, the progressive narrative could hold. But when it implies the replacement of household appliances with shorter lifespans but flashier interfaces, then one begins to doubt. One can also doubt the progressive narrative of capitalist growth when observing or experiencing this process from the ecological boundaries of capitalist society. It is to this problem we shall now turn.

3. The Biophysical foundations of capitalist accumulation

Economic growth can be experienced as an ever increasing amount of new forms of commodities entering into circulation, or as access to commodities and services which in the past were reserved to wealthy elites (such as air travel for commuting purposes, so-called luxury cruises or disposable single dose pods packed with exotic varieties of coffee beans). It is also experienced as new productive processes, as new employment opportunities, as seemingly more productive machines and tools (when it is the productivity of labor that is multiplied, machines are not productive per se). Lately, it is also experienced as the appearance and wide diffusion of an ever more diverse and complex array of "smart" electronic devices and objects. This leads to growth being also experienced as *angst* over the concern that automation threatens to wipe out many jobs that we take for granted today.

The phenomenon of growth is also experienced in a more immediate fashion as a material change in the way space is organized around us. Buildings get higher, suburbs sprawl, highways get wider and automobile traffic more dense. Concrete and steel structures grow faster than the trees planted to decorate them, deeper and ever more vast container commercial ports saturate coastlines and penetrate estuaries. In huge areas of the Global South and parts of the countryside in the Global North, complex and diverse agroecosystems are replaced by growing fields of monoculture crops designed to feed livestock or to provide staples to the global agro-food industry: soy beans in the Brazilian savanna, organic "fair trade" Quinoa on the Andean plateau, palm oil plantations in Malaysia, shrimp farms in Thailand's Mangroves, and GMO corn in the North East of America. While children of the privileged capitalist core still learn at a young age that chickens, hens and pigs are barnyard animals, this bucolic mythical existence hides the fact that the metabolism of most societies today rests on massive stocks of caged animals living short cramped miserable lives on industrial farms where they are stuffed with imported feed for a couple of weeks before being hauled off in masses to slaughterhouses. Other communities experience growth as the unrelenting and largely irreversible transformation brought upon their lived environments by an ever growing demand for energy and minerals. Coal pits swallowing forests in Germany, tar sand pits eating away at Muskeg wetlands in Canada, pastures in Dakota littered with oil rigs flaring gas, car factories taking peasant's land in India, whole watersheds poisoned by mine tailings in Brazil, equatorial forests illegally cleared in the Congo basin by European Timber corporations, fields covered with shiny solar panels, hills and stretches of sea crowded with wind farms.

This other *Landnahme* side of capitalist growth has long been condemned by romantic critics of industrial capitalism from an aesthetic and cultural perspective. Degrowth has shifted the basis of this critique with the development of a new language borrowed from biophysical and ecological economics.[8] Growth appears as flows of energy and matter passing *through* societies and in doing so sustaining bodies, human or animal, as well as the material artifacts that populate our world. The latter are known as "stocks" and they need flows or "throughputs" to be maintained. From an ecological "materialist" perspective there can be no "output" of goods and services, no build-up of productive capacity in "inputs" without this throughput of energy and matter. From this insight follow three propositions: growth of output implies growth of throughput; throughput flows define the boundary between society and nature; because capitalism is a monetary production economy, in a capitalist society throughput flows are veiled. This is where the socio-ecological contradictions of capitalism are lodged.[9]

Throughput and the socio-ecological contradictions of capitalism

In capitalism, this throughput must be extracted, it must be harnessed in useful form, put to work or absorbed in some manner and eventually as waste excreted in a cycle from "source" to "sink." Sources and sinks are the points of contact, entanglement and contradiction between nature and capitalist society. This linear process is the material basis of all the social relations in a capitalist monetary economy. From a biophysical perspective, the idea that accumulation could be "immaterial," or that a good or a service could be dematerialized is completely ridiculous. Even dreams must be embodied in living, breathing, sleeping, eating and excreting beings.

For the throughput to flow there must be extraction, which

has important ecological as well as biogeochemical effects and consequences, from depletion to ecosystem colonization and simplification by agriculture. The throughput must also be externalized as waste and absorbed into ecosystems and returned to biogeochemical cycles. This dimension of waste also has consequences and effects, ranging from surplus production (e.g. waste food) to the waste stream embedded in the production process or running through households. But by far the most problematic waste streams that capitalist societies produce today are liquid and gaseous emissions of the basic elements out of which life has sustained itself on our planet: carbon, nitrogen, phosphorous, as well as the toxic substances that we produce and externalize. Absorption of these wastes means, from a biophysical and ecological perspective, forcing the biogeochemical cycles and regulatory mechanisms that maintain the climate, water, and soil systems as we have experienced them since the last glaciation or even beyond.

Throughput and capitalist production

Throughput as a concept captures all the materials of organic and inorganic origin as well as energy forms that are transformed during the economic process. It is a linear flow subject to biophysical laws and constraints such as the laws of thermodynamics. One of the most important ones, foundational to degrowth thinking, is the "law of entropy": as matter and energy moves through society and through successive transformations, its entropy increases, and this is an irreversible process of dissipation in which high quality energy becomes heat, minerals are dispersed, metals corrupted.[10] But it is only through these same successive transformations that basic staple commodities become more complex artifacts, producers' goods and then consumers' goods destined for final use and eventually these use-values become waste.

As value is added in capitalism considered as a monetary

production economy, entropy rises in the same sphere considered as biophysical economy. The higher the growth rate of the former, the faster the throughput must flow, the more intense the dissipation of matter and energy, the more this throughput forces sinks and sources in ecosystems and biogeochemical cycles. This is the inescapable materiality of a capitalist economy. Furthermore, the higher the growth rate of a monetary production economy, the larger it becomes, both in terms of fixed capital and of income and output flows implied in its expanded reproduction, which also has important throughput implications.

The accumulation of capital is mirrored in the ever growing mass of productive artifacts the throughput must reproduce through inputs of energy and additions of matter. Resulting expanded output and incomes have their own throughput implications in the sphere of consumption.

Throughput and capitalist consumption

In a capitalist society consuming the output also mobilizes a massive throughput of energy and matter. Environmentalists are quick to blame hedonistic individuals for ecologically unsustainable lifestyles based on overconsumption. But advanced capitalism, because of the growth dynamic outlined above, is constantly faced with the specter of overproduction and of unabsorbed surplus capacity – literally idled fixed capital or uninvested profits.[11] This barrier of over-accumulation can be (and has been) surmounted, by managing the consumption of the output. Commodities, even the most basic, are designed to maximize output consumption: they don't last long, they are overwrapped, they are disposable or they depend on energy and matter thirsty artifacts that households must collect to enjoy them. Vast social resources, labor and creativity, as well as the underlying material throughput processes needed to sustain these resources, are pooled to condition demand by creating a "waste form" of the output. And even the apparently most dematerialized of consumer products, such as internet based video games, have their material signature in smartphones with a targeted churn rate of 18 months. It is not only that the output must be absorbed and consumed, but it must be consumed in such a way as to make room for the absorption of a continuously expanding output. This is growth. And in this economy, overconsumption is not a psychological pathology, it is the constrained mode of consumption imposed on those that must buy commodities to subsist and flourish, because it is embedded in the form of the output. The throughput effects of mass consumption on sinks and sources arise from this determined mode of existence of the output, what we called the "waste form" of commodities and of the consumptive artifacts that mediate their flow. Through the dynamic coupling of overproduction to overconsumption, growth in advanced capitalism is forestalling an always immanent crisis of over-accumulation.

4. Concluding thoughts

As the scale of the economic process grows in the form of an expanding monetary production economy – more output, more income, more capital fixed in artifacts – material throughput growth is multiplied as are the ecological and biophysical effects on sinks and sources through entanglements between nature and society. A critical theory of accumulation captures the social dimension of capitalism: unequal income distribution, alienating labor processes, exploitation, class domination. A critical theory of growth captures capitalism's appearance in the material world and the socio-ecological contradictions its expansive nature implies.[12] But as we stated in the beginning of this chapter, growth is more than just a material process, it is a central legitimating device and culturally hegemonic idea in modern capitalist society. Furthermore, as a functional property of capitalism as an economy, it is also a stabilizing device. And thus the socio-ecological contradictions produced by capitalist growth tend to find growth based answers.

This is a first reason why a critique of growth, in the form of degrowth, is needed to open up the horizon of alternatives beyond growth. A second is that the more radical movements that have actively contested capitalism developed alternatives premised on profound change in the social relations of production, distribution and even power that rested on the material continuity of the growth based society they were challenging. Degrowth's ecological materialism opens a space to critically examine the material base of contemporary capitalist society and consider the biophysical scale and form of a future society that is ecologically embedded and limited after capitalism and after growth. Finally, because it has progressively developed an autonomous critique of capitalism through the critique of growth, degrowth contributes in an original and specific way to the renewal of critical approaches to capitalism in both theory and practice. The challenge for degrowth is to translate this into concrete alliances with more traditional anti-capitalist and progressive social movements and actors.

Endnotes

1 D'Alisa et al., 2014.
2 Klein, 2014.
3 Muraca, 2013.
4 Dörre et al., 2009.
5 Fraser, 2016.
6 Biesecker and Hofmeister, 2010.
7 Salleh, 2017.
8 Fischer-Kowalski and Haberl, 2015.
9 Brandt and Wissen, 2018.
10 Georgescu-Roegen, 1971.
11 Foster, 2005.
12 Kramm et al., 2017.

Literature

Biesecker, A., & Hofmeister, S. (2010) "Focus: (Re)productivity Sustainable relations both between society and nature and between the genders," *Ecological Economics*, vol. 69, pp. 1703–1711.

Brandt, U. and M. Wissen (2018) *The Limits to Capitalist Nature. Theorizing and Overcoming the Imperial Mode of Living*, London, Rowan and Littlefield.

D'Alisa, G., Demaria, F., and Kallis, G. (eds.) (2014) *Degrowth: A Vocabulary for a New Era*, London, Routledge.

Dörre, K., Lessenich, S., and Rosa, H (2009) *Sociology, Capitalism and Critique*, London, Verso.

Fischer-Kowalski, M., Haberl, H (2015) "Social metabolism: A metric for biophysical growth and degrowth," in: Martinez-Alier, J. (ed.), *Handbook of Ecological Economics*, Cheltenham, Edward Elgar, pp. 100–138.

Foster, J. B. (2005) "The treadmill of accumulation: Schnaiberg's environment and Marxian political economy," *Organization and Environment*, vol. 18, no. 1, pp. 7–18.

Fraser, N. (2016) "Contradictions of Capital and Care," *New Left Review*, vol. 100, pp. 99–117.

Georgescu-Roegen, N. (1971) *The Entropy Law in the Economic Process*, Cambridge, Harvard University Press.

Klein, N. (2014) *This Changes Everything: Capitalism vs the Climate*, London: Penguin.

Kramm, J., Pichler, M., Schaffartzik, A., and Zimmermann, M. (2017) "Societal Relations to Nature in Times of Crisis—Social Ecology's Contributions to Interdisciplinary Sustainability Studies," *Sustainability*, vol. 9, no. 7, pp. 1042.

Muraca, B. (2013) "Decroissance: A Project for a Radical Transformation of Society," *Environmental Values*, vol. 22, no. 2, pp. 147–169.

Salleh, A. (2017[1997]) *Ecofeminism as Politics: Nature, Marx and the Postmodern*, London, Zed Books.

Chapter 2

Assembly during the 15M protests (Image: CC BY-SA 2.0, David Martín :: Suki_ ::)

15M: Strategies, Critique and Autonomous Spaces

Eduard Nus

The whole text is written from the personal standpoint of the author. He tries to distinguish between the interpretation of the 15-M movement and the ideas that the autonomous current has. He writes with a perspective amid the 15-M movement in the city of Barcelona. This particular or current branch, can be summarized by one of the 15-M's motto *"ningú ens representa"* (nobody represents us). Eduard is a member of the *Autonomy Reflexion Group* and of *"La Base: ateneu cooperatiu"* in Poble Sec, Barcelona. He is currently starting to build autonomous bases in semi-rural places around Can Tonal de Vallbona.

1. A heterogeneous movement with a common denominator

The 15-M movement was very heterogeneous. Nevertheless, the participants of the 15-M movement shared the following ideas as a common denominator:

- A critical stand on existing institutions (We are not commodities in the hands of politicians and bankers, nobody represents us, etc.).
- Opposition to the antisocial measures of the economic policies implemented by the government and, in a deeper sense, criticism of the commodification of life, the need to express outrage and the need to find responses to the crisis.
- Opposition to the competitive principle and the need to put an end to the alienation and individualization of life, to which this system condemns us. With the words of our friend Pablo Molano, who has recently left us: A lot of people say that 15-M was an act of protest. It is true, but it was not just that. It was, and is, an encounter, a recognition and the abolition of personal and ideological barriers. We were one, because we were all and each with their own quirks, accepting each other.

To sum up, we can say that the central idea is that society and the people must be placed on top, and that political and economic institutions must be subordinate to them.

The context

The 15-M movement in Spain developed out of a long series of protests following annunciations by the central government with regard to major wage and labor cuts, more privatization of public services and a drastic erosion of the welfare system. In response to this, and seeing that the major trade unions failed to call for a general strike and were instead negotiating with the established powers, people started to demonstrate and organize themselves. In Barcelona, the Barcelona Assembly was created, a gathering of activists who wanted to unite everyone who was affected and oppressed by the neoliberal measures implemented by the government. At the same time, other collective platforms such as "Democracia Real Ya" (Real Democracy Now) also emerged online as a way to express the people's outrage and their discontent with the governing elites. The following motto, which hung on the walls of an important squat building in Barcelona just a few days before the general strike, which then in September 2010 was called upon by the trade unions, nicely summarizes the collective mood of the time: "Banks suffocate us. Employers exploit us. Politicians lie to us. CCOO and UGT[1] trade unions sell us. Fuck off!"

In the same vein, "Democracia Real Ya," whose main motto was "We are not commodities in the hands of politicians and bankers," called for large demonstrations in all major Spanish cities on May 15th. These demonstrations, apparently without prior planning, turned into permanent camps which occupied major squares in the main Spanish cities and thus starting a long series of protests. This plural and diffuse movement of citizen's assemblies, which formed during the camps, was the beginning and the most important moment of what we know as the 15-M movement. In Barcelona, the camps remained there for several weeks until they were forcefully evicted by the Catalan police. Following this controversial act, they re-grouped in the neighborhoods as part of a decentralization strategy. This consolidated existing projects and gave rise to new ones, but meant losing participation in town square occupations.

Some of the most important elements were the collective learning, the organic functioning, the general fraternal attitude and the almost forgotten feeling of having something in common. Again, something happened that had the force to unite us beyond the discourses of mass media and its alienating show. It was something that we, the people, shared, outside of the boundaries and regulations defined by the elites to avoid sectarian divisions and the prevailing individualism.

From the squares to the neighborhoods

After the squares were evicted, the movement rooted in the neighborhoods. At this time, two different projects started to emerge more clearly: one that wanted to plant the seeds for a new self-ruled society and the other that talked about a new constitution and the creation of new alternative political parties. The supporters of the first ones were few and without enough clear ideas or bases to create an anti-systemic movement or to change everyday life; so they continued to work in local projects as usual but with renewed energies and more people. To them, 15-M was a climax, but not a shifting point. The others, the majority, fell easily into a dynamic of demands, denouncement, compromise and cultural events. Requests to politicians were watered down to preserve the rights and welfare system of the previous years, as if this were possible.

If we are very optimistic, we can consider 15-M as a turning in the context of a series of demonstrations and as part of a wider project that could become an alternative to the current system. The collective consciousness of the collapse in which we are immersed was not yet very distinct. The crisis was still very "new" and the claims of the time were therefore very strongly focused on not losing what had been achieved until then. This meant ignoring that we were in the middle of a changing era, a civilizational shift. After many affluent years, when all came down, people felt lost and upset, even betrayed. There weren't any clearly discernible alternatives, let alone an organization to support them. Therefore, it was easiest to try to return to what people already knew.

The autonomous perspective within 15-M

As already mentioned, 15-M was a heterogeneous movement. The autonomous perspective within 15-M is an autonomous and local approach that existed before the 15-M mobilizations, and like many others, participated and was reinforced by it. From my point of view, 15-M was a climax in this current, not a shifting point. Also, like other currents it is not an explicitly self-recognized movement.

This current shares the common points we've listed before, but we don't think that the problems we have to face are bad rulers or evil bankers, but that it is something inherent in the capitalism-state system. To solve it we have to go to the roots of the system and deactivate it.

Autonomy and Heteronomy in history

We can analyze history as a struggle between autonomy and heteronomy. In a political sense, autonomy is the self-determination of the communities and heteronomy is the opposite. We understand autonomy in a broader sense, not only as a political regime, but also as a way of life, with regard to how we use time or resources, how we relate to each other and so on.

The history of the movement for autonomy goes back to Antiquity. It is the history of self-organization, of the commons, of neighborhood assemblies, of countless revolutions. During history, different movements have continued the heritage of their predecessors, as we try to do nowadays. In Catalonia we are heirs of the libertarian movement of the first decades of the 20th century, and the workers struggle during the 1970s. We are also heirs of feminist, ecologist and anti-globalization movements, who influenced and nourished our practices, analyses and discourses.

In our country, the movement almost disappeared due to draconian repressions during the Franco dictatorship. After the end of the dictatorship, the resistance and any revolutionary approaches were minimized, especially during the period 1980-2000 and due to the growth of the welfare state. In the first years of the new millennium, it started awakening, little by little, especially within the anti-globalization movement. In the years before and during the 15-M movement, this autonomist movement became more visible, and neighborhood assemblies started to form. Thanks to 15-M and the work that was done during the following years, as well as the relentless strengthening of the dynamics of the capitalist system, this current is more present now and starting to gain strength.

Today it is obvious that heteronomy is winning the struggle, and that we are facing a multidimensional crisis (social, economic, ecological . . .). We are not only damaging the planet and other forms of life, we are even risking the survival of humanity.

In addition, it is clear that we must overcome capitalism not only as an economic system but also as a world view, a set of values and its associated lifestyles (or, should we rather say lifeless-styles?). Personal interest, selfishness, and commodification are central elements that permeate our relationships and attitudes. So if we want to change this system, we need to thoroughly rethink our strategy, proposals, discourses and practices: We need a new cosmovison of ourselves and the world.

The alternative

The consensus of the 15-M movement was to regain sovereignty over our lives. However, there are different proposals and visions on what sovereignty means and what could be the strategy to achieve it. In some cases, the proposals are revolutionary and in most cases, they are reformist.

From the perspective of which I feel a part, the alternative is a society that is self-determined, self-managed and based on communal life and sovereign public assemblies, without the state or any dominating power. The alternative also implies another worldview, our relationships with each other, with time, with nature. We think of communities rooted in a territory, self-reliant, mainly living off their own resources, and confederated with other communities. In this context, we find the ideas and practices of Democratic Confederalism[2] interesting, ideas which are currently applied by a majority of the population in Kurdistan.

The idea of societal change, to achieve this alternative, is to build and defend a common life, another lifestyle with another worldview, and a political and social movement that can spread, coordinate and defend this communal life. The idea is that this movement can also challenge the current system of domination with enough power to replace it, and to end it.

There are different points of view on how to accomplish this shift from the existing system to this new stateless form without capitalism and other forms of domination. The most feasible for us is a transitory process allowing the new forms to be tried and tested within the current system; the construction of a "parallel society," not only to create this "new world" here and now in a small scale but also to have enough power to resist and disable the existing one.

2. Concrete local and political action

We can identify three levels of participation within the 15-M movement:

- The core, consisting of the most committed and persistent activists. There are a few thousand of them all over the country and they are in charge of planning and coordinating actions.
- The active citizenship (hundreds of thousands), who participate in the multiple forms of collective expression.
- Outraged or unhappy citizens (two thirds of the population) who somehow sympathize with the aims and actions of the movement.

The movement is organized around specific actions, working areas and groups that are organized in committees and a general assembly (no matter how large[3]).

After the 15-M demonstrations and square occupations different projects and initiatives arose. In the beginning, all the initiatives were based more on local and horizontal projects. With the new electoral processes after the 15-M mobilization came new parliamentary political projects in addition, which are considered to be the heirs of the 15-M movement. So we can differentiate two groups in the evolution of the movement practices:

Firstly, those who decided to participate in state institutions. Most of them think that the problem has to do with bad rulers (such as the political party *Podemos*), and some of them think that the problem is the system itself, but it is important to be in state institutions in order to slow the system dynamics (such as the political party *Candidatura de Unidad* (CUP) or some parts of *Barcelona en Comú*). It comprises a few thousand activists who are active on these platforms and the millions of people who vote for them in elections.

Secondly, there were those who refuse to participate in state institutions and continue with direct local work (many local projects, cultural centers, cooperatives, etc.). There are a few thousand activists who participate in these projects, and it is difficult to determine how many people sympathize with them. The 15-M was a nourishing moment for existing projects and also for the creation of new ones. It was a moment that energized existing activists but also brought a lot of new people to the existing groups. Most of them became inactive a few weeks/ months after the square occupations, but the few who remained considerably strengthened the projects.

The organization of this second option is very ephemeral, not formally organized and operates on two interrelated levels: On the one hand, projects with a local perspective (what unites them is a territory), which aim to defend the neighborhoods, to strengthen communities and breathe life into the commons. And on the other hand, thematic projects with a more broad territorial perspective. What unites them is a common perspective, a struggle, an area of activity etc. Regarding such projects, it's worth noting that in recent years there have been several organizational proposals (Process Embat, Apoyo Mutuo . . .) to come together and give voice to the second kind of groups, the more autonomist ones. Also, during the last two or three years there have been a number of gatherings to generate thought and reflection or simply to get organized. Awareness is growing about the need to build a more organized and coherent movement.

The strategy also consists in acting on these two levels, by looking at the long-term aspect (building a new world and ending with the existing order), but making everyday actions. We think that strategic awareness is of key importance in determining the fate, evolution or stagnation, of different projects, and to give purpose and strength to each action.

3. Advancing and implementation of degrowth ideas

We can talk about the 15-M as a movement of movements. Most importantly, all the social movements in Spain participated in it. The degree of involvement varied; some of them participated more actively, more enthusiastically or more skeptically, but we can say that everybody was there. Most of the social movements sympathize with the 15-M movement.

The 15-M movement was influenced directly by the degrowth movement. However, due to the heterogeneity of the movement, and the fact that the degrowth perspective was shared only by a minority, it didn't have an important presence. It is very difficult to describe the relationship between the two, as it was non-coherent and not continuous. From what I know, it had a clear presence in some committees and working groups and no relationship with others.

The most distinct influence of the degrowth movement consisted in bringing in the awareness of peak oil and environmental problems. However, this turned into something like an ecological label, rather than being established as a movement within 15-M.

In Catalonia the degrowth movement started around 2007, with an activist approach. After two years, a crucial part of the activists moved on to other frameworks or created broader movements, which considered the strongest degrowth ideas, but took them further.

We want to highlight the *Cooperativa Integral Catalan* (Catalan Integral Cooperative) which started and is still supporting a lot of self-managed projects – it was created by degrowth activists – and the *Democràcia Inclusiva* (Inclusive Democracy Action Group), an action group for inclusive democracy, which was also initiated by degrowth activists. From my point of view, in Barcelona, the academic section grew stronger than the activist section of the degrowth movement over the last years.

We believe that many of the basic ideas of the degrowth movement are related to the autonomous approach of which I feel a part. Practices related to the degrowth movement have been gaining strength as well. We can say that we were inspired by ideas and practices from degrowth in significant nuances, and we are therefore interested in the debate that might arise around those ideas. We very much welcome this publication because it allows us to delve into that debate.

4. Growth is not the only problem and lifestyle change is not a solution

From my point of view, the role of the degrowth movement has to be to participate in and contribute to other movements or struggles, but I don't think of it as "The movement" of social transformation. We don't want an ecological movement with a holistic perspective, but a holistic movement with a strong ecological view. In order to achieve this, we think that it is also important that the degrowth movement doesn't turn into a mainly academic movement.

The 15-M movement has implicit proposals in its practices that can be interpreted and applied to any social movement whatsoever, including the degrowth perspective. Above all, we think that the degrowth perspective could learn from the 15-M movement concerning the multiple faces of the system and its ways of oppression, and how this translates to specific problems for the people. This knowledge can help to carry out an analysis and to broaden the perspective, allowing us to consider the fact that the strategy to overcome such oppressions can't just consist of reforms.

I have identified a number of contributions from the degrowth perspective that the 15-M movement would benefit from adopting. You can probably find more with deeper and more extensive knowledge of the degrowth movement than I have. The most important ones I can identify are the following:

- To understand and accept the planet's physical limits, and the relationship between economy, ecology, energy, resources, etc.
- To understand the consequences of economic growth.
- Voluntary simplicity and changing our own lives.
- To offer people who are concerned about the specific environmental or economic crisis a certain anti-systemic perspective, a broader view and analysis, including different struggles or problems within a common analysis, identifying a common root.

From our point of view, I would like to propose the following issues to the degrowth perspective:

1. Growth is a problem, but not the main issue: The degrowth

perspective sees growth as the main problem of the system. Hence, we ask: Why do we have a growth economy? This is the key question. Growth is a big problem, but it is just an inherent feature of the current economic system. Growth is the consequence of a competitive scheme, the purpose of which is the concentration of power in the hands of private interests. In the words of Ted Trainer: "We are dealing with extremely important initiatives, which are heading in directions that are admirable […] but which are unfortunately mistaken regarding the nature of the global problem and the way out of it."[4]

2. A market system implies growth: Growth is not only a consequence of a growth ideology, it is also caused by the dynamics of a market economy. This is obvious for projects such as some cooperatives. They don't follow the growth ideology but have to grow to survive in a market economy.

3. Degrowth and capitalism: Degrowth within capitalism, particularly in a globalized economy, is an oxymoron. Capitalism requires growth to reproduce itself. When growth is not possible, there is an economic crisis or a war, and a restructuring takes place, which usually implies more concentration of power, more inequality, and also more oppression towards the environment and/or the population.

Proponents of the degrowth perspective have to ask themselves which social organizing system could cause a reduction in material consumption? Which social organizing system could reintegrate human life with nature? We think that this is impossible in a market economy. Which system could also end most structural oppression? We don't think that this can be done if we maintain the nation-state system in which elites and hierarchies are a precondition for survival, as they control most of the things we need to survive: food production, health centers, energy production. All this implies that the growth economy cannot be overcome with reforms, nor with isolated projects.

We need both a new collective imaginary and new values, as

well as new institutions and public spaces, which can reinforce and maintain these values. These institutions must have structural elements such as self-reliance and local assemblies, and be empowered through direct relationships within the neighborhood, as well as direct relationships with the things that sustain life.

4. It is not only a lifestyle manner: In order to end the problems of growth and the current system, it is ineffective that we think of it only as a matter of lifestyle, or as if we could solve those problems only by having a "better" lifestyle. We have to change our lifestyle, but if we want to achieve a societal change, we have to make this change of lifestyle part of a political strategy. We need a broader social change strategy capable of connecting all actions we develop for establishing new social institutions and replacing the existing ones.

5. Open-minded discussions and local projects for deconstructing the current system

Our wish is to integrate practices and some analytical viewpoints from degrowth which could cohere into a broader common movement, with the aim of changing society from its roots, to end domination in all its forms (political, economic, ecological, social . . .).

Although we learned many things during the 15-M demonstrations, it wasn't enough for the changes we want and need. Our opinion is that the 15-M movements didn't go further because there weren't enough clear ideas, practices, resources, examples, etc. There wasn't enough focused strength that would change people's everyday lives, which in turn would enable the building of a broader movement that could change the world as we know it.

Therefore, our proposal is to continue working in two main areas: Firstly, to share spaces of open-minded discussion, to build common narratives of how we analyze the world and also how we want to live in it. Secondly, we propose the creation of local projects in which we can try out the world that we envision, and from where we can showcase and rethink our ideas, from where we can defend what we are doing and where we can establish a common life that has the power to disable and deconstruct the current system.

Endnotes

1 CCOO (Comisiones Obreras) and UGT (Unión General de Trabajadores) are the main workers union of Spain.

2 Democratic confederalism is a libertarian socialist political system developed by Abdullah Ocalan, and currently applied by the Kurds, especially in the Kurdish part of Syria. It is based on direct democracy and on a grass-roots approach. It is open towards other political groups and factions. It is flexible, multi-cultural, anti-monopolistic, and consensus-oriented.

3 During the occupations there were, for example, daily assemblies on site, with the participation of thousands of people. These daily gatherings were obviously far from being actual democratic assemblies as there was neither the culture nor the technique for meetings with such participation. They were not very relevant because the discussions weren't sustained through several sessions; each daily gathering was an isolated event, and the communities were not empowered, and had no common basis to be managed by the assemblies . . . they suffered from "assemblitis," the making of a procedure into a way of life, rather than using assemblies for self-governance.

4 Trainer, 2010, p. 1.

Links

Decocracia Real Ya platform website: democraciarealya.es

15-M article in the 15-M Wikipedia: 15mpedia.org/wiki/15M

Can Batlló project website: canbatllo.wordpress.com La Base project website: labase.info

CanTonal project website: cantonal.net

The Autonomy Reflexion Group: grupreflexioautonomia.org

Literature

Barcelona Assembly (2010) *Statement about the Bank squat in Catalunya square (Barcelona).* Available at assembleadebarcelona.wordpress.com/2010/09/26/la-manifestacio-del-25-s-ocupa-el-banc-espanyol-de-credit-en-pl-catalunya (Accessed 23 January 2019).

Dalmau, B. (2012) *15M balance towards emancipation.* Available at www.rebelaos.net (Accessed 23 January 2019).

Fotopoulos, T. (2005) "Multidimensional Crisis and the Inclusive Democracy project," *The International Journal of Inclusive Democracy*, special issue. Available at inclusivedemocracy.org/journal/ss/ss.htm (Accessed 23 January 2019).

Fotopoulos, T. (2007) "Is degrowth compatible with a market economy?" *International Journal of Inclusive Democracy*, vol. 3, no. 1. Available at inclusivedemocracy.org/journal/vol3/vol3_no1_Takis_degrowth.htm (Accessed 23 January 2019).

GADI (Editorial Team of the Catalan ID Group) (2010) "Spain: Beyond the general strike," *The International Journal of Inclusive Democracy*, vol. 6, no. 4. Available at inclusivedemocracy.org/journal/pdf%20files/pdf%20vol6/Spain%20-%20Beyond%20the%20general%20strike.pdf (Accessed 23 January 2019).

Trainer, T. (2010) *De-growth is not enough*. Available at dieoff.org/_Economics/De-growth%2014.11.10.doc (Accessed 23 January 2019).

Chapter 3

The Clandestine Insurgent Clown Army in action, G8 protest, Scotland 2005. (Image: CIRCA)

Artivism: Injecting Imagination into Degrowth

John Jordan

Labelled a "domestic extremist" by the police and "a magician of rebellion" by the press, John has spent the last 25 years merging art and activism. He has worked in various settings, from *Tate Modern* to squatted social centers, from international theatre festivals to climate camps. He co-founded *Reclaim the Streets* and the *Clown Army*, co-edited *We Are Everywhere: The Irresistible Rise of Global Anti-Capitalism* (Verso, 2004), and co-wrote the film/book *Les Sentiers de l'Utopie* (Editions Zones, 2012). He now co-facilitates the *Laboratory of Insurrectionary Imagination* (*Labofii*) with Isabelle Fremeaux and lives on the liberated territory of the ZAD of Notre-dame-des-landes, against an airport and its world.

1. Artivism, merging the boundless imagination of art and the radical engagement of politics

Artivism is not really a movement. It's more an attitude, a practice which exists on the fertile edges between art and activism. It comes into being when creativity and resistance collapse into each other. It's what happens when our political actions become as beautiful as poems and as effective as a perfectly designed tool. Artivism is the *Clown Army* kissing riot shields to push the police away; it's the *Yes Men* secretly infiltrating the world's media pretending to be corporate mouthpieces; it's when flocks of flamenco dancers shut down banks promoting austerity in Spain; it's when the *Brandalism* collective hacks hundreds of bus shelters in the midst of a state of emergency and replaces the adverts with radical messages. What it's definitely not about is making *political* art, art *about* an issue, such as a performance about the refugee crisis, or a video about an uprising. It is not about showing new perceptions of the world, but about changing it. Refusing representation, artivism chooses direct action.

Proponents of direct action believe that in order to change things, it is best to act directly on the matter instead of asking others to do things for us. It is the opposite of lobbying and protest marches. Direct action is about transforming the world in the here and now, together. By breathing the spirit of art onto direct action, we can come up with irresistible forms of resistance. If you see a bulldozer cutting down a forest to build a new airport, you don't write a song about it, you put your body in its way (maybe while singing!). The most beautiful thing, however – the aesthetic goal – is *winning:* enabling the survival and continued abundance of the living forest and its ecosystems. With artivism, the beautiful and the useful overlap.

Artivism as an indiscipline

Some might prefer to call it "creative resistance," and some "art activism." Others, following the words of the German artist and co-founder of the Green Party Joseph Beuys, might call it "social sculpture." The authors of *Artivisme: Art, Action Politique et Résistance Culturelle,* however, simply say that artivism is an "indiscipline," something with refusal rooted in its heart.[1] In fact, it refuses to be contained by the problematic discipline of art or by the separate identities of "artist" and "activist" – labels that assume that artists have a monopoly on creativity and activists on social change, suggesting that somehow other people are neither creative nor involved in changing the world!

Artivism treats social movements as a material. Their forms of action and alternatives are forms that our collective imagination can change and reinvent. In the same way that an artist might work with wood or paint, artivism might look at plans for direct action to shut down an open-cast coal mine and imagine how it could be made more powerful and theatrical. It might involve designing the layout of a climate camp so that it is more convivial and open as a place to welcome new people. It might involve inventing new ways of holding horizontal assemblies or designing a shared ritual before going out to sabotage a military base with your affinity group. When, as Gerald Raunig writes, "art machines and revolutionary machines overlap," we get a moment of artivism.[2]

2. A rich, diverse and colorful movement, which can bring down empires in the most unexpected ways

The strategies employed by artivists depend on the political context of their work and are too numerous to fit here, but one brilliant handbook and website of tactics, theories and principles is *Beautiful Trouble.* One example from the book is how to create protests that do not look like protests as a key strategy for those working in repressive regimes or during states of emergency where public dissent is banned. The *Orange Alternative* did this wonderfully during martial law in Poland in the late 1980s. Despite protest bans, they called for a "Gnome" gathering, to demand better "Gnomes' rights." When faced with thousands of young people wearing orange gnome hats, the regime's soldiers did not know what to do, and the generals did not call the tanks in. For the first time since martial law was declared, a mass of people had taken public space back, had a great time doing it, and managed to spread a sense of confidence far and wide. Within a few years the whole of Eastern Europe was out in the streets. Some historians claim that the movements that brought down the Soviet Empire began with artists, guerrilla theatre and musicians opening up space for dissent.[3] Humor has often been at the center of artivist tactics.

Another common tactic is reverse-engineering, which asks the hacker question: "What can this thing do?" This involves hacking a daily object and turning it into a machine of resistance. You can reverse-engineer anything, including laws: Students at the University of Texas fought back against the new campus carry gun law by strapping on dildos! The organizers of Cocks Not Glocks explained that, although it is illegal to openly carry dildos on campus, they are "just about as effective as [guns in] protecting us from sociopathic shooters, but much safer for recreational play." This also illustrates the principle of "put your target in a dilemma position," which means that you put your opponent in a situation where they are forced to respond to your action. But whatever they do, they lose, by appearing either ridiculous or violent.

Those involved in artivism are as diverse as their tactics: some went to art school, others to theater academies, some simply managed to avoid having their creativity sapped from them at school and want to apply it to political action. Artivism's greatest strategies are perhaps innovation and confusion, as repeating the same tactics – the A to B march, the picket, the internet meme, the blockade, the protest camp, the riot – can quickly lose its impact. The most successful actions are often those where new forms are invented that manage to take the authorities by surprise. That is why movements need to constantly innovate their tactics faster than the authorities are able to respond to them; including, of course, tactics to protect protesters from police violence. In the last decade we have seen a range of creative shields, from the book-block shields made from giant book covers (the image of a cop beating George Orwell's *1984* is unforgettable), to the Climate Camp's shields with beautiful photographic portraits of those affected by the climate breakdown pushing through police lines to shut down the builders of a new runway.

Many popular tactics were originally invented by artivists, including Denial-of-Service (Dos) attacks for blocking the websites of opponents, now infamously used by Anonymous.

Creativity and the crafting of new forms needs time and attention, but given the urgency and speed of activism this is never easy. The spirit of art thus also brings a different rhythm to activism, one that is much more in keeping with the aims of degrowth; a de-accelerated, slower, more considered approach, but no less passionate.

3. Opening up the space to dream: nurturing collective creative thinking and the spirit of play within the degrowth movement

At the moment, it feels as though artivists have made fewer connections with the degrowth movement than with other movements such as refugee support, climate breakdown, anti-austerity, alter-globalization, etc. Why this is the case is hard to fathom.

Climate and the concept of the Anthropocene are huge themes in the art world at the moment. However, much of it is sadly part of a corporate elite using culture as a cheap research and development tool and an effective public relations exercise to promote green capitalism. Volkswagen consultants working with artists and ecologists during the Über Lebenskunst project at Berlin's art center *Haus der Kulturen der Welt* (2010-2012) to look at the future of transport is just one of many examples. At the recent COP21 (2015) in Paris, many big name artists played the role of "artwashers" by creating work for a corporate greenwash event, *Solutions COP21*, which brought together some of the world's biggest polluters, from fossil fuel corporations to car manufacturers, from industrial agriculture giants to builders of airports and motorways, for a fair to demonstrate that they had the real solutions to the crisis.

Business-as-usual events like this love to use art as a mask to hide their corporate crimes and give themselves an air of contemporary sophistication. "Artwashing" cleans their logos, and makes us forget that they are destroying living communities of people and ecosystems for profit. An important strategy of artivism is to critique artists and institutions who collaborate with "artwashing," using what Foucault termed *parrhesia*, the act of a person taking the risk to "say everything," to speak the truth dangerously against what the majority believe. Since 2010, the *Liberate Tate collective* has been doing this with stunning interventions in the art museum against BP funding. (These interventions were ultimately successful, as in March 2016 BP announced that starting in 2017 it will no longer fund the Tate). If more artists were involved in movements such as degrowth that strive towards coherence between ideas and ways of living, fewer artists would be busy feeding the suicide machines of capitalism with one hand and claiming progressiveness with the other, and maybe more would be encouraged to apply their creativity to social movement forms.

Participatory pedagogy

The fact that the degrowth conferences of 2014 included an art thread together with scientific, economic and social threads is encouraging. More of these initiatives should be developed so as to break the "academic" conference mold and include more creative forms of knowledge sharing as well as a more holistic approach. Artivists' teaching practices tend to be more horizontal and based on participatory popular education models that seek to develop the shared critical knowledge already present, rather than a "top down" knowledge transfer (via PowerPoint or a conference) from the knower to the students. Artivists tend to go beyond mere talking and listening —working and playing with the body and materials; engaging head, heart and hand equally. This should be a key pedagogic strategy —perhaps a return to the pedagogic idea of the "polytechnic," where learning philosophy was no different from learning how to make a chair.

The process of making things together can be a good mobilizing tool for developing strong affinity groups and bringing people into movements for the first time. After all, it may be a lot less frightening for first-time activists to attend a workshop to learn – as in the case of *Tools for Action* – how to make giant inflatable silver cobblestones for an action, rather than taking part in a big assembly discussing a campaign against a new fracking license.

Setting up transdisciplinary solutions workshops/ laboratories around particular topics, where artists/designers would be brought in not as the "aesthetic communicators" of the ideas, but as creative participants trying to find solutions in collaboration with other disciplines, would be an important step towards merging the degrowth movement with the spirit of artivism.

Creating spaces that nurture such creative thinking and playing as part and parcel of a movement process is key. The degrowth movement, despite its at times overly academic tone, could have the capacity and sensibility to embody this spirit, because at its heart are notions of a change in our culture towards qualitative rather than quantitative ways of being. Degrowth has been called "an example of an activist-led science."[4] Perhaps one day we will be able to say that it was an activist-led art as well.

4. Making degrowth irresistible: the role of desire and fantasy in creating a new culture

I write as someone living in a wood-heated yurt in a small commune on an organic farm in France, where degrowth is at the center of our collective's values. For us, degrowth is coupled with good living. As the French slogan goes: *Moins De Biens, Plus de Liens* – Fewer Things, More Relationships. But in popular mainstream culture degrowth is often misperceived as an activity that involves self-control (stop shopping, stop driving, stop flying, etc.) and privation (don't want or buy new things, etc.), that calls for a return to the past (stop using fossil fuels/new technologies, etc.) where life was hard (grow your own vegetables, make your own bread, stay local, etc.) and happiness rare. In addition, degrowth is usually framed within an apocalyptic timeline of a planetary life support system collapse – not exactly making it the most desirable of movement imaginaries. Such caricatures of degrowth are a far cry from notions of abundance, pleasure and play that are often present in artistic processes and that are concepts that capitalism has taken away from us.

As with most traditional progressive politics, degrowth has a tendency to work in a scientific, "reality"-based manner. Much of the work seems to be passing on information, statistics, facts, economic analyses, etc. It often feels overly academic and heady and ignores emotions – Where is the dreaming and fantasy? While there have been spaces for other forms of intuitive learning, celebrating, etc. at the recent degrowth conferences, this is often seen as merely an addition to the "rational" lectures and workshops.

Stealing fantasy back from capitalism

Capitalism has captured our fantasies with the spectacle of

consumerism; its celebrities have become our mythological heroes, its video games our wild adventures. It promises us the fantasy of a better life that can always be even better. Fantasy itself is the fuel of the entertainment business, popular culture and most religions, and yet we fear it as a tool of politics. We distrust anything that might seem irrational and relegate it to the "arts program."

Artivism, however, recognizes that politics has always been about fantasy, because at its heart is imagining what kind of future world we want. We have been able to use such tools, steal them back from popular culture and create what Stephen Duncombe, author and founder of the Centre for Artistic Activism, calls "ethical spectacles." There, we collectively perform our dreams via imaginative participatory actions, creating new realities via symbols and stories that construct a truth together rather than waiting for it to set us free. The degrowth movement could learn from this and acknowledge that successful politics are as much an affair of desire and fantasy as of reason and rationality. To leave all these powerful tools in the hands of capitalism is a mistake. As long as capitalism's lures are perceived to be more fun and more able to speak to our desires than degrowth, we will fail to make the radical cultural changes that are so necessary, and buying an iPad will still be way cooler than riding a donkey.

Instead of artists flocking to apply their creativity to the movement, they continue to work in the advertising industries and other machines that reproduce capitalism's desire traps. Without their creativity degrowth will remain a beautiful set of ideas rather than a new culture. The questions we must ask are: How do we learn to educate each other to desire differently? How can degrowth become as sexy as capitalism? And how can small really become beautiful? And, last but not least, how can we begin to sense the inherent violence of industrial civilization, to really, deeply feel the crimes against life that it perpetuates, to shake off the anaesthesia, the numbness, and return to aesthesia, the senses?

More coherence is needed

What degrowth can bring to artivism and especially to the art world is the drive for coherence between thinking and living. Separating what we believe in from how we act in the world inevitably leads to suffering, and confusing role models. With many in the cultural field there is a chasm between their politics, aesthetics, ethics and everyday life. Many artists and cultural producers fly from conference to biennale, to carry out work about climate change, while others exhibit anti-systemic work in museums sponsored by banks. Not considering their life as a material to work on, a concept Foucault articulates as "a technique of life, an art of living," they reproduce separations of capitalism. Instead of applying their creativity to questions of how we could travel without causing climate breakdown, how we could organize without domination, how we could grow our food without destroying our soil systems, how we might build new communes, they continue to live in constant contradiction between what they believe in and how they behave. Degrowth's focus on holistic practices could change this.

5. Building a culture of resistance where art and activism are no longer separate from everyday life

One of the most urgent tasks is to build a *culture of resistance*. I don't believe that we will be able to put in place solutions to the ongoing social and ecological catastrophe without acts of resistance. Those who profit from the present economic system will not relinquish their power. We need movements that are able to show desirable alternatives while being prepared to resist the current system. Without a shared set of values and behaviors, without a culture where acts of resistance (from protest to sabotage) are supported by a wider population than that which is actually ready to take part in them, we will not have the systemic change necessary to achieve justice and avoid the collapse of our life support systems on this planet.

That is why things like bringing degrowth and a climate camp together are key, because not everyone is going to be suited for the front line of resistance. But all these people need to feel part of a shared culture. Yet movements so often forget this and don't see the importance of creating the material infrastructures and affective sensibilities that support resistance in the long term. Unfortunately, many in the transition town networks – or in other cultures of ecological alternatives such as permaculture et al. – while thinking long term solutions and material infrastructures, seem to think that our culture will be able to magically transition from capitalism to "something nicer, greener, etc." without resistance. I don't believe this culture will somehow undergo a voluntary transformation to a sane, equitable and sustainable way of living. I think we have to undo much of this culture and rebuild entirely different ways of being and sharing our worlds and that this is what resistance is: confronting and dismantling unjust structures of power to make way for other cultures to flourish.

This is what a culture of resistance looks like

A culture of resistance is one based on sharing our material and emotional support with those involved in a movement of resistance.

A culture of resistance is when in winter 2015 in France citizens opened up their homes and farms to the 200 people in the tractor and bike convoy that rolled up from the *zad* occupation (an autonomous resistance zone against a planned airport in western France) to the COP21 in Paris, despite the state of emergency and bans on their movements. A culture of resistance is *not* the so-called "ecological" philosopher Bruno Latour refusing to sign a letter against the building of the same airport because he fears his name being associated with radical ecologists.

A beautiful example of a culture of resistance was the underground railroad that enabled slaves to escape the southern United States. It's *not* the French government evicting refugees from their self-made Calais camps to force them into a prison-like set-up with no communal space. At the heart of a culture of resistance is refusing a culture of domination in favor of a definition of love that enables the other to be free.

Breaking down the separations

In the end I think that in the new culture that will come after the culture of capitalism and domination, the role of art and activism will change radically. Art as a thing separate from everyday life, a thing for the rich to collect and profit from, a thing to watch or to own, done by others, will be over. It will be seen as a verb rather than a noun; a way of doing, a certain quality of paying attention that anyone can practice in everyday life, not just the "artists."

Perhaps the notion of the activist as someone who is a specialist in transforming society will disappear too, as in a society of the commons, run with local assemblies and a confederation of commons rather than the hierarchical state, in which everyone will feel part of a process of social transformation, part of a practice of politics. In this society, politics will not be separate from ethics anymore. Aristotle saw the pursuit of the good of the political community as a branch of ethics, the pursuit of human good as a whole. This pursuit he called *Eudaimonia*, meaning "the good life," and he believed that it was the ultimate goal of all human beings. 2300 years later, perhaps the degrowth movement will bring us closer to this dream than ever before.

Endnotes

1 Lemoine and Ouardi, 2010.

2 Raunig, 2007.

3 Horáková and Vuletic, 2003.

4 Demaria et al., 2013, p. 191.

Links

The Centre for Creative Activism, based in New York: artisticactivism.org

The Laboratory of Insurrectionary Imagination (Labofii): labofii.net

Interview with its co-founders John Jordan and Isabelle Fremeaux: transitionnetwork.org/news-and-blog/isabelle-fremeaux-john-jordan-and-the-rise-of-the-insurrectionary-imagination

Pockets of Resistance: A documentary, directed by Ralf Christensen: youtube.com/watch?v=Ncb-Akm9dgs

Beautiful Trouble – a Tool Box for Revolution: beautifultrouble.org

Liberate Tate collective: liberatetate.org.uk

Literature

Demaria, F., Schneider, F., Sekulova, F. and Martinez-Alier, J. (2007) "What Is Degrowth? From an Activist Slogan to a Social Movement," *Environmental Values* vol. 22, no. 2, pp. 191–215.

Duncombe, S. (2007) *Dream: Re-imagining Progressive Politics in an Age of Fantasy*, New York, The New Press.

Horáková, P., Vuletic, D. (2003) *Writer Padraic Kenney discusses his book "A Carnival of Revolution" and the events of 1989 in Central Europe,* Radio Prag. Available at radio.cz/en/section/talking/writer-padraic-kenney-discusses-his-book-a-carnival-of-revolution-and-the-events-of-1989-in-central-europe (Accessed 23 January 2019).

Lemoine, S., Ouardi, S. (2010) *Artivisme: Art, Action Politique et*

Résistance Culturelle, Location unknown, Alternatives.
Raunig, G. (2007) *Art and Revolution*, Los Angeles, Semiotext(e).
The Laboratory of Insurrectionary Imagination (2011) *A Users Guide to Demanding the Impossible,* Minorcompositions, London. Available in different languages at demandingimpossible.wordpress.com (Accessed 23 January 2019).

Chapter 4

Together for an unconditional basic income at the UBIE (Unconditional Basic Income Europe) meeting in Hamburg, Germany in 2016. (Image: CC BY-SA, Glenn Slotte)

Basic Income: Unconditional Social Security for All

Ronald Blaschke

Ronald is the co-founder of Netzwerk Grundeinkommen (the German Basic Income Network) and has been a long-standing member of the network's council, a collective body that represents the interests of members between general members' meetings. He is also the co-founder of the Unconditional Basic Income Europe network (UBIE), co-editor of several publications on basic income and author of numerous articles covering poverty, basic income, feminism and growth criticism.

1. The basic income is a way of unconditionally securing every person's existence and allowing each person to participate in society

Behind the notion of a basic income is the conviction that every person has a right to an unconditionally ensured material existence and social participation. The basic income is the monetary side of this security. The four criteria that identify the unconditionality of the basic income are as follows. A basic income should:

- Be guaranteed to all people as a legal individual right
- Ensure the existence of all people and enable their social participation
- Not be subject to means testing, and
- Not be tied to any obligations to work or provide other services in return.

In addition to the basic income, there are also non-monetary ways of unconditionally securing every person's material existence and allowing them to participate in society, such as a free access to goods, infrastructure and services. These can complement the basic income or can be introduced and developed without a basic income.

Basic income – a long history

The idea of a basic income was first established by English author Thomas Spence in 1796. He combined it with other ideas such as the (re)communitarization of the shared natural goods from human life, the securing of public infrastructure, the development of democracy, and the equal involvement of women.

In the 19th century, there were several proposals for a basic income in Europe, such as from Victor Considerant, from Belgian Egalitarians and from Joseph Charlier. These suggestions were always embedded in more general notions of social change, which included developing a democratic system and a cooperative economy, guaranteeing political freedoms and social rights, or nationalizing important companies, among others. However, these proposals mainly referred to what can be considered a partial basic income. They are not true basic incomes that would secure existence and enable social participation.

During the 20th century, the circle of suggestions for basic incomes or partial basic incomes widened enormously in Europe and the USA (e.g. on the part of Bertrand Russell, Dennis and Mabel Milner, Erich Fromm, Martin Luther King, Philippe van Parijs, Herwig Büchele and Lieselotte Wohlgenannt, André Gorz, Michael Opielka, Georg Vobruba and Claus Offe, among others). Their arguments in favor of such a notion were varied, and in almost all cases, their basic income proposals were a part of other social change concepts. Subsequently, the second half of the 20th century has seen a deepening of ties between the basic income debate and ecological and feminist issues.

In 1976, Erich Fromm published *To Have or to Be,* stating the need for further fundamental socio-political changes, in addition to the introduction of a guaranteed basic income that he had propounded since the mid-1960s. According to Fromm, it is necessary to overcome all patriarchal forms of dominance, and in order to put an end to the irrational concepts of economic growth, the power of determining the aims of production must be radically democratized.[1] In 1978, a group of Danish intellectuals proposed in the bestselling book *Revolt from the Centre* (Niels I. Meyer, Kristen Helveg Petersen, Villy Sørensen) a form of basic income they referred to as a "citizen's wage," together with a more equal distribution of income and a democratically and ecologically oriented society and economic system. In addition, the authors stated that household and family-related work has the same importance as other forms of work. The book was widely discussed and since then the topic of a basic income has periodically returned to the country's political agenda. In France at the end of the 1970s, there was a significant public debate surrounding André Gorz's criticism of a growth-oriented economy and of paid work, as well as of his later publications stating the need for a different way of producing, a radical shortening of work times and a basic income.[2] In Germany, the Alternative-Green discussion on basic income in the mid-1980s was tied to an overall criticism of industrial society. Previously, the independent unemployed movement in Germany had ignited the debate about the basic income – called *Existenzgeld* (subsistence allowance) – together with a basic criticism of wage labor and power.

Basic income – criticism of existing relationships of power in the economy, state and partnerships

The principles behind the idea of a basic income, incorporating a criticism of the principles of power of current societies *and* current forms of partnership arrangements, are as follows: Nobody must do anything against their free will or make themselves available in exchange for something due to material poverty if they do not want to — be it on the jobs market or in a partnership. Furthermore, every person has the right to participate in the democratic organization of public affairs, including the economy, and in the organization of partnership arrangements, without fear of facing material blackmail. In order to make these principles a reality, freedom from material poverty is necessary – as *unconditional* material security. Conditional material security (or its complete lack) opens the floodgates to misery, poverty, marginalization, despotism and dependence on the state and partners, as well as stigmatization and discrimination.

2. A heterogeneous and networked basic income movement – international, national and regional

The basic income movement is as heterogeneous as other social movements. It includes libertarians, socialists, communists, feminists, critics of growth, critics of globalization, trade unionists, self-employed persons, unemployed persons, business people and representatives of solidarity-economic co-ops, academics, religious and non-religious people, party members and non-party members. It is not currently possible to formulate a reliable quantitative statement about their structure or their belonging to certain social classes.

On a global scale, those in favor of the basic income are organized as part of the Basic Income Earth Network (BIEN, founded in 1986). At a European level, they are part of Unconditional Basic Income Europe (UBIE, founded in 2014). They are also organized in national, regional and local networks and initiatives, as well as cross-regional organizations and associations that work towards achieving the implementation of a basic income. Some examples of their activities:

In India, in 2011 and 2012, the Self Employed Women's Association (SEWA) carried out basic income pilot projects in rural areas with the support of BIEN. The accompanying study showed significant improvements in the health and socioeconomic situation of the people in the villages where a basic income was provided, compared to the control villages with no basic income.[3]

In Europe in 2013, various initiatives and organizations started a European Citizens' Initiative in favor of a basic income. Even though the required number of signatures was not reached, the initiative was still a success, as it led to the creation, especially in eastern and southern Europe, of networks and initiatives campaigning for a basic income, as well as the founding of UBIE.

In Germany, the largest network is the *Netzwerk Grundeinkommen* (Basic Income Network, founded in 2004), which currently unites 131 larger member organizations and smaller regional initiatives as well as over 5,000 individual members. It is also the largest national basic income network in the world. The Netzwerk Grundeinkommen is one of BIEN's partner organizations. Alliances and networks supporting a basic income within the Die Linke, Bündnis 90/Die Grünen and the Pirate Party political parties also influence the debate.

What is clear is that there is no "single" basic income movement and no "single" basic income concept. (Just as there is no "single" degrowth movement or concept.) However, within both movements – provided their supporters feel committed to an emancipatory aim[4] – there are concurring or similar views that could be fruitful for shared political engagement.

3. The basic income movement is active within other social movements, including the degrowth movement

The basic income movement is involved in demonstrations, public political campaigns, debates and educational programs, political lobbying work and (popular) academic conferences and publications. The supporters of a basic income take part in discussions, conferences and campaigns with or of other social movements.

For example, basic income promoters were involved in preparing the *Citizens' Manifesto for European Democracy, Solidarity and Equality*, which was introduced to the public debate in Europe by *European Alternatives* and other social movements. It contains specific suggestions for political changes within the European Union, was compiled by European citizens in a participatory bottom-up process and was presented to members of the European Parliament in Brussels in December 2013. It also included the suggestion of a basic income. A further example of joint activities with other social movements is the joint organization of the campaign and founding conference for the Care Revolution network and an international feminist workshop on the topic of "Feminist and post-patriarchal demands for a basic income" in 2014.

In the international degrowth and growth-critical debate, the concept of a basic income has been the repeated object of discussions and ideas regarding its potential to both counter growth and to provide social security to the members of a post-growth society. This has been the case, for example, at the international degrowth conferences in Barcelona (2010),[5] Leipzig (2014), Budapest (2016) and Malmö (2018). In the international basic income debate, for its part, degrowth, the criticism of growth and the socio-ecological transformation of society are recurring topics, whether at the 14th BIEN Congress in Munich (Germany) in September 2012, the 16th BIEN Congress in Seoul (South Korea) in July 2016 or the 18th BIEN Congress in Tampere (Finland) in August 2018.

In 2018, several hundred academics published an open letter in *The Guardian* and other European newspapers, calling on the European Union and its member states to plan for a post-growth future in which human and ecological well-being is prioritized. Their proposals include limits on resource use and progressive taxation to decrease social inequality and reduce working time:

> Resource use could be curbed by introducing a carbon tax, and the revenue could be returned as a dividend for everyone or used to finance social programs. Introducing both a basic and a maximum income would reduce inequality further, while helping to redistribute care work and reducing the power imbalances that undermine democracy.[6]

The German basic income movement is also involved as part of the national and international degrowth movement, particularly since the "Beyond growth?! Ecological justice. Social rights. Good life" congress in Berlin in 2011 and the Degrowth conference in Leipzig in 2014. Cooperation with the degrowth movement comes through working in organizational bodies, through joint publications, debates and educational programs. In May 2016, mutual understanding was further strengthened at a European-wide conference in Hamburg as part of a participatory process dealing with "unconditional basic income and degrowth." Content-related overlaps between the basic income movement and the movement critical of growth were discussed (see below).

In the context of these joint processes, the basic income movement has: firstly, emphasized the unconditional material security of all people as an essential requirement for individual freedom *and* true solidarity – i.e. a solidarity that feels committed to people's needs and to reinforcing their autonomy – as well as its importance for other social movements; secondly, tested out basic income concepts to see whether they help or hinder the concerns of other social movements; thirdly, highlighted that a social, economic, ecological and cultural transition of society is not a monothematic concept, but one that brings together and makes necessary a range of different approaches. One such example is the identification of content-related overlaps between the basic income movement and the degrowth movement.

Overlaps between the basic income movement and the degrowth movement

Concurring or indeed similar political approaches are shared across four areas within both movements:

1. *Social security and redistribution*: The basic income movement believes that a basic income is part of a concept of reliable, preventative and, most importantly, human rights-based social security for all. This presupposes a comprehensive redistribution of social wealth. One concept proposed is an ecological basic income or eco-bonus as an independent basic income or as part of the financing of a basic income. This could be a measure to achieve social compensation or redistribution and it could be financed, for example, through an eco-tax. This concept is included in certain basic income models discussed in Germany.

The degrowth movement believes that a good life for all is not possible without unconditional social security for all members of society. People's fear of losing their livelihood, as well as precariousness and social division, block important transformation processes, including ecological ones.

Furthermore, the relationship between climate change and poverty in the Global South is discussed in both approaches. Just like the degrowth movement, sections of the basic income movement that are critical of globalization see a relationship between the prosperity of the Global North and poverty in the Global South, namely as a consequence of the Global North's economic imperialism. They are therefore pleading for an alternative international economy and division of labor, as well as for redistribution to poor countries.

2. *Democracy*: The basic income movement believes that a basic income will promote people's political and democratic participation in all public-political opportunities, including the economy. In the first place, recognizing that the basic income is a transfer payment to which everyone is entitled means recognizing every individual as an equal member of the community. Secondly, it allows everybody to participate politically and democratically, without any form of material blackmail. Of course, the basic income must be introduced democratically, which would require a high degree of social acceptance.

The degrowth movement assumes that the transition to a society that uses significantly fewer natural resources and does not damage the environment is only possible via democratic means, and that sustainable production and consumption require democratic organization.

3. *Alternative and solidarity-based economy:* Sections of the basic income movement that are critical of capitalism in particular have discussed how it is possible to produce beyond the principles of profit and competition, and how production and distribution can be democratic and solidarity-based, so that they are oriented towards the common good and the needs of people. Social security and individual freedom arising from a basic income would promote social and democratic participation

and an attitude based on solidarity – including in the economy. Furthermore, a basic income would ensure material security and free time for development and activities in line with an alternative and solidarity-based economy.

Some in the degrowth movement argue that – in contrast with profit and competition-driven economies – it is only possible to stop excessive consumption of resources and environmental damage by democratically organizing production and consumption, i.e. through a solidarity-based economy. Moreover, the necessity of having time for different types of cooperative individual work in the informal, unpaid sector has been discussed. Practical approaches will need to be tested out.

4. Individual and collective time sovereignty: The basic income movement assumes that the basic income enables your own and the collective working time and lifetime to be handled confidently, since fundamental material security and social participation are a given. Time sovereignty can be seen as both quantitative and qualitative: Quantitative refers to the duration, such as how long you are in gainful employment; whereas qualitative time sovereignty is determined based on the (aims of the) activities which are (achieved or) performed in a specific period of time. The concept of time sovereignty is therefore closely linked with the social security of people, together with the question of democracy and approaches to a solidarity-based economy – also in their respective gender-specific dimension.

The degrowth movement believes that shortening the period of gainful employment and having more time available for other activities is part of the transition towards a degrowth society. Many feminist approaches combine the question of time with ecological and democratic questions, as well as with the revaluation and redistribution of work.

4. Achieving unconditional material security and halting the exploitation and destruction of the natural bases of life are necessary for a social-ecological transition

Representatives of the basic income movement frequently state that achieving a social-ecological transformation is impossible without an emancipatory concept of social justice. Forms of social justice that do not include the unconditional material security of all individuals fall short of humanistic and democratic principles for organizing society and cohabitation. A sustainable ecological transition to a society that uses significantly fewer natural resources and does not damage the environment cannot be achieved through a dictatorship, nor through the existential blackmailing of people, nor in a socially divided society. For its part, the following growth-critical principle is important for the basic income movement: A good life and unconditional material security for all cannot be sustainably achieved by exploiting, depleting and destroying natural resources.

In a globalized world, these principles of social justice and ecological care can only be implemented politically through a global social movement that takes both of the aforementioned aspects into account.[7]

5. An emancipatory social movement is possible

Human emancipation could be an aim shared by the basic income movement and other social movements: Emancipation (understood as self-empowerment) cannot be the result of compulsion, violence or power. It must rely on solidarity, which recognizes the needs and autonomy of individuals – an autonomy that nevertheless incorporates dependence on others. The same solidarity-based principle must prevail between individual countries around the world and between groups of people. Emancipation calls for an inclusive democracy that does not exclude any person, group of people, or country. Undemocratic global and continental institutions, which currently exert power over the economy, trade and social matters, must give way to legitimate democratic bodies. In turn, the solidarity-based relationship between individuals, groups of people and countries is inconceivable without a relationship between people and nature where human beings are seen as a part of nature, and nature as the foundation of human life. Or in feminist terms: Treating one another carefully and treating nature carefully are two sides of the same coin.

On the basis of these principles, economic-imperial, nationalist and racist aspirations, the exploitation and destruction of nature, discrimination against women, as well as physical and psychological violence against human beings are to be rejected.

A truly emancipatory social movement is both plural and bound by these principles. It seeks commonalities and acceptable solutions for each (sub)movement, as anything else would weaken it. There are no simple solutions for complex social problems. There can be no sustainable social change without different strategies that promote one another. That is also the conclusion drawn by many academics and activists named above: For them, a basic income is *one* part of a concept promoting a social-ecological transition within society/societies.

Translation: Ellen Worrell

Endnotes

1 Blaschke, 2012.

2 Gorz, 1997.

3 SEWA, 2015.

4 There are (market-)liberal and conservative aims that could be associated with a partial basic income or a criticism of growth systems, but they have no basis in either movement. One example of a basic income from a neo-liberal point of view is a concept devised by Thomas Straubhaar, which is based on the partial-basic-income approach devised by

Milton Friedman. The specific structure of each basic income concept, as well as its association with other social changes, will make clear whether an emancipatory or a (market) liberal/conservative approach is being taken (Blaschke, 2012).

5 See for example the final Declaration of Barcelona: degrowth.info/wp-content/uploads/2015/05/Degrowth_Declaration_Barcelona_2010.pdf (Accessed 23 January 2019).

6 See theguardian.com/politics/2018/sep/16/the-eu-needs-a-stability-and-wellbeing-pact-not-more-growth (Accessed 23 January 2019).

7 Blaschke et al., 2016.

Links

Basic Income Earth Network: basicincome.org

Unconditional Basic Income Europe: ubie.org

Basic Income Network Germany: grundeinkommen.de/english

Unconditional Basic Income and Degrowth conference: ubi-degrowth.eu

Literature

Andersson, J. O. (2010) *Degrowth with basic income – the radical combination*, available at basicincome.org/bien/pdf/munich2012/andersson.pdf (Accessed 23 January 2019).

Blaschke, R. (2012) *From the Idea of a basic income to the political movement in Europe – development and questions*, Berlin, Rosa Luxemburg Foundation. Available at rosalux.de/fileadmin/rls_uploads/pdfs/rls_papers/Papers_Basic-Income_Blaschke-2012pdf.pdf (Accessed 23 January 2019).

Blaschke, R, Praetorius, I., Schrupp, A. (eds.) (2016) *Das Bedingungslose Grundeinkommen. Feministische und postpatriarchale Perspektiven*, Sulzbach/Taunus, Ulrike Helmer.

Gorz, A. (1997) *Misères du présent. Richesse du possible*, Paris, Galilee.

SEWA Bharat (2015) "Madhya Pradesh unconditional cash transfer project. Executive summary." Available at sewabharat.org/wp-content/uploads/2015/07/Executive-summary.pdf (Accessed 23 January 2019).

Skidelsky, R., Skidelsky, E. (2012) *How much is enough? Money and the good life,* New York, Other Press.

Chapter 5

Dance to honor Pachamama (mother nature) on the big seed exchange fair in Pedro Mocayo (Ecuador). (Image: Author)

Buen Vivir: A Perspective for Rethinking the World

Alberto Acosta

Alberto is an Ecuadorian economist and was previously Minister of Energy and Mining, president of the Ecuadorian Constituent Assembly and a presidential candidate in the Republic of Ecuador.

1. What is *Buen Vivir*?

"We will never create a perfect world.
And we should be aware of that."
Carlos Taibo, 2015

This chapter outlines the scope and limits of Buen Vivir, which can be translated as "good life" or "good living." This "good life" has always been a pluralistic concept, namely "buenos convivires": different ways of "living well together." It is therefore not about opening the gates to a single, homogeneous, unrealizable good life but far more about people living well together in a community, different communities living well together, and individuals and communities living well with nature.

The good life should be considered as something that is undergoing a constant construction and reproduction process. It is not a static concept, and certainly not a backward one. Buen Vivir is a central element of the philosophy of many societies. From this perspective, it is a design for life that has global potential despite having been marginalized in the past.

In some indigenous communities, there is no concept analogous to the "modern" Western concept of development. There is no concept of a linear life with a former and subsequent state (in this case underdevelopment and development). Nor are there concepts of wealth and poverty based on the accumulation or lack of material goods. As such, Buen Vivir entails a world view that differs from the Western world view in that it has community and not capitalist roots. It breaks both with the anthropocentric view of capitalism as the dominant civilization and with the different manifestations of socialism to date. The latter must be rethought from a socio-biocentric position and cannot be updated by simply changing the name.

The good life entails a process of decolonization, which should also involve depatriarchalization.[1] This necessitates a profound process of intellectual decolonization on political, social, economic and cultural levels.

Ultimately, Buen Vivir is highly subversive. It is not an invitation to return to the past or to an idyllic but otherwise non-existent world. It should also not become a kind of religion with its own commandments, rules and functions, including political ones. We can understand Buen Vivir to be persons living in harmony with themselves, with other people in the community, harmony within the community and between humans and nature.

Reciprocity practices in the Andean and Amazonian regions
There are many examples of economic practices involving reciprocity, solidarity and responses based on social action in the Andean and Amazonian region. Without asserting their transferability or generalizability, the following is a brief list of some forms of economic relations in indigenous communities:

- *Minka* (*minga*): A mutual aid institution in the community setting. It guarantees labor that serves the common good and meets the collective needs and interests of the community, for example, in the execution of projects, such as the construction and maintenance of an irrigation canal or road. It is thus a form of collective work.
- *Ranti-ranti*: Unlike the specific one-off barter economy found in the economic systems of some mestizos, here barter is part of a chain that leads to an endless series of transfers of value, products and work days. This is based on the principle of "giving and taking," without delimiting this to time, actions or space, and is linked to certain ethnic, cultural and historical values in the community.
- *Uyanza*: This is a call for communities to live together and in unity. *Uyanza* also offers the opportunity to thank Mother Earth for her ability to regenerate and provide humans with her produce. It is also an institution of social aid, including families who have made their labor available on loan.
- *Uniguilla*: Bartering to supplement food and useful objects. This enables improved nutrition, with products from other

regions and different ecological niches.

- *Waki*: In a person's absence, his agricultural land is allocated to other communities or families, who cultivate the land. The produce is divided between the two families or communities. This system is also used for animal care and breeding.
- *Makikuna*: A form of support that involves the whole community, extended family, friends and neighbors. It is a type of moral support at the time a family requires it most, particularly in unexpected situations and emergencies.

2. Buen Vivir: Indigenous movements fighting for alternative ways of life

The origins of Buen Vivir

The thoughts surrounding Buen Vivir have only recently entered public discourse, particularly in Ecuador and Bolivia; their emergence can be explained by the battles of indigenous communities, which particularly gained strength at the end of the 20th century. Associated values, experiences, practices and world views in general already existed before the arrival of the European conquistadors. However, they were silenced, marginalized or openly opposed. One should not forget that the good life is not unique to Latin America but has been practiced in many different epochs and regions of Mother Earth.

The best-known linguistic references to the good life take us back to the original languages of Ecuador and Bolivia: in the former, there is "*Buen Vivir*" (Spanish) or "*Sumak Kawsay*" (Kichwa) and in the latter "*Vivir Bien*" (Spanish) or "*Suma Qamaña*" (Aymara), "*Sumak Kawsay*" (Quechua), "Ñande Reko" or "*Tekó Porã*" (Guarani). Similar notions exist in other indigenous cultures, such as those of the Mapuche in Chile, the Guarani in Paraguay, the Kuna in Panama, the Shuar and Achua in the Ecuadorian Amazon, and the Maya in Guatemala and Chiapas (Mexico). The African term *"Ubuntu"* (sense of community) and the Indian *"swaraj"* (radical ecological democracy) are other examples.

This diversity has resulted in numerous movements that further the ideas of the good life. However, one cannot speak of a single good life movement as such. Some groups, despite favoring, defending, articulating and promoting Buen Vivir, do not fly the Buen Vivir flag. Moreover, this is about experiences, values and practices that already exist in different parts of the planet and about gaining strength from different perspectives. There has so far been no effort to organize these processes in a more institutionalized way, in order to avoid rigid dogmatic visions and proposals, which ultimately suffocate the creativity needed to construct *buenos convivires*. In Bolivia and Ecuador, the concept of Buen Vivir has constitutional status, being included in the 2008 Constitution of Ecuador, and the 2009 Constitution of the Plurinational State of Bolivia.

The Ecuadorian constitution contains several fundamental ideas that emerged simultaneously and in a unique way in this small country: for example, the recognition of the rights of nature and of the fundamental right to water, which bans any form of privatization of this essential resource, and the idea of leaving crude oil in the Amazon below ground. The constitution's preamble sets out the aim of building a "new form of public coexistence, in diversity and in harmony with nature, to achieve the good way of living, the *sumak kawsay*."

At the same time, we must be wary of falling into the "trap" of accepting Ecuadorian and Bolivian official propaganda on the good life. At the government level, this concept has been compromised by being ranked below demands for concentrating power and disciplining societies, while capitalism has been modernized.

Buen Vivir in the context of Latin American history

Understanding the good life requires an understanding of the history and current situation of indigenous peoples and nations, fundamentally a process based on the principle of historical continuity. Buen Vivir is part of a long quest for alternative lifestyles, forged by the passionate battles of indigenous peoples and nations. What is remarkable about these alternative proposals is that they come from groups that have long been marginalized, excluded, exploited or even destroyed. Their long-disregarded proposals invite us to break with a number of concepts that have been taken for granted until now.

The proposals of Buen Vivir are gaining traction in a moment of crisis in the Latin American oligarchic national State, which is rooted in colonialism and neoliberalism, thanks to the growing organizational efforts of indigenous and other grassroots movements. The idea of being in harmony with nature, characterizing Buen Vivir, promotes discussion on environmentally friendly alternatives.

The indigenous community in the broadest sense is pursuing a collective project for the future. The utopias of the Andes and the Amazon are currently shaping discourse, political projects and social, cultural and economic practice. This approach should not be exclusionary, however, and should not result in dogmatic visions. It must be expanded with perceptions from other regions of the world, connected to one another spiritually, and potentially also politically, in their fight for a transformation of civilization.

Yasuní-ITT Initiative – on the difficulty of achieving global utopias

In addition to theories regarding large-scale change, there are also concrete examples, even at a global level. The Yasuní-ITT Initiative's proposal to leave oil under the ground in the Ecuadorian Amazon was and remains an excellent example of global action that was started by the civil society of a small country. It should not be forgotten that the Ecuadorian

Amazon region has been impacted by oil extraction for decades. Consequently, many indigenous people living in voluntary isolation have left the extraction regions for the last remaining forest areas. The indigenous population is concentrated and increasing in an ever smaller area that has already lost some of its original biodiversity. This has led to increasing resistance from these groups to oil extraction, which, in turn, has stimulated growing support from other movements in Ecuador and around the world.

In view of the highly complex situation, the Yasuní-ITT initiative has four aims: 1. To protect the land and thus the lives of the indigenous peoples who live in voluntary isolation; 2. To preserve the national park's unique biodiversity (the Yasuní National Park has the highest biodiversity recorded on the planet); 3. To protect the global climate by not exploiting large amounts of crude oil, thus avoiding 410 million tons of CO_2 emissions; 4. To take a first exemplary step toward a post-fossil fuel era in Ecuador.

And that is not all. In addition, there could be a fifth aim: That we humans find concrete solutions to the critical global problems resulting from climate change caused by us, and worsened by the latest period of global capital expansion.

In return for the Yasuní-ITT initiative Ecuador expected a financial contribution from the international community, with other countries, especially the more prosperous societies, taking on their share of the responsibility, depending on the environmental destruction they had caused. This was not conceived as compensation for continuing to act in line with the traditional concept of development (*desarrollismo*). Instead, the payment was meant to be the starting point for the creation of a new scenario in which the severe global imbalances caused by extractivism and economic growth would be stopped and reversed. Unfortunately, the initiative has failed because rich countries have not shouldered their responsibility and Ecuador's government did not respond sufficiently to the revolutionary challenge from civil society.[2]

Nevertheless, one legacy of the initiative should be underlined: The emergence of a strong social movement of young people committed to defending Yasuní, who were well organized and united in their call for a transformation of civilization.

Currently, there are many concrete alternative proposals, not to be discussed here for reasons of space. What is important is that these ideas have spread considerably in recent years, even beyond national borders,[3] and that this dissemination is part of the long and complex emancipation process of humanity.

3. Furthering degrowth's horizons with Buen Vivir

Degrowth in the Global North, post-extractivism in the Global South

We now face the essential challenge of ending the frenzy of economic growth or even achieving degrowth, particularly in the Global North. On a finite planet, there is no room for permanent economic growth. If we continue down this path, we will reach a situation that is no longer environmentally sustainable and is increasingly socially explosive. Overcoming this creed of economic growth, particularly in the Global North, must be accompanied by abandoning extractivism in the Global South. This means that we must develop and pursue post-extractivist strategies.

The relation between these two processes of degrowth and post-extractivism in the global context is obvious: If economies in the North are no longer to grow, demand must fall. In this case, it would no longer make sense for countries in the South to base their economies on exporting raw materials to the North. For this reason, and many others, it is important for poor countries to also take on degrowth in a responsible manner.

However, the convergence of the visions and actions in post-extractivism and degrowth does not mean that poor countries should sacrifice an improvement in their living conditions in order that rich countries continue their unsustainable level of consumption and waste. Not at all.

Criticism of capitalism as a common denominator

The common denominator in these two perspectives is a severe criticism of capitalism, which involves the increasing commercialization of societal fabric and nature. Exponents of both degrowth and Buen Vivir agree that the fundamental problem is the way in which progress, development and economic growth are understood and implemented. Both approaches complement each other conceptually: degrowth is a "missile word," destructive, not constructive, while Buen Vivir is constructive at its core.[4]

A move away from capitalism involves transition through a variety of alternative practices. There are many such non-capitalist practices around the world. These include examples with utopian objectives that call for the harmonious co-existence of humans and the environment, combining the good life with degrowth efforts. This is ultimately about abandoning the failed attempt to pursue production-oriented development as a mechanistic one-way street of economic growth, a global mandate and a straight line. This is a radical change. It is not about implementing examples that have allegedly been successful in industrial countries in the Global South. Firstly, this is impossible. Secondly, these examples have not in reality been successful.[5]

4. Achieving a utopia in the indigenous world

The indigenous world was a victim of the *conquista* and colonization. These exploitative and repressive processes continue to impact the current situation, colonial and capitalist influence still being evident in many different forms, precluding the possibility of a romantic approach to indigenous reality. The good life, as the sum total of practices that oppose colonialism and its consequences, encourages a certain way of life in indigenous communities - particularly in those that have not been absorbed by capitalistic modernity or that have decided to isolate themselves from it. There are also elements of Buen Vivir in communities that have "succumbed" to modernity. Even in regions that are not directly connected to the indigenous world, community lifestyles are being developed that promote harmony among members and with nature.

In politics, or rather, in political decision-making, a different form of governance is being practiced with Buen Vivir at community and *ayllu* level in broad areas of the Andean and Amazonian region with the aim of creating a horizontal society.[6] This requires direct democracy, direct action and self-management instead of new forms of top-down and, even more importantly, an individual "enlightened" leader. With broad and participative debates, a consensus is reached by the community.

A key element here is that the solution is not the State, and even less the market. Rather, another type of State is needed —a plurinational State as proposed by the indigenous movements in Bolivia and Ecuador— which is not hierarchical or authoritarian, and which is controlled from below at the community level.[7] The big question that now arises is how politics can be regained as a dynamic space within society.

Our democracy can learn a lot from these experiences.

Buen Vivir in the urban space

Buen Vivir is not restricted to the countryside, although it originated there. However, today's urban spaces are very far from dealing with the environment respectfully and with solidarity. One of the greatest and most complex challenges is to conceptualize the good life for and in cities.

In this respect, it should not be forgotten that many migrants living in cities maintain close ties to their original communities. One such example can be seen in the groups that have joined forces to [re]construct forms of Buen Vivir in the Bolivian city of El Alto. In other areas of the world, there are also many interesting practices and approaches. An example from the growing number of alternatives is transition towns, the aim of which is to hand over control to communities in order to survive the challenge of climate change and create a post-fossil fuel economy. This movement is active in many countries and has much in common with Buen Vivir.

5. Buen Vivir: An inspirational and diverse approach

Buen Vivir integrates various humanist and anti-utilitarian approaches from different regions (at least in theory). Since the beginning of the 21st century in particular, increasing and diverse protest movements opposing the classical understanding of development have gained momentum. The growing environmental movement should be highlighted here in relation to environmental destruction and the signs of exhaustion in nature.

Buen Vivir approaches from the indigenous Andean and Amazonian region can be combined with other approaches to community life, for example, those of the Zapatistas or Kurds, as well as those of feminist, farming and environmental struggles. They all have many things in common with the flourishing degrowth movement.

The primary lesson is that there is no one true approach. Buen Vivir is not a synthetic, monocultural proposal. Rather, the good life takes on contributions and knowledge from other cultures that question the implications and requirements of the dominant form of modernity. It thus does not reject modern technologies as long as these are compatible with the creation of harmonious community relations with respect for nature. Solidarity with both nature and the community is needed

New ethics are needed to organize life in self-managed community spaces without power relationships. The emerging society should be horizontal, open and non-sectarian. An economy based on these ethics will promote the reproduction of life and not capital, will secure the existence of all creatures and move beyond the current human-focused reality, in which humans are the rulers of the universe, in all its variants.

If we are moving beyond the exploitation of nature for the purpose of accumulating capital, there are even more reasons to stop exploiting human beings. We will have to recognize that human beings are creatures that are not individuals by nature but rather part of a community, and that we are that community. These communities, peoples, nations and countries should live in harmony with one another.

This dual solidarity - with nature and within the community - requires that we take the civilizing step of recognizing applicable human rights and the rights of nature without restrictions.

Translation: Anonymous

Endnotes

1 Kothari et al., 2015.

2 Acosta, 2014.

3 The following examples should be highlighted among many others: In Ecuador, the different groups who joined forces in the Unidad Plurinacional de Izquierdas (Plurinational Unity of Left Wing Groups) proposed a governmental plan on the basis of Buen Vivir or Sumak Kawsay. See Acosta, 2013; and the program *RAIZ – Movimiento Cidadanista* in Brazil, 2016, available at www.raiz.org.br (Accessed 31 January 2019).

4 Unceta, 2014.

5 Tortosa, 2011.

6 *Ayllu* refers to the entirety of families by blood or by marriage.

7 Bolivia has not come far in this regard, and Ecuador even

less so.

Links

Buen Vivir at Beautiful Solutions: solutions.thischangeseverything.org/module/buen-vivir

Video on Buen Vivir: degrowth.info/en/dim/degrowth-in-movements/buen-vivir

Literature

Acosta, A. (2009) *La maldición de la abundancia,* Quito, Abya-Yala.

Acosta, A. (2014) *Iniciativa Yasuní-ITT – La difícil construcción de la utopía.* Available at rebelion.org/noticia.php?id=180285 (Accessed 30 January 2019).

D'Alisa, G., Demaria, F., and Kallis, G. (eds.) (2014) *Degrowth: A Vocabulary for a New Era,* London, Routledge.

Gudynas, E. (2015) *Extractivismos – Ecología, economía y política de un modo de entender el desarrollo y la Naturaleza,* La Paz, CLAES/CEDIB.

Kothari, A., Demaria, F., Acosta, A. (2015) "Buen Vivir, Degrowth and Ecological Swaraj: Alternatives to Sustainable Development and the Green Economy," *Development* vol. 57, no. 3, pp. 362-375.

Schuldt, J. (2005) *¿Somos pobres porque somos ricos? Recursos naturales, tecnología y globalización,* Lima, Fondo Editorial del Congreso del Perú.

Taibo, C. (2015) ¿Tomar el poder o construir sociedad desde abajo? Un manual para asaltar los infiernos, Madrid, Catarata.

Tortosa, J. M. (2011) *Mal desarrollo y mal vivir – Pobreza y violencia escala mundial,* Quito, Abya-Yala.

Unceta, K. (2014) *Desarrollo, postcrecimiento y Buen Vivir,* Quito: Abya-Yala. Available at rosalux.org.ec/producto/desarrollo-postcrecimiento-y-buen-vivir (Accessed 30 January 2019).

Chapter 6

Moved care revolutionaries (Image: Netzwerk Care Revolution)

Care Revolution: Care Work – the core of the Economy

Matthias Neumann and Gabriele Winker

Gabriele and Matthias are writing as activists in the German-based Care Revolution Network, which they have been involved in since 2014, including as members of the Freiburg regional group. The views and opinions expressed in this article are theirs. Gabriele is the author of the book *Care Revolution. Schritte in eine solidarische Gesellschaft* (Care Revolution. Steps towards a society based on solidarity) and is Professor of Sociology of Work and Gender Studies at the Hamburg University of Technology. Matthias is a supermarket employee and political scientist.

1. Care Revolution wants to shape care and self-care according to needs with a fundamental change in societal direction

Care Revolution activists are working for a good life in which all people's needs can be met in full without excluding anyone or exploiting others. Building on insights from feminist politics, Care Revolution puts the fundamental significance of care work at the core of its social critical analysis and political action. From birth, people are dependent on the care of others, without which they could not survive. Beyond childhood and youth, and times of sickness and frailty, people are also dependent on others in their everyday lives. The possibility of getting help and support in a difficult situation is an important criterion for a good life. This also applies to the possibility of being able to care for others without having to be disproportionately disadvantaged.

Care work is an activity that all people carry out. They care for themselves, for their health, for their education, they cook for themselves or for other people, bring up children, advise friends, and care for relatives who need support. Some care work is paid, for example, that carried out by carers or nursery school teachers. Most of this work, however, is done within families by women and is unpaid; often it is not considered to be work at all.

Currently in Western Europe as in other industrialized countries, more and more people face the increasingly difficult task of mastering the balancing act between employment and unpaid care work for themselves and others. They live with the constant threat of failing to meet demands. In their employment, they are confronted with increasing demands on flexibility from the company, continually rising performance pressure, as well as salaries, which are often too low compared to the cost of living. According to the neoliberal credo of individual responsibility, each individual is required to combine high professional requirements with increasing self-organization tasks and the growing demands of familial care work.

This situation is aggravated by the fact that, in order to reduce costs, many state welfare services, for example, in the health or education system, are being cut rather than expanded. It is primarily many women who suffer in this deficient state infrastructure as they carry out most of the socially necessary care work in the home alongside their paid employment. In high-earning families, part of this work is passed on to poorly paid migrant domestic workers who do not have social security. In this way, high earners solve their problems on the backs of those for whom even this precarious work means an improvement to their catastrophic position. State tolerance of these working conditions in private households, which fall below societal minimum standards, is aggravating a global division of labor that ignores the basic needs of care workers from countries in Eastern Europe and the Global South.

Care Revolution as a political strategy

The obvious response that meets needs is to organize and carry out the work needed in families and institutions together and without discrimination. For those in the Care Revolution network, attending to people's needs, space for empathy and solidarity, as well as genuine democracy in politics and the economy are essential. With the following steps, it is possible to come closer to the aim of good care and a good life:

- Sufficient income for all in order to secure a sustainable livelihood: This primarily means a substantial minimum wage without exceptions, an unconditional basic income and a significant improvement in pay for work in care careers.
- Sufficient time to be able to care for one's close ones and oneself alongside paid employment, and maintain time for leisure. This primarily means a considerable reduction in working hours for full-time workers, special arrangements

for people with a lot of care responsibilities, and a non-discriminatory division of care work between men and women.

- A social infrastructure that truly supports care and self-care: This primarily means an expanded and free education and health system, affordable accommodation, free local public transport and support for self-help networks and commons projects. This can be realized by redistributing societal wealth.
- Real involvement in societal decision-making: This means comprehensive self-governance, starting in the care sector. This can be effected via a council system that enables national coordination and democratic control. Many care projects, such as health centers, nurseries or educational establishments can also be organized decentrally with local self-governance in districts or neighborhoods.
- Non-discriminatory society: This means that there is no exclusion, no discrimination and no privileges owing to one's ethnic origin, nationality, gender, sexual orientation, physical ability or occupational skills.

Care Revolution's aim is a society based on solidarity. Those in the Care Revolution network understand this to be a radically democratic society, oriented towards human needs and, in particular, towards caring for one another. In a society based on solidarity, the needs of all people in their diversity are met, without people from other global regions being discriminated against. Correspondingly, Care Revolution means that it is no longer profit maximization but human needs that are the focus of social, and thus also economic action.

2. *Care Revolution network* actors call for more time and resources for paid and unpaid care work

In the *Care Revolution network* there are initiatives from different areas of society and with different political priorities. These include organizations of caregiving relatives, disability groups, parent groups, migrant groups, *ver.di* and *GEW* trade union site groups in the field of care and childcare, social movement organizations, queer feminist groups and radical left-wing groups. In March 2014, sixty such initiatives came together in Berlin for the first time to prepare and hold a conference, which 500 people attended. Shortly after this, these and other initiatives founded the *Care Revolution network*. Currently, the network is limited to Germany, Switzerland and Austria. Therefore, the problems it tackles and the struggles it is involved in are those of capitalist countries in the Global North. Racism and the global division of labor are important to us, if we are concerned, for example, with the situation of migrant live-in nurses or global care chains. But our viewpoint is affected by who we are and where we live. So, later on, we hope to learn in cooperation with political movements in other countries. At the moment, we are not there yet.

Examples of groups represented in the network

A significant proportion of the initiatives represented by *Care Revolution* come from a feminist or queer feminist background. Some have fought since the 1970s, as part of the second wave of feminism, for a revaluation of unpaid reproductive work. Today, older and younger activists in the Care Revolution network again want to comprehend the feminist agenda as a more general form of social criticism, including through their struggles for improved care resources. Here, priorities are quite varied. Some highlight the gender gap in care work and demand recognition of this socially necessary work. Others are active in groups that combine anti-capitalist and feminist positions and discuss their own life circumstances in relation to structural crises. The latter involved Care Revolution in the Blockupy protests.

Women in Exile, which also participated in the first *Care*

Revolution conference, calls for refugees to be housed in apartments rather than in camps where there is no privacy or protection against attacks. The initiative is demanding this for women and children as a matter of urgency but also calls for all camps to be dissolved. The initiative combines its public relations activities for this aim with informing refugees about their rights, and positions against racism and the migration regime.

In recent years, labor disputes regarding paid care work have made the headlines. These disputes have been innovative in various ways. For example, the *ver.di* site group and the staff council at Charité – Universitätsmedizin Berlin demanded a collective agreement regarding minimum employee coverage from the company that operates Berlin's university hospitals. This labor dispute was supported by the association *Berlinerinnen und Berliner für mehr Personal im Krankenhaus* (Berlin Residents for More Hospital staff) with actions to demonstrate solidarity; it did this explicitly in the interests of potential patients. On 1 May 2016, this collective agreement was achieved after over four years of disputes. A second example are the disputes in German municipal nurseries. In the 2015 strikes, there were calls for a societal revaluation of care work in nurseries and social services, as well as an increase in pay to reflect this. There were increased and partially successful efforts to gain parents as allies for this cause.

There are also labor-managed companies that support Care Revolution's ideas. One example are the carers at *Lossetal care center,* which is a working part of the *Niederkaufungen commune.* Other members of the commune, neighbors and relatives are involved as much as possible in the care facilities for care-dependent individuals and people with dementia in particular. This should improve quality of care. It is also an expression of the social objective that people in neighborhoods should provide each other with mutual support. The care center complements this with the required professional input.

In familial care work, the initiative *Armut durch Pflege* (Poverty Through Care) can be mentioned. This initiative created the association *Wir pflegen – Interessenvertretung begleitender Angehöriger und Freunde in Deutschland* (We Care – Interest Representation for Accompanying Relatives and Friends in Germany). The aim of the initiative is to give a voice to those affected by difficult situations and their demands, and to bring about material improvements for relatives who are carers, for example, through a substantial care allowance. As such, the association's demands also relate to the human dignity of the people being cared for, which should not be dependent on their ability to pay. The organization *Nicos Farm* pursues the same aims by different means: Children and young people who are dependent on lifelong care owing to a disability should also be able to have a dignified life if their parents themselves are in need of care or are deceased. The organization aims to implement a project involving accommodation, employment opportunities and therapy at Lüneburger Heide in Germany.

Framework conditions for joint action

The *Care Revolution conference* in March 2014 was a moment where mutual interest, as well as the different needs and difficult situations were as evident as the desire for a joint explanation regarding the social suffering experienced. At the conference, the widespread weakness in the implementation of the individual initiatives became evident, as did the reasons for this: because no economic pressure can be established in that kind of care work, because the work is frequently carried out by isolated individuals, and because, in neoliberal discourse, completing care tasks is the responsibility of the individual. Above all, the conference underlined a desire to address these issues through joint action.

Cooperation between the different initiatives is not easy: There are real, varied struggles and alternative projects on care work. There is recognition of the similarities between them and the desire to support one another. However, individual, often existential battles are necessarily at the heart of the initiatives' work. Activists' lack of flexibility due to care responsibilities, precarious living conditions, and lack of time and money further impede joint action. Additionally, there is still a lack of experience of joint action actually resulting in more success. All of this is currently preventing Care Revolution from gaining more of a public presence.

3. Care Revolution and degrowth can fight for a society based on solidarity together

In terms of content, we see an important link between Care Revolution and degrowth in the fact that both concepts relate to prospects for a good life. This also applies, as far as we can judge, to the other movements that are represented by and brought together under the *Degrowth in Movement(s)* banner.

At first glance, there appears to be a fundamental contradiction in that degrowth places emphasis on "less": It is about combining less use of resources with a good life for all where everyone's needs are met. In this scenario, a necessary decrease in economic growth should not be a threat to standards of living but rather represent an opportunity. In contrast, Care Revolution is ultimately seeking more: More time, a more supportive social infrastructure and more material security are unavoidable prerequisites for an improvement in the position of care workers. For the health, care, education and childcare sectors, it is also about more employees and higher wages.

It gets politically interesting when these two aims are combined: less use of resources by society and more care resources. Then this is about reducing all areas that are destructive to humans and the ecological foundations of human life. Examples include armaments manufacturing, coal power stations or the current structure of individual transport. At the same time, it is about growing specific areas that are necessary for self-care and care for one another and creating the conditions for this. It is about developing concepts for how a reduction in soil sealing can be combined with an expansion of nurseries, how a reduction in the consumption of consumer goods can be combined with more material security and support for relatives who are carers, how more employees in healthcare and education can be combined with a societal reduction in working hours. In general, it means thinking about how a society can be structured to meet people's care needs and preserve the ecological foundations for human life at the same time.

We believe that bringing together degrowth and Care Revolution is worthwhile because of the parallels between the two concepts. Both make one uncompromising demand of a desirable society: It must make a good life possible for all people globally and for subsequent generations. This premise brings with it the idea that a society that cannot guarantee this should be changed. Against this backdrop, degrowth and Care Revolution can meet precisely where they both place a pointed emphasis on anti-capitalism. For the degrowth approach, there is the central idea that an increase in the efficiency of energy and resource usage is not enough to sufficiently reduce consumption. Not only must production processes change but the production scope and the way one uses consumer goods must too. Mobility, access to washing machines, tools or libraries, as well as the use of gardens, will have to be much more collectively managed in order to enable access for all. If successful, such a transformed economy would not mean a sacrifice, but would mean having other, richer social relations. This equally positive reference to the interdependence of human beings is very similar to Care Revolution's thinking on care and care work. To be dependent on one another is a fundamental part of human life. As such, it is also immensely important to focus on human collaboration and solidarity in political actions and in the development of societal alternatives.

A joint effort with other movements is an especially attractive notion, as is fighting together. Both Care Revolution and degrowth can identify with the topic of "a society based on solidarity, a life based on solidarity," which touches on the need for changes in societal institutions as well as changes in one's own lifestyle. Both analyze the destruction of the human being as a social being and ecosystems in capitalism and contrast this with the principles of a society based on solidarity. As such, both are anti-capitalist projects at their core. If this is true, then both movements also pose questions about social transformation: How do individual struggles, experiments and political changes intensify to the point that an alternative to capitalism, based on solidarity, becomes reality? We consider the search for transformation strategies to be part of a joint project for needs-oriented social movements.

4. Care Revolution's strength is that very heterogeneous initiatives are calling for comprehensive social change together

One strength of the initiatives under the Care Revolution banner is their heterogeneity, as the topic of care speaks directly to people from different backgrounds with different political ideas, life concepts and desires. At the first conference in March 2014, it was impressive to see how this diversity was combined with mutual respect and curiosity.

We believe this relates to the fact that care has reference points in all social and political settings. Care addresses vital needs, which underlines the absurdity of wanting to treat, teach, advise or care for people according to the principle of maximum profit. People with different life experiences and different life situations are coming to the conclusion that society must be entirely redesigned, at least with regard to care. It is relatively easy to imagine alternatives in care as the necessary social infrastructure can largely be realized decentrally, in local districts or villages.

Nurseries, healthcare establishments and social centers can be organized with forms of direct democracy. All those directly affected by negotiations regarding care institutions can be involved. This is primarily possible because care workers of different kinds are meeting on a level playing field: both those for whom care is a career, and those who are involved in care within families or self-care. They can meet each other as experts who are pursuing the same aim of organizing care well with different skills and interests. Experiences in the care sector and in struggles for better care conditions can also make comprehensive socialization, which goes beyond the care sector, appear more realistic and more desirable. Freeing all areas of production and how we live together from the framework of valorization and market competition is also a condition for protecting the ecological foundations of life.

With regard to commons projects, we believe Care Revolution activists can learn a lot from movement approaches such as those who participate within the *Degrowth in Movement(s)* project. Unlike in the care sector where initial efforts are being made, there are already multiple projects there, where people are jointly developing and living out part of a more liveable future on a small scale. We are thinking here of community repairs, fab labs (public workshops equipped with 3D printers), communal gardens or the many projects in community-supported agriculture.

5. Needs-oriented movements can develop a liveable alternative to capitalism together where they combine their alternative projects and transformation strategies

The different movements and practices under the *Degrowth in Movement(s)* banner have certain features in common: The centrality of human needs, attentiveness to life in general, the importance of real social relationships and fair social framework conditions make up a shared core, with quite different emphases. From this core, the consequences of capitalist development, which destroy the ecosystem as much as human beings as social creatures, may be criticized. Projects promoting a life based on solidarity can be brought together in discussion and in practice. Individual efforts can be linked and societal alternatives developed.

Strengthening these links to one another is perhaps what is most urgent. This involves the different movements developing a liveable alternative to capitalism through exchanging ideas. It is also about them finding a shared focus in their projects and in their solidarity-based lifestyle. If this is successful, the movements can achieve something together that each individual cannot.

Partial movements also have something to contribute. For example, if migrants are caring for people at home in miserable working conditions, this creates an opportunity for a needs-oriented movement based on solidarity with different reference points: the right of the person requiring care to be well cared for, the right of the relatives to not be solely responsible for care, the rights of the migrant carers to good working conditions and good pay, the rights of the migrants' children or relatives and the people in their home countries who care for them. It is necessary to account for all these justified demands, which affect the care system here, as well as the unfair distribution of work globally. If movements focusing on migration, care or the global division of labor work closely together, they can support each other with a comprehensive overview of the situation.

Redesigning towns and villages based on solidarity also requires joint action. Organizing a collective social infrastructure in districts entails removing the care sector from valorization. Communal gardens require free access to land. Experiments in co-living, shared repair workshops, community kitchens or policlinics should not be restricted or impeded by the fact that their rental payments have to generate sufficient returns. Reducing private car use requires a correspondingly developed local transport network and thoughts on how urban sprawl and the spatial separation of housing and paid work can be addressed. By bringing together the many individual projects, a new, more strongly contoured image of liveable towns could emerge; discussing necessary conditions should enable us to determine more clearly how a societal alternative could function. By the very different activists from different individual movements meeting and becoming politically active together, they can support each other in thinking of and practicing alternatives without old and new exclusions.

Translation: Anonymous

Links

Care Revolution homepage: care-revolution.org

Text on Care Revolution in English: transform-network.net/en/publications/yearbook/overview/article/yearbook-2016/care-revolution-a-feminist-marxist-transformation-strategy-from-the-perspective-of-caring-for-each

Video documentation of Care Revolution action conference in Berlin in 2014: youtube.com/watch?v=C3k_kjLqVCU

Literature

Biesecker, A., Wichterich, C., Winterfeld, U. v. (2012) *Feministische Perspektiven zum Themenbereich Wachstum, Wohlstand, Lebensqualität*, Berlin, Rosa-Luxemburg-Stiftung. Available at rosalux.de/publikation/id/6177/femi nistische-perspektiven-zum-themenbereich-wachstum-wohlstand-lebensqualitaet (Accessed 30 January 2019).

Fried, B., Schurian, H. (eds.) (2015) *Um-Care. Gesundheit und Pflege neu organisieren*, Berlin, Rosa-Luxemburg-Stiftung. Available at rosalux.de/publikation/id/8432/um-care (Accessed 30 January 2019).

Praetorius, I. (2015) *The Care-Centered Economy. Rediscovering what has been taken for granted*. Berlin, Heinrich-Böll-Stiftung. Available at: boell.de/en/2015/04/07/care-centered-economy (Accessed 30 January 2019).

Winker, G. (2015) *Care Revolution. Schritte in eine solidarische Gesellschaft*, Bielefeld, Transcript.

Winker, G. (2018) "Care Revolution. Interview by Brigitte Aulenbacher and Birgit Riegraf," *Equalitiy, Diversity and Inclusion*, vol. 37, no 4, pp. 420-428.

Chapter 7

2014 People's Climate March NYC, (Image: Stephen Melkisethian)

Climate Justice: Global Resistance to Fossil-Fueled Capitalism

Tadzio Müller

Tadzio has been involved in the climate justice movement for a decade and was active in the alterglobalization movement before that. As an activist, his main area of focus is the organization of mass civil disobedience, for example, the successful *Ende Gelände* protests against lignite coal mining. He currently works as an expert on climate justice and energy democracy at the Rosa Luxemburg Foundation in Berlin.

1. We are not all in the same boat: The climate crisis as a crisis of justice

What is climate change about? First and foremost, justice! The best symbol for this process is not the sad polar bear, but New Orleans destroyed by Hurricane Katrina in 2005. There, the majority of the wealthy *white* population succeeded in fleeing from the floods and the ensuing chaos, because they (for the most part) owned their own cars, which they could use to leave the city. The mostly poor black population largely remained behind, and was subjected to the government's incompetent and repressive disaster management for several weeks. Burned into our minds are images of African-Americans standing on rooftops, signaling to the helicopters flying over the city that they need help – and yet being wantonly ignored.

We often think of ourselves as being all in the proverbial "same boat." Unfortunately, this is not true. If we are all in the same boat – let's say, the (space)ship Earth – then there are several classes on this ship, and in the event of an accident, the lower decks are flooded first. And just like on the *Titanic*, there are lifeboats available for those who can afford them. Another example is rising sea levels. They are rising for everyone, but in Bangladesh people are being flooded, while in Holland floating cities are being built with resources accumulated there while using the global environment as a dump, all without a second thought.

In summary: On average, those who have contributed least to climate change suffer the most, while those who have contributed most suffer the least. The latter usually have sufficient resources to protect themselves from the effects of climate change. They have accumulated these resources, this wealth, precisely through those activities that have driven climate change. This central fact, which, by the way, applies to almost all so-called "environmental crises," is perhaps best described as "climate injustice." That is why the call for mere climate protection does not go far enough. What we need is *climate justice.*

2. From the environmental justice movement to the climate justice movement

In order to understand the demands and requirements of the climate justice movement, it is worth taking a look at the history of social struggles, in particular the emergence of the environmental movement in the USA in the 1960s, which was first and foremost a movement of the *white* middle class for the *white* middle class. It originated in relatively privileged "white" city districts and towns, and fought to keep these communities free from air pollution and to prevent the inhabitants' children from being poisoned by chemical plants and power plants. As understandable as these demands were, they had a regrettable effect. Instead of such plants being closed down, they were simply moved; from the richer communities to the poorer ones, populated mostly by African Americans, Hispanics, Native Americans and other marginalized groups. The struggles of the liberal environmental movement did not lead to the solution of the problems they had criticized – instead, they were simply shifted a few steps further down the ladder of social power.

Resistance to environmental and climate racism

The communities of color, suddenly oppressed by a whole range of polluting industries, did not merely become passive victims. Instead, they organized themselves, accused the environmental movement of "environmental racism," and began their own movement for environmental justice. Analytically, this means: If apparent environmental problems are not seen as social problems, if there is no awareness of how a single polluting factory is embedded in broader social structures of domination and exploitation, not only are these problems impossible to solve, but existing social inequalities will be exacerbated.

In the 1980s, as the debate on climate change began to gain momentum, the idea developed that the problem was above all *technical* – that the concentration of greenhouse gases in the atmosphere had to be reduced and eliminated through certain mechanisms. In the 1990s, this in turn facilitated the development of so-called market mechanisms to combat climate change. Without opening up the entire critical debate on these impressively ineffective environmental policy tools, they are based on a technical logic that does not take social structures into account; i.e. that because every CO_2 particle is the same, it does not matter who saves CO_2 where and under what conditions.[1]

In economic terms, it is actually best to save CO_2 where it is cheapest, and that is easiest in the Global South, where everything is cheaper on average. So, we could give money to development aid organizations to protect forests from deforestation, in order to protect the climate, while we in the Global North continue to burn fossil fuels. However, this idea has a huge catch: the forests which were suddenly to be saved from excessive deforestation were often home to indigenous peoples who have excelled at sustainable forest management for thousands of years. And these peoples were threatened by expulsion from their ancestral lands, so-called "green grabbing" through the market mechanisms negotiated in the 1990s as part of the Kyoto Protocol. In the context of these negotiations, the story of environmental justice was once more taken up. In response to the "climate racism" of official climate policy, American activist for indigenous peoples and founder of the *Indigenous Environmental Network* Tom Goldtooth, who himself comes from the environmental justice movements, for the first time formulated the demand for climate justice. Thus began the fight to construct climate change as a question of human rights and justice.

The next step in the development of the climate justice narrative was the publication of the Greenhouse Gangsters vs. Climate Justice report.[2] The report focused on fossil fuel energy companies; and instead of suggesting solutions at the individual level (for example, ethical consumption), it focused on major structural transformations. In addition, the struggle for climate justice was quite explicitly described as a global struggle. The report also put forward the movement's most important policy framework to date, namely a critique of the Kyoto Protocol's market mechanisms as "false solutions."

A global movement for climate justice is created

In Bali in 2002, the organizations that would later become the core of the movement, and articulate the Bali Principles of Climate Justice, met for the first time. In 2004, several groups and networks which had long been working on a critique of market mechanisms in general, and emissions trading in particular, came together in Durban in South Africa and founded the *Durban Group for Climate Justice*. The final breakthrough came at the 13th Climate Change Conference in Bali in 2007. The aforementioned network of critical organizations provoked an open conflict with the politically more moderate *Climate Action Network*, whose cozy lobbying strategy had been shown to be something of a flop. One result of this conflict was the founding of the *Climate Justice Now!* network in 2007. The press release announcing the formation of this new actor articulated a number of claims which still apply to the climate justice movement today. Later translated into a sort of founding manifesto, the press release demanded:

- that fossil fuels be left in the ground, and replaced with investment in suitable, safe, clean and democratic renewable energies;
- the drastic reduction of wasteful overconsumption, especially in the Global North, but also in terms of southern elites;
- a massive transfer of funds from North to South, under democratic control, based on the repayment of climate debt (. . .);
- resource conservation based on human rights and enforced under indigenous land rights, with control of energy, forests, land and water driven by these communities;
- sustainable, small-scale farming and food sovereignty.

To achieve these goals, the movement has made use of a wide range of instruments, from the publication of clever reports and day-to-day political work in communities particularly affected by climate change, through civil disobedience (for example, coal mine blockades), to the militant struggles of the Ogoni in the Niger Delta.

In summary: the climate justice movement is a descendant of the environmental justice movement. Like the environmental justice movement, the climate justice movement originated in the Global South (see below), and aims to focus less on technical change and more on basic social structures. I would venture the following definition: Climate justice is not so much a state of affairs – e.g. the fair distribution of the costs of a potential solution to the climate crisis – but more a process, namely the process of struggling against the social structures which cause climate injustice.

If we heed this broad definition, we can even say that many of the struggles for climate justice are not necessarily being fought under the banner of climate justice, but are represented as struggles for land, water, and other basic needs and human rights.

USA: Indigenous peoples and communities of color as supporters of resistance

The fact that the climate justice movement arose in the US also structures the way that the project's social base is viewed. On average, alleged "environmental problems" hit the most socially vulnerable the hardest. In the US, this usually means the communities of color, among which Native American communities are once again generally the most marginalized. The groups designated in the USA and Canada as First Nations see themselves as part of a global indigenous network which is most affected by environmental disasters. In addition to this, they live (on average) in places where the highest biodiversity is concentrated, and their socio-ecological practices —for example, forest use— are highly sustainable. Our survival may also depend on them, as learning from them could mean learning real sustainability. This is why so-called "frontline communities" or "affected communities" (often indigenous communities) are the main supporters of the resistance, the famous "revolutionary subject" of the climate justice movement.

These "frontline communities," often communities of color in the USA, thus join forces with typically white and/or otherwise privileged "allies."[3] With regard to these activists, we tend to find the social milieus we have been expecting in this part of the world since the emergence of the so-called "new social movements" from 1968 onwards: younger, more mobile, better educated, and often slightly more "alternative" than the social average.

The view of Europe: The role of allies, and differences from the environmental movement

The European wing of the movement, which does not have the US's tradition of environmental justice struggles to fall back on, and which is dealing with different social structures, is significantly more represented by the *white* and privileged than the movement in the US. This is quite logical to a certain extent: in the Global North, there are simply fewer affected groups or "frontline communities" —with a handful of exceptions, such as the villages in the Lusatia region and the Rhineland which still fall victim to the madness of lignite mines. Most of us act, globally speaking, in the role of allies.

In Europe, the climate justice movement differs from the broader environmental movement in two main elements: firstly, through its conceptual anti-capitalism, including a clear rejection of all varieties of green capitalism (green market economy); and secondly, through its focus on the tactics of civil disobedience (often mass civil disobedience) and deliberate rule-breaking, in contrast to the more legalistic tactics of traditional environmental organizations. Examples of this type of climate activism in the

Global North are the civil disobedience campaigns at the climate summits in Copenhagen (2009) and Paris (2015), but above all sit-ins and blockades of coal power plants and coal mines, airports and other places where climate change is generated. Of the above-mentioned key demands made by the climate justice movement, the central one is: "Leave it in the ground!" – fossil fuels must be left in the ground!

3. Climate justice and degrowth: United against fossil capital!

There is a positive, fairly close relationship between the climate justice movement and the degrowth movement, something which should come as no surprise to anyone after the Degrowth Summer School at the Rhineland Climate Camp in 2015. The reason for this is obvious: they have a common enemy, namely the fossil fuel-based energy system.

On the side of the climate justice movement, the argument is quite clear: Climate change, as explained above, is a deeply unjust phenomenon. Behind this are a number of social structures, but the key driver of climate change is an energy system that has been based on fossil fuels since the Industrial Revolution. After the COP21 climate summit in Copenhagen in 2009 demonstrated to the climate change movement and its more radical climate justice wing that little should be expected from "the powers that be" in the fight against fossil fuels, they began to focus on local and national energy struggles.[4] The core of the climate (justice) movement now consists of fighting for a rapid phasing out of fossil fuels, opposing fracking and the development of gas infrastructure, and campaigning for the development of democratically controlled, largely decentralized renewable energies.

From the perspective of degrowth, the argument is a little more complicated, since there is a wide range of political positions within the degrowth spectrum, some of which are more critical of capitalism than others, and some of which concern themselves with environmental issues to a greater or lesser extent. Nevertheless, Eversberg and Schmelzer describe degrowth as having a perspective of transformation which is predominantly "critical of capitalism," and which has abandoned the idea that sustainable development is possible in the context of a capitalist economy.[5] Although there are also non-ecological reasons to be interested in the topic of degrowth, it appears that many people become involved with the issue due to the constantly escalating socio-ecological crises with which we have been confronted in recent years.

And so we come to the crux of the matter: If the post-growth movement is first and foremost about the destruction of our natural resources, then it also has to be about capitalism, because capitalism has an in-built microeconomic compulsion towards infinite growth. The growth dynamics of capitalist production are not explained through oft-cited metrics such as gross domestic product, but through the microeconomic behavior of individual companies, which are driven by market forces to invest money today in order to make more money tomorrow – companies that don't achieve this don't survive. If this is not mere speculation, then the result is the following correlation: money => commodity production => consumption => more money, followed by the re-investment of at least part of this money. Or in summary: M => C => M′. This microeconomic equation represents the general formula for capital, and it expresses the compulsion to act felt by each businessperson every day. From an ecological point of view, this means that this necessary additional daily profit must come from somewhere "in nature." If every day more workers convert more raw materials into commodities by using more energy, then M => C => M′ also means a continuous rise in global resource consumption. This is the nature of capitalism.

And capitalism would not have developed in this way, perhaps would never have arisen at all, if it had not entered into a quasi-symbiotic relationship with fossil fuels (coal at that time) in 18th century England. I do not believe that a form of capitalism based on renewable energies is impossible, but the capitalism which exists today, and which has already passed several "environmental limits," could never have existed without fossil fuels. Whether we speak of fossil capital or fossil-fueled capitalism, capitalism is the root of our global need for growth, and its motor runs on fossil fuels – precisely those fossil fuels which are also driving climate change.

4. Better together: The weaknesses of one are the strengths of the other

Accordingly, the climate justice movement can provide the degrowth movement with something that the latter occasionally lacks: a common, antagonistically structured field of practice. This has nothing to do with the now somewhat tedious question of whether degrowth is a movement or not, given that it has no identifiable opponents. I accept the argument of Eversberg and Schmelzer that the target of the degrowth movement is not a single sector or institution or external process, but the "imperial mode of living" as a whole, which we in the Global North have —at least to a certain extent— internalized. This is not about the academic definition of a movement, which is ultimately irrelevant anyway, but about the motivation of the people involved, and the need to create conflicts so that the movement can develop transformative potential beyond articles in the culture section and niche day-to-day living practices. In 2015, the *Ende Gelände* campaign brought more than 1,000 people together (and over 4,000 people in 2016!) in an act of mass civil disobedience, namely the peaceful occupation of a lignite mine. This action created a conflict which the campaign then won, thus generating an enormous sense of collective empowerment (The Laboratory of Insurrectionary Imagination 2015). It is this collective empowerment that enables the creation of a type of antagonistic identity construction, without which major social transformation is almost certainly impossible.

In turn, the degrowth movement can offer the climate justice movement something that it lacks: a narrative that will have strong appeal in parts of Europe and the Global North. *Exhibit 1:* The fourth Degrowth Conference succeeded in gathering together approximately 3,000 people in Leipzig, while no other social movement I am aware of can muster more than 2,000 (even in Berlin); I would hazard that a conference on climate justice would find it difficult to attract even 1,000 participants. Doubtless this success is in part due to the amazing work of the organizers. But it is also an indicator that the degrowth narrative is attractive to more than just the "usual suspects" who attend social movement events. (This impression is reinforced by the fact that many of the participants had never been to a social movement conference before.) *Exhibit 2:* The culturally important (albeit politically somewhat irrelevant) German parliamentary commission of inquiry on "Growth, Prosperity, Quality of Life" from 2011 to 2013 shows that criticism of growth has even "infected" conservative and liberal cultural milieus. *Exhibit 3* (from my own experience): When I try to convince my conservative grandfather of the climate justice narrative, and of the fact that the wealth we have accumulated in the Global North is —in reality— a great debt that we should return to the Global South, he usually ignores me. When I present him with perhaps the central point of degrowth reasoning, namely that you cannot have infinite growth on a finite planet, he is forced to agree. On this basis, we can then start a conversation critiquing capitalism. In this story, my grandfather is representative of many people in the Global North who have little interest in "climate justice," but who share the unease that the degrowth movement is able to formulate.

5. Strategy, strategy, strategy!

Politically speaking, the climate justice movement reached a new peak in May 2016. In the second round of *Ende Gelände*, this time held as part of a global campaign entitled *Break Free from Fossil Fuels*, which led actions against fossil fuels and in favor of energy democracy on five continents, we achieved a number of significant successes. By gathering together approximately 4,000 participants in a highly tactical and strategic act of civil disobedience in the field of climate action, we have set new standards; the level of international participation in the act itself, and the international coordination of the act in the context of the Break Free campaign are reminiscent of the degree of internationalization which made the alterglobalization movement so inspiring. More important, however, is the fact that this time we did not remain in the coal mine; instead we reacted to the tactical and political retreat of our opposition from the pit (Vattenfall and the Brandenburg Ministry of Interior) by playing off our political and moral strength and setting up the blockade on the tracks. "On the tracks" here refers to the railway tracks in the Lusatia region that supply the coal-fired Schwarze Pumpe (Black Pump) power station with lignite from three opencast mines. This rail blockade was of prime importance because we in the Global North do more damage to the planet through expanding our industrial and service sectors than through primary resource extraction (such as lignite mining): this primarily refers to power plants, factories and server farms, not to gold mines and coal mines.

Why am I writing about this at the end of this text? Because this time something happened that very rarely happens in the social movements that I have experienced: They assessed their own strength realistically, and developed tactics and strategies which related this strength realistically to the scale of the challenge. So if I could articulate a wish to both movements (a somewhat strange task, I might add, as for me the two are not unrelated), it would be: Let us plan strategically, let us act wisely, and not merely expressively, because we are few, with scarce resources, and we have an enormous task ahead of us (the abolition of capitalism, saving the climate etc. . . .). Consequently: strategy, strategy, strategy. Without strategy, it's all bullshit.

Translation: Kate Bell

Endnotes

1 Moreno et al., 2015.

2 Bruno et. al., 1999.

3 Moore and Kahn-Russel, 2010.

4 Brand et al., 2018.

5 Eversberg and Schmelzer, 2018.

Links

Ende Gelände: ende-gelaende.org/en

Climate Justice at the Rosa-Luxemburg-Stiftung: rosalux.de/en/dossiers/climate-justice

Beautiful Trouble – A Toolbox for Revolution: beautifultrouble.org

Literature

Brand, U., Bullard, N., Lander, E., Mueller, T. (2018) "Contours of Climate Justice: Ideas for shaping a new climate and energy politics," Special issue of *Critical Currents*, vol. 6, no. 9. Available at tni.org/files/download/contoursofclimatejustice.pdf (Accessed 30 January 2019).

Bruno, K., Karliner, J., Brotsky, C. (1999) *Greenhouse Gangsters vs. Climate Justice*, San Francisco, Transnational Resource and Action Center. Available at corpwatch.org/sites/default/files/Greenhouse%20Gangsters.pdf (Accessed 30 January 2019).

Eggers, D. (2011) *Zeitoun*, London, Penguin Books.

Eversberg, D., and Schmelzer, M. (2018) "The Degrowth Spectrum: Convergence and Divergence within a Diverse and

Conflictual Alliance," *Environmental Values*, vol. 27, no. 3, pp. 245–267.

Focus on the global south (2007) *What's missing in the climate talks? Justice!*, available at focusweb.org/node/1301 (Accessed 30 January 2019).

The Laboratory of Insurrectionary Imagination (2015) *Drawing A Line in the Sand: The Movement Victory at Ende Gelände Opens up the Road of Disobedience for Paris*, available at labofii.wordpress.com/2015/08/23/drawing-a-line-in-the-sand-the-movement-victory-at-ende-gelande-opens-up-the-road-of-disobedience-for-paris (Accessed 30 January 2019).

Moore, H., Russell, J. K. (2011) *Organizing Cools the Planet: Tools and Reflections on Navigating the Climate Crisis*, Oakland, PM Press.

Moreno, C., Speich Chassé, D., Fuhr, L. (2015), *Carbon Metrics. Global abstractions and ecological epistemicide*, Berlin, Heinrich Böll Stiftung.

Müller, T. (2012) "Of energy struggles, energy transitions, and energy democracy," *LuXemburg*, vol. 1, pp. 6-15. English translation available at zeitschrift-luxemburg.de/of-energy-struggles-energy-transitions-and-energy-democracy1 (Accessed 30 January 2019).

Chapter 8

An Occupy Wall Street activist. (Image: CC BY 3.0, David Shankbone)

Commons: Self-organized provisioning as social movements

Johannes Euler and Leslie Gauditz

Johannes and Leslie are active in the Commons-Institute which, among other things, promotes the production of knowledge and education about the Commons. They are in their early thirties, have a middle-class background and make a living working in academia. They were brought together by the fact that they both practice, reflect on, and write about commoning. This text draws on the collaboration of many Commoners, who received earlier drafts and contributed with very helpful comments. Nonetheless, the final version reflects the personal views of the authors and is shaped by their specific position within the Commons movements and the discourses that circulate within it.[1]

1. Commoning: a different way of living and acting together – within capitalism but with the aim to go beyond it.

Commons are products and resources that are created, cared for and used in a self-organized manner – this is what we call self-organized provisioning. The concept and the associated practices are very old and constantly created anew at the same time. There exist many names for what the term commons describes today, some of them older, some more recent. The English term stems – at least – from the Middle Ages. Commons exist in a great variety of forms and in all parts of the world.[2] With the development of knowledge-centered digital commons – such as Wikipedia – and of free software – such as GNU/Linux and LibreOffice – the debate around the commons has become more vivid in recent years.

Also the 2009 Nobel Prize in Economics that was awarded to Elinor Ostrom for her research on the commons contributed to the spread of general awareness on these themes. The political scientist studied the governance regimes of communities that were successfully sharing their resources. She collected best practices for long-lasting "self-governing institutions." Those include, for example, that communities decide on their own about the rules they want to follow, that these rules are congruent with local social and environmental conditions and that the conflicts that may arise are resolved within the community itself.[3]

While Ostrom focused mainly on the rules in place, other writers focus on the social practices at hand. They argue that the most important underlying feature is commoning.[4] From this perspective, which is the one that we come from, commoning can be understood as self-organized provisioning that is conducted by peers who aim at satisfying needs. This is done with the aim to satisfy needs taking into account the needs of all those affected including the more-than-human (for example, plants).[5]

This way of producing, reproducing and using is indifferent to the logic of commodity production predominant in capitalist societies.[6] Commodity production aims at making profit and mainly takes into consideration the needs of humans in terms of money. Instead of wage labor and trading goods, where only those can take part that have money, commoning relies on voluntary contributions.[7]

In capitalism, reproductive activities – that is, caring for other people and the environment – and productive activities take place in separated spheres, just as production and use. Ideally, this division is not upheld by commoning. This is the idea which we try to get across when we talk about provisioning. What commoning is can be seen, for example, in community gardens. There, food is usually not produced for profit and with the help of a lot of pesticides but in an ecological manner and sometimes for cooking, eating and celebrating together. This does not mean that the logic of exchange and profit and the divisions prevalent in capitalism are completely absent from commons associations. However, commoning works predominantly according to different principles, as just described.

Clearly, there are no universal blueprints, no panaceas as Ostrom used to say, for organizing the commons. Commoning adapts to the local social and environmental circumstances that may be very different and change over time. However, Habermann names four core principles which we want to mention here: contribution instead of exchange; actual use (possession) instead of property;[8] share all that you can; and use all that you need.[9] So commoning is about sharing and voluntary contributions, as we have already described. On top of that commoning is not merely about the management of what one might call "collective property." Holding the legal titles of property might be useful for some commons associations so that they can protect their activities from outside threats. But actually, exactly this possibility of excluding others with the help of legal and coercive powers is in contradiction with the inclusive logic of the commons[10] which is about factual, real enactment. It is inclusive whenever possible and as long as the *needs* of those involved in and affected by the commoning processes are taken into consideration.

The perspective of the commons focuses on ways of living together where people can actually influence their very living conditions and environments. They can choose how they want to take part in the world-making processes depending on what gives them pleasure, what they need and wish, what they find useful and necessary.[11] This is how Wikipedia was created, for instance. People found the free access to knowledge to be important and liked writing articles and organizing the necessary processes. Even though hierarchical, coercive and exclusive organizational structures and practices may and do exist within such projects, they are ultimately in contrast to those kinds of motivations and tend to create tensions and harm those projects.[12]

2. The social movement and the movements of commoning

There is not one single umbrella organization when it comes to commons. However, there are several networks that are more or less visible. There is, for example, the Commons-Institute in Austria, Germany and Switzerland. At the global scale there are the P2P-Foundation and the Commons Strategies Group and in the academic world the flagship of the Ostrom school is the International Association for the Study of the Commons. Which kinds of people are actually fostering and dedicated to promoting the world of the commons is hard to say due to the lack of systematic studies. Thus, this text is not least a possibility for us as authors to reflect upon the question whether or not there is something we might call a commons movement. We definitely do not claim to give a comprehensive overview; even less so about what is happening outside the so-called "western world."

Commoning can be found in any imaginable social context and in connection with various resources – such as air, seeds and water but also caring for those in need, digital technology, housing, cooking, art and music, modular bicycle construction and knowledge production. This is possible because it is not the resource or product that determines whether or not it is a commons. Instead of being rooted in the very nature of the matter in question being a commons depends on the way people interact with it and with each other.[13] Looking at the prevailing definitions of social movements gives the impression that there are mainly two points that are agreed upon. On the one hand, a self-image or identity that connects the different actors seems to be crucial. On the other hand, directing the activities intentionally towards a political goal or societal transformation seems to be of importance. Movements are commonly classified according to the means of protest they deploy.

Currently, there are many smaller or larger movements all over the world who try to protect commons, resist enclosures and establish new spaces for commoning. They protest, write pamphlets, use social media and petitions, go to court and sometimes act outside the legal boundaries. Additionally, there are commoners who are consciously acting on the verge, outside or even against the capitalist logic of commodification, private property and profit. All those commoners who are intentionally active in a political way could be considered "commons activists" and might be considered as being the backbone of the "commons movements." They aspire for a transformation of the world according to the principles of commoning, organize themselves in respective groups and networks and engage politically.

However, for many commons activists it is more important to prefiguratively set an example than to protest on the streets.[14] Prefigurative actions follow the principle "In my own life I practice what I want to see in the greater whole." This means that those who make up the commons movement may also be interested in creating alternative spaces through their own actions, for example, in interpersonal relationships and collective decision-making processes. But those actions of creating and upholding alternative spaces do not necessarily go together with the intentional aim to change the world at large. Many commoners do not explicitly pursue an ideal of transformation or a critique of capitalism. They might not network as political activists do, they might not even use or know the term commons and they might not describe themselves as commoners. However, those people *move something*. As the social practices of commoning and their rationale undermine the capitalist logic, this specific way of "moving something" is in itself changing society. Thus, what we deal with is more than "just" social movement. We might differentiate between the commons movements, which involve the intentional engagement towards political changes, and the movements of the commons, which are about bringing the change into the world through the very social practices deployed.

Commoners are normally active locally, some of them internationally or even globally connected. If anything like a commons movement exists, it is a global one that builds on actions "on the ground." However, for achieving political changes on both local and larger scales, the different groups struggling for the commons might need to make reference to the commonalities of their struggles. A common self-image does exist partly and is on its way. It may help to build alliances and see unusual connections across sections, boundaries and cultures. Why not merge the struggles for open source software with those for open source seeds? Activists might need to identify themselves more explicitly as part of a greater movement of the commons that has the potential to and in part explicitly aims at a fundamental transformation. Building alliances with other movements that strive for the establishment of alternative economies might be just as crucial. Because even if a lot is already moving in the direction of the commons, the bigger picture will hardly change as long as the commonalities of all those activities are not perceived, thought, practiced and communicated.

3. The commons and the degrowth movement contain each other, but differ in focus and strategy

When we were asked if we wanted to write an article for a book project that might give the impression that commons are a part of the degrowth movement, we asked ourselves about the strategic implications of this. And is it not (also) the other way around? Might degrowth be actually a part of the commons movement? It is a matter of interpretation, framing, and scale: which theme is overarching and which ones overlap? Why is this even important?

We assume that a commons world would be a world beyond the capitalist growth imperatives – but does the degrowth movement also automatically include commons into its considerations? If degrowth means that we have to free ourselves from the bonds of the growth imperative, and if commons activists advocate more commoning in the world, we have to ask: which growth do we need to free ourselves from? What do we need more of? How could this come about? Who is promoting it? On the level of the activists there seems to exist a high degree of mutual recognition and sympathy between degrowthers and commoners. Especially the critical part of the degrowth movement appears to fit well with the part of the commons movement. Both aim at breaking with those patterns that represent the logic of today's social system and have effect into (and through) the people's individual acting and thinking. Degrowth denounces growth imperatives and the commons movement criticizes the profit pressures in the present society. It seems obvious that these are two sides of the same coin.[15]

As degrowth was formed as a counter-movement criticizing the growth model, an idea for an alternative of its own was initially not at the center of attention. Considering commoning however, one can imagine a world in which our living conditions are (re)produced in a non-capitalist way, beyond the growth imperative. Hence commoning may be and is often seen as an integral part in framing a post-growth society. Especially the considerations on "Buen Vivir" – living well – that are often drawn upon in the context of degrowth show remarkable similarities with the Commons concepts and principles (see Chapter 5 in this volume).

However, we can also point out differences. Degrowth focuses more explicitly on resilience and sufficiency. The planetary ecological boundaries are usually implicitly included in commoning but not necessarily explicitly discussed among commons activists. From a commons perspective one can argue that parts of the degrowth movement are not critical enough of the commodity logic, and that they put too much faith in the state as promoter of regulations and change. The discrepancies in focus might, at least in part, be explained by the differences with respect to the question of how to achieve a transformation of the society at large and what an alternative might look like.

4. Learning from each other: ecological cycles, critique of state and domination, sustainable technology and freedom

How can the commons and degrowth movements be inspired by each other's perspectives? The description and analysis of local and practical knowledge is strong and deeply founded with commoners. Yet, degrowth scholars are stronger in emphasizing planetary boundaries and global ecological cycles. Particularly regarding the pursuit of a commons society as a possible reality, exchange on issues of global sustainability would be fruitful and possibly prevent inappropriate and unrealistic optimism.

The commons perspective, on the other hand, could also bring inspiration to the degrowth movement. Degrowth often focuses on abstract indicators on CO_2-emissions, economic growth and resource depletion. The movement derives its critique of consumerism in the Global North from such indicators. From a commons perspective, qualitative differences between practices as well as necessities for changes on the structural level come to the fore. The commons movement's critique points to consumption that does not fulfill needs, but instead aims for status or out of profit motives. Commoning relies on the general assumption that a fulfilling and enjoyable life is achievable for everyone. This means that the primary target is not individual renunciation but rather finding answers to the questions of who produces what, how, why and with which effects, and who uses it (up).

The commons discourse fundamentally criticizes the logic of money and exchange with the alternative principle of "contribution instead of exchange." There is a discussion on whether a reform of the monetary systems helps to transgress this logic or rather strengthens it. In our view, a long-term commons vision would be a social system that frees itself from exchange as a societal mode of mediation.[16] In addition, there is a critical attitude towards state institutions – not only because both markets and states play a substantial role in various enclosures, but also because commons do not work in a centralized way. This is also a significant delineation of the commons movement against a state-centered communism. Locating commons beyond markets and states infers that commons activists want to break with the principles of the market economy as well as the nation state.[17] It can be said that their normative foundation is a fundamental rejection of any form of domination. A greater consideration of such critical debates of states and markets as socially determining institutions could enrich the degrowth movement and it would contribute toward shedding light on structural obstacles to a post-growth society.

A fundamental critique of technology – oftentimes building on the work of Ivan Illich – is both present in the degrowth contexts and used constructively within contemporary debates around the commons. Commoners ask: "Which form of technology corresponds to human needs, and who benefits from that technology, and with which aims?" The strong roots in the digital world and a great participation of tech-savvy people from hacker- and maker-spaces, as well as the Open Hardware circles, form the basis of a certain optimism towards technology. Critique of technology and optimism go hand in hand: while the first deals with current-day technologies that are seen as problematic, the second develops new ones that work according to different principles like modularity, repairability or resource conservation – principles that are also compatible with degrowth demands. For example, the project "Open Source Ecology" has taken it upon itself to develop fifty industrial machines that a small village needs for its inhabitants to lead a sustainable, yet relatively self-sufficient good life.

As mentioned in the beginning, there seems to be a lot of degrowth in the commons, and a lot of commons in degrowth. Similarly, other currents that are united in this book find themselves sharing a lot with these two movements. Many of these inspirations are discussed and put in practice in places of commoning. For instance, perspectives on equality between humans and nature are brought from environmentalist and animal-welfare circles; justice discourses play a role; so does the aim of human equality inborn in the No-Border movement, which aspires to a world without national borders. Many sovereignty movements – for example, for food sovereignty – share principles with the commons movement, as their aim is to regain the power to determine one's own living conditions.[18]

However, sometimes commons activists relate to other transformation efforts fairly critically; for instance, when the means suggested for implementation stand in contrast to the respective aims – as when hierarchically organized political parties start promoting commons. Similarly, they criticize approaches and practices that improvidently reproduce or manifest the logics that need to be transcended – equivalent exchange, commodification and money – as well as problematic hierarchies and oppressive conditions.

5. Together on the way to a post-capitalist world: emancipatory, need-oriented, resource-conserving and without growth compulsion

A transformation perspective that envisions the path to a commons society is described as the "germ form model."[19] This approach offers an important reference point, especially in the German-speaking debate; it entails the idea that a consistent practice of commoning can spread in the here and now while it could – due to the current crisis-prone societal system – be able to become the logic that determines society in the future. Hence the potential of a commons society is already present with current commoning practices. This is the "seed" that such a society could be grown from.

One vision of post-capitalism is that of a world that is non-hierarchical but rather self-organized through polycentric networks of functionally differentiated connection nodes: a world in which everyone's needs are predominantly met through commoning.[20] This world would also be marked by autonomous and responsible activities that give joy and meaning without over-using resources or destroying eco-systems. The commons movement puts its trust in the human potential and translates the concept of sustainability into the language of human needs: There is a need to preserve the planet that can only be met if we organize our individual and collective satisfaction of needs in accordance with the boundaries of the planet. Commoning is a practical way to deal with human and more-than-human natures that is not built on abstract growth compulsion, but rather acknowledges that we humans are a (re)productive element of the earth.[21]

Commons may not solve all of the world's problems, neither in the long run and less so here and now. But we live in the final stages of capitalism in which polarities tend to become more emphasized and conflicts are fought out constantly and ever more brutally. Commons associations and other alternatives are always in danger of being usurped. Fights to defend, re-establish and negotiate commonly managed spaces, resources and products are necessary as long as the hierarchical nation state and the capitalist market with their respective logics are dominant. These struggles will be more successful if they take place in the context of a strong emancipatory movement that builds on shared visions.

Therefore, it is of particular importance to create positive perspectives, formulate and – above all – practice a vision of solidarity. For the future we think it is desirable that the movement remains polycentric but finds a coordinated direction. Summed under the term convergence, such processes of building alliances – of which many currents present in this book also partake – are already taking place. At the same time, disputes regarding content should be intensified in order to discuss strategic questions and differences in analysis and vision openly and controversially. This is the only way to avoid the different currents remaining separated. Instead, what would be needed is a *connectedness in diversity*. The term "socio-ecological transformation," understood as emancipatory and transcending capitalism, could offer a shared umbrella. It can capture the shared horizon of the different currents.

Translation: Maike Majewski

Endnotes

1 Heartfelt thanks to Fiorenza Picozza for help in revising this text.

2 Bollier & Helfrich, 2015.

3 Ostrom, 1990.

4 For example, see Bollier and Helfrich, 2015; De Angelis, 2017; Weber, 2013.

5 Euler, 2018.

6 Meretz, 2017.

7 Habermann, 2016.

8 This refers to the German legal distinction between *Besitz* (posession) and *Eigentum* (property). Here possession is determined by concrete physical access, control and use while property refers to the abstract ownership and right to sell, rent or destroy something. However, in everyday language, both are often confused. We are not certain about the equivalents in other languages and states, but would be interested in discussions and exchange about it.

9 Habermann, 2016.

10 Meretz, 2017.

11 This should not be confused with an impulsive, "pure" pleasure principle. It explicitly includes a long-term assumption of responsibility and dealing with the necessities of life.

12 In fact, they seem not to stem from the logic of the commons but to be a result of the way the encompassing social environments are structured.

13 Helfrich, 2012.

14 Maeckelbergh, 2011.

15 Euler, 2018.

16 Meretz, 2017.

17 Ostrom, 1990.

18 In this context we explicitly exclude nationalist and other movements, which also positively refer to the term

"sovereignty" but aim primarily at the exclusion of others.

19 Meretz, 2017, p. 442.

20 Meretz, 2017; Euler, 2018.

21 Weber, 2013.

Links

The Peer to Peer Foundation: blog.p2pfoundation.net

Creative Commons: creativecommons.org

The Commoner – A Web Journal for different Values: www.commoner.org.uk

Homepage of the German Commons Institute: commons-institut.org/thema/english

On the Commons: onthecommons.org

Sprout of Change – a blog: keimform.de/category/english

Social Network Unionism: snuproject.wordpress.com

Literature

Bollier, D., and Helfrich, S. (eds.) (2015) *Patterns of Commoning*, Amherst, Off the Common Books.

De Angelis, M. (2017) *Omnia sunt communia: On the commons and the transformation to postcapitalism*, London, Zed Books.

Euler, J. (2018) "The Commons: A Social Form that Allows for Degrowth and Sustainability," *Capitalism Nature Socialism*, pp. 1–18.

Habermann, F. (2016) *Ecommony: UmCARE zum Miteinander*. Sulzbach am Taunus, Ulrike Helmer.

Helfrich, S. (2012) "Common Goods Don't Simply Exist – they are Created," in: Bollier, D., and Helfrich, S. (eds.), *The Wealth of the Commons: A World Beyond Market and State*. Amherst, Levellers Press, pp. 61–67.

Illich, I. (1973) *Tools for Conviviality*, New York, Harper and Row.

Maeckelbergh, M. (2011) "Doing is believing: Prefigration as Strategic Practice in the Alterglobalization Movement," *Social Movement* Studies, vol. 10, no. 1, pp. 1-20.

Meretz, S. (2017) "Peer-commonist Produced Livelihoods," in: Ruivenkamp, G. and Hilton, A. (eds.), *Perspectives on Commoning: Autonomist Principles and Practices*. London, Zed Books, pp. 417–461.

Ostrom, E. (1990) *Governing the Commons: The Evolution of Institutions for Collective Action*. New York, Cambridge University Press.

Weber, A. (2013) *Enlivenment: Towards a fundamental shift in the concepts of nature, culture and politics*. Berlin, Heinrich-Böll-Stiftung.

Chapter 9

Demonstration "enough is enough for all" at the final day of the Degrowth Conference 2014 in Leipzig. (Image: CC-BY-SA, Klimagerechtigkeit Leipzig)

Degrowth: Overcoming Growth, Competition and Profit

Corinna Burkhart, Dennis Eversberg, Matthias Schmelzer and Nina Treu

We write this contribution as editors and coordinators of the *Degrowth in Movement(s)* project, together with Dennis Eversberg. We all consider ourselves part of the degrowth movement in Germany and Europe. Corinna first discovered degrowth during her studies through an internship at *Research & Degrowth* and met the others while working for the *Konzeptwerk Neue Ökonomie* (Laboratory for New Economic Ideas). She is now a PhD student in Human Geography at Lund University, Sweden. Dennis is a sociologist and researcher at the Research Group on *Post-*

Growth Societies at the University of Jena. His recent research has focused on the social composition, motivations and practices of activists in the degrowth movement. Matthias is an economic historian and activist, works at *Konzeptwerk Neue Ökonomie* and is a permanent fellow with the same research group. Nina co-founded *Konzeptwerk Neue Ökonomie* in 2011 in Leipzig and has been engaged in activism around degrowth since 2014.

1. Overcoming growth, competition and profit – for socially and ecologically sound, globally fair economies and ways of life

Degrowth is a term relatively recently introduced into academic and scholarly debates. It aims to challenge the hegemony of growth. And degrowth proposes as an alternative a radically democratic reorganization of the political and economic structures of industrialized societies, aiming at drastic reductions in resource and energy throughput while furthering a good life for all. Degrowth proposals are rooted in the conviction that a good life for all without exceeding ecological thresholds has to overcome growth, competition and profit. The now guiding economic and social principle of constantly striving for "more" enforces an order of permanent competition in all areas of life. On the one hand, this generates imperatives of social acceleration that overwhelm and exclude a great many people. On the other hand, this obsession with economic maximization destroys the natural conditions for human life and the habitats of plants and animals.

As a transformative vision for society, degrowth requires fundamental changes in everyday social practices as well as a profound cultural, social and economic transformation that overcomes the capitalist mode of production. Degrowth is not a predefined model of an alternative, or a plan to be implemented from the drawing board. At its heart, it is about re-politicizing sustainability debates and, more broadly, all of the central aspects of our lives and economies, in order to jointly conceive of, experiment with and fight for alternatives. The shared values underlying these transformative endeavors are awareness, solidarity and cooperation.

Primarily, the degrowth debate is a debate from and for the early industrialized countries of the Global North, even though social movements from the Global South are important allies and partners – for example, discussions about *buen vivir*, post-extractivism and the grassroots ecological movements of the poor. Rich countries must reduce their consumption of raw materials, resources and land, as well as their emissions and waste production, to a level that is sustainable in the long run and that allows the countries of the South to have equal access to opportunities for material flourishing.

Rejecting a policy focus on economic growth does not imply a dogma that nothing in the economy must expand. Rather, the opposition is directed against a specific narrow-minded understanding that equates increases in the Gross Domestic Product with greater social well-being and affirms the corresponding societal institutions and imaginaries, ranging from capitalist accumulation to consumerism and acceleration. In the degrowth vision, certain fields of economic activity may very well expand, while others that are socially or environmentally objectionable need to be phased out (see below). The point is that, either way, this is to be made the subject of conscious democratic decisions, based on a thorough assessment of the social and ecological consequences.

Alternatives envisioned by the degrowth movement

While degrowth activists and like-minded scholars broadly agree on the critical tenets outlined above, there are ongoing intense debates on the principles of the "good life for all" to which the movement aspires. The following principles are common, widely accepted reference points in these debates:[1]

- A focus on a good life for all, and therefore on the satisfaction of concrete human needs. In contrast to dominant ideas reducing prosperity to material wealth, this includes concepts such as "time prosperity" and conviviality. The good life is thus defined by the quality of human relationships and the greatest possible freedom from all forms of domination.
- An insistence that social orders can be changed, and that they need to change towards greater sufficiency — instead of a fixation on technological innovation and increased efficiency — as strategies for solving ecological problems. From a degrowth perspective, an absolute decoupling of economic growth from resource use and emissions is an illusion, since it is technologically, politically and historically highly implausible. This implies a need for alternatives beyond the concepts of ecological modernization and green growth.
- A belief in a collective and inclusive political process as the only fair way to make decisions on which products and services are needed, what types of economic and social activity should expand, and — most of all — what there should be less of in the future. Candidates for shrinking or being dismantled include the fossil-fuel and nuclear sectors, the military, the arms industry or the advertising sector, as well as individual motorized transport or air travel. Conversely, expansion may be an option for social and collective infrastructures, an ecological circular economy, decentralized and renewable energy sources administered as commons, care work, education and a solidarity economy.
- An affirmation of the necessity for redistribution of income and wealth on a national and global level, and for a transformation of social security systems. In addition to an unconditional basic provision granted as a right —

not necessarily only as a monetary income, but including expanded social infrastructures — many also demand a maximum wage.

- A notion of economy that puts the reproduction of life front and center, in which the production and processing of goods is subordinate to human welfare and the wellbeing of nonhuman nature, instead of the other way around. A first step in this direction would be a radical reduction in hours of wage labor for all.
- A concern with liberation from the one-sided Western development paradigm, as a precondition for enabling a self-determined shaping of society and a good life in the Global South.
- A call for expanding democratic forms of decision-making in all areas of life, including the economy, in order to enable full and equal participation in society. Experimenting with and practicing grassroots and consensus-oriented processes is fundamental to the movement.
- A recognition of the need for regionally based, but open and interconnected economic circuits. As international trade deepens social divisions and thwarts ecological sustainability, degrowth advocates believe in the need for de-globalizing economic relations – without promoting cultural isolation, homogeneous "bioregions," or economic protectionism for the sake of competitiveness. Instead, they call for open forms of democratic re-localization.

In all of these dimensions, change towards a socially just and ecologically sustainable society and economy at a global level is only conceivable as the result of a combination of different strategies: In this sense, science and research are just as important as activism and practical projects that seek to provide alternatives in the here and now. Conservative, racist-nationalist and sexist currents of thought may also criticize growth – but they go against the essence of degrowth and its fundamental orientation towards a good life and equal rights and freedoms for all human beings worldwide. There is no place for them in degrowth.

A brief history of the degrowth movement

Now an international movement, the beginnings of *degrowth* can be found in France in the early 2000s. However, the concept of economic growth has been the subject of criticism for almost as long as it has existed. In particular, since the 1970s, both the widely-read study *Limits to Growth* (1972), and the work of a range of intellectuals and economists such as André Gorz, Ivan Illich or Claudia von Werlhof have contributed significantly to the development of this current of thought. In 1972, French political theorist André Gorz first used the term *décroissance* in a positive and normative sense, posing the question that remains fundamental until today: "Is the earth's balance, for which no-growth – or even degrowth – of material production is a necessary condition, compatible with the survival of the capitalist system?"[2] However, it was only in 1979, when the French translation of a collection of papers by ecological economist Nicholas Georgescu-Roegen appeared under the title *Demain la Décroissance: Entropie – Écologie – Économie*, that the term was established in its more specific meaning: as an alternative to the ideas of "steady state" and "zero growth."[3]

These French origins reveal the twofold conceptual tradition that the term has carried from the outset: It merged a scientifically based ecological critique of growth and of mainstream economic thought with a strand of socio-cultural criticisms of the escalatory logic of late capitalism.[4] In 2002, a special edition of the French magazine *Silence* on the subject of *décroissance* sparked a new wave of debates, leading up to the first *International Conference on Degrowth for Ecological Sustainability and Social Equity* in Paris in 2008. It was through this event that the English word "degrowth" was established as a broadly used term, leading to its subsequent adoption in international scientific debates. Further international conferences on degrowth have since taken place in Barcelona (2010), Venice and Montreal (2012), Leipzig (2014), Budapest (2016) and in Malmö, Mexico and Brussels (2018). Over the years, the number of participants has continued to rise, now including scientists from a wide range of disciplines as well as activists and practitioners. The conferences are a meeting point and a place of debate, learning and networking for the degrowth movement, and they regularly generate wider public attention for the topic in their host countries.

2. Critical self-reflection as a path to anti-capitalism: socially homogeneous, but driven by diverse concerns – and critical of capitalism

Degrowth-related groups or movements are highly decentralized, normally possessing neither a formal network nor an organizing center. Rather, they are composed of a great diversity of individual and collective actors.

Internationally, since the first conference in Paris in 2008, the collective *Research & Degrowth (R&D)*, which is active in Spain and France, has become a central node. *R&D*, mostly based in and around Barcelona, seeks to promote the dissemination of degrowth ideas in the academic world.

In France, the movement mainly revolves around the periodicals *Silence* and *La Décroissance* as well as the *Parti pour la Décroissance* (Party for Degrowth), which, although organized as a party, is considered by most of its members as more of an instrument of political communication than of achieving or exerting power. In Italy, the group *Associazione per la decrescita* (Degrowth Association) engages mostly in academic debates, while the *Movimento per la Decrescita Felice* (Movement for Happy Degrowth), strongly rooted in local groups, promotes the idea of voluntary simplicity and seeks to provide examples of an alternative, "good practice." In Germany, degrowth ideas are promoted by a plurality of civil society organizations such as *Konzeptwerk Neue Ökonomie* (which hosts the degrowth web portal at degrowth.info), *Netzwerk Wachstumswende* or *Attac,* and many ecological economists also engage with degrowth. Eastern European groups and researchers working on degrowth, such as the *Institute for Political Ecology* in Zagreb, have received increased attention and acquired momentum thanks to the 2016 degrowth conference in Budapest. In similar fashion, the 2018 conference in Malmö has sparked the founding of new networks and groups in Scandinavia, including the *Institutet för nerväxtstudier* (Institute for Degrowth Studies) in Malmö.

Groups promoting degrowth also exist in North and South America, India, the Philippines, Tunisia and Turkey. Furthermore, there is an ever-increasing range of research, in addition to small-scale practical projects in various countries (e.g. *Can Decreix* in France) more or less closely related to degrowth.[5] Experience has shown that progress in building up a local degrowth movement is often crucially advanced by the practical grassroots process of collectively organizing degrowth events such as the International Conferences and Summer Schools.

Publishing and practicing

Degrowth is, on the one hand, a proposal for profound societal transformation; and in this sense, much of the work focuses on spurring societal and academic debates through all sorts of publications, events and conferences. On the other hand, degrowth is also a common logic to a great many hands-on projects, which manifests itself through their concrete political and everyday practices. It is thus not a contingent choice that larger degrowth events are organized collectively by grassroots teams, catered with food that is regional, organic, vegan and prepared collectively, and financed exclusively by politically progressive organizations. Typical practices in degrowth circles are, for example: consciously restricted mobility practices (refraining from flying and traveling by car), participation in vegetable co-ops, living in alternative housing projects, working in the solidarity economy, cooperatives or community projects, and participating in direct actions.[6]

Who are the grassroots degrowth activists, and what are their beliefs?

A survey carried out among 814 participants of the 2014 Leipzig degrowth conference – the biggest one so far, at 3,000 attendees – allows us a glimpse at the social composition as well as the ideas and ideals of activists at the grassroots level of the degrowth spectrum. The results show that degrowth recruits its supporters mainly from the ranks of students, academically educated and urban middle-class groups. For many younger activists, degrowth seems to be a crucial issue for their politicization. With this sociodemographic makeup, degrowth is, in socio-structural terms, quite typical for the "new social movements" that have sprung up time and again since the 1970s around issues of emancipation and ecology.

In terms of their core beliefs, the survey identified a basic consensus that is, despite all disagreements about the details, shared by a large majority of "degrowthers." This vision can be summarized as follows: Growth without environmental destruction is an illusion. Therefore, in the industrialized countries shrinkage will be inevitable. This implies that we will have to refrain from certain amenities we have become used to. The transformation towards a degrowth society needs to be peaceful and emerge from below, it amounts to overcoming capitalism, and gender equality must be a central issue in the process.[7]

Beyond these shared core beliefs, however, the survey has also revealed that there are crucial differences and disagreements between what one might call five main currents within the degrowth spectrum. (1) The eco-radical *Sufficiency-oriented Critics of Civilization,* who believe in a coming collapse of modern society and whose activities focus on building up resilient alternative communities; (2) the moderate *Immanent Reformers,* who try to achieve a change toward greater sustainability within the existing political institutions; (3) a young, probably transitory group of *Voluntarist-Pacifist Idealists,* who imagine a degrowth transition as a peaceful process in which people realize their "real interests" and voluntarily choose to refrain from their destructive behavior; (4) the *Modernist Rationalist Left,* geared to effecting revolutionary change through classical mass organizations and socialist policies, after having thoroughly analyzed the situation based on a sound theory; and (5) the *Alternative Practical Left,* bridging many of the divides between the other currents in a radical approach to theory and practice inspired by anarchist thought (for details, see Eversberg and Schmelzer, 2018). This illuminates how diverse the conference attendees are in many respects, including:

- core issues and perspective (between emotional attachment to nature, techno-optimism and radical anti-capitalism);
- forms of organization (between large organizations, alternative projects and associations of scholars and activists);
- political practices (between petitions, direct actions, and the founding of alternative communities);
- and political backgrounds (from "weakly" political local practices through NGOs and classic left-wing organizations to radical activist circles).

3. What degrowth is – and what it is not

The potentials and weaknesses of degrowth are a matter of intense debate. The contributions assembled in this book show that even among broadly sympathetic movements and groups, there are widely differing, even partly contradictory, understandings not only of what degrowth is, but also of its potentials and limits. These different perspectives are due as much to the individual views and experiences of the authors as they are to their respective movements' relationships to, degree of overlap with, or disagreement with core tenets of degrowth. In the spirit of mutual learning, (self-) critical reflection and collaboration, this section summarizes three typical fault lines and points of contention raised by different contributors. We hope that the emerging degrowth movement takes these challenges as lessons.

Degrowth: Between individual sufficiency and abstract theory?
Many contributions criticize that degrowth focuses too much on individual consumption, sufficiency and voluntary simplicity, that it individualizes societal problems and does not sufficiently take structural power relations into account. This reductionist and individualist (mis)understanding of degrowth might result from the dominance of sufficiency-oriented currents in the German-speaking post-growth discourse, which focus on consumptive restraint and individual sacrifice. In addition, many contributors to this volume reproach post-growth/degrowth for only seeking a reduction in GDP, rather than presenting alternatives or a positive vision for society. As initiators of the dialogue documented in this book, and in line with our work at *Konzeptwerk Neue Ökonomie,* we share this critical view of the limitations of a narrowly sufficiency-oriented degrowth discourse, and consciously aim to advance a more comprehensive and structural understanding of degrowth.[8]

A related critique revolves around the strategic focus of degrowth with regard to theory and practice – albeit with contradictory intentions. While some state that degrowth is too theoretical and academic, lacking a proper practice, others perceive degrowth as mainly an activist current or multiplicity of small-scale alternative projects without a proper theoretical analysis. Some say that degrowth should not only carry out a "communication offensive," but should also take part in practical conflicts. Still others think that degrowth should be more specific regarding its theoretical implications and its theory of change. These contradictory critiques, we suggest, point to the importance of developing and organizing the emerging degrowth movement in a direction, in which these elements – theory and practice, analysis and action – are key elements, with equal weight. Degrowth should not become merely an academic research paradigm, for which there are some initial signs, but should also develop strong currents working on practical alternatives and strengthen its links to social movements.

Framing degrowth and growth

Another set of charges levelled against the degrowth concept addresses its focus on growth, as well as against the term "degrowth" itself, as a dissonant word that does not resonate with many people. Some object that growth is the wrong choice of target for critique, arguing that growth, even economic growth, is not necessarily in itself a bad thing – for example, for societies in the Global South or for desirable fields of economic activity such as the care sector. For several contributors, the concept of growth still has a positive connotation. They therefore argue that we should not focus on "less," but on a "more" that is to be achieved in different, immaterial, non-destructive dimensions. In addition, certain currents that are themselves critical of growth consider it merely a secondary manifestation of the core problem of capitalism, and therefore view degrowth as insufficiently fundamental in its critique. Still, most contributors do not suggest discarding the term and concept. Rather, they suggest defining and using it more clearly and unambiguously. Emphasis should be placed on principles such as solidarity, democracy, participation, equality of rights and social inclusion to constructively complement the critical perspective. We see these arguments as important contributions to the ongoing discussion about the benefits and pitfalls of the term "degrowth."[9] Even if we think the term is still useful – precisely because it is a provocative slogan or "missile word" – we would also suggest using other terms in our cooperation and common struggles with other social movements.

Closeness to degrowth

Opinions also vary in terms of the perceived intensity of the relations between degrowth and the authors' own movements, or in other words: of where authors would place both their own movements and the degrowth movement within the mosaic of social movements. The contributors from the anti-coal movement, for example, locate their struggle in close proximity to degrowth. The ecovillages movement in their contribution see themselves as part of degrowth. While the free software movement sees its struggles as one of the struggles of the degrowth movement. And while degrowth clearly played an important role in the occupations of public squares in Spain (15M), it was only one perspective out of many in this "movement of movements." Others see degrowth as another part of a common whole (post-extractivism), as a common goal (transition towns), or as another manifestation of an overarching current (urban gardening).

A related point of friction seems to be the — actual or desired — role of degrowth within the broader spectrum of movements. Some are clearly worried that degrowth is too dominant, or that it establishes certain (taboo) topics, thus leading to a monoculture. In this context, the contributors from the solidarity economy movement raised the pertinent question of whether it is intellectual competition that causes many movements to proclaim whatever makes them unique. Looking at the self-reflexive analyses offered by the contributions, however, what strikes us is precisely the absence of such competition — at least in any conspicuous form. Rather, what pervades many of them seems to be more of a desire to continue cooperating and co-developing together.

4. A future for degrowth and degrowth as a future

Degrowth has in the last decade played a key role in questioning growth- and technology-centered future narratives, strengthening the search for systemic alternatives, and bringing together diverse actors from social movements and alternative economic currents. For the next years, fundamental challenges arise at all these levels. Even though the development of degrowth as an academic research paradigm is particularly impressive, there is still a long way to go before the degrowth hypothesis – that it is possible to live well in another social system without growth – has entered the mainstream of most disciplines, especially economics. On the conceptual level, there are a multitude of open questions, and it is highly important to discuss these in a socio-political and thus politicizing debate, not as an individualizing discussion about voluntary simplicity. Finally, confronted with strengthened right-wing politics, brutal border closures and export-oriented growth politics, degrowth faces the challenge of organizing majorities for a political project that is based on universal and internationalist values and that is diametrically opposed to ruling interests.

Translation: Santiago Killing-Stringer

Endnotes

1 D'Alisa et al., 2014; Muraca, 2013; Kallis, 2018; Schmelzer and Vetter, 2019.

2 Cited in Kallis et al., 2014, p. 1.

3 On the history of degrowth, see Muraca and Schmelzer, 2017.

4 Latouche, 2010.

5 Kallis et al., 2018.

6 Schmelzer and Vetter, 2019.
7 Eversberg and Schmelzer, 2018.
8 Schmelzer and Vetter, 2019.
9 Kallis, 2018.

Links

Degrowth-Webportal, including a media library, an event calendar, a blog, a map of degrowth initiatives as well as basic information on degrowth: degrowth.info

Research & Degrowth, an academic association dedicated to research, training, awareness raising and events organization around degrowth: degrowth.org

Education methods "Beyond Growth": endlich-wachstum.de/kapitel/materials-in-english

Information and communication networks for degrowth: degrowth.net

Literature

Brand, U., and Wissen, M. (2018) *Limits to Capitalist Nature: Theorizing and Overcoming the Imperial Mode of Living,* London, Rowman & Littlefield.

D'Alisa, G., Demaria, F., Kallis, G. (eds.) (2014) *Degrowth: A Vocabulary for a New Era,* New York and London, Routledge.

Eversberg, D., and Schmelzer, M. (2018) "The Degrowth Spectrum: Convergence and Divergence within a Diverse and Conflictual Alliance," *Environmental Values*, vol. 27, no. 3, pp. 245–267.

Kallis, G. (2018) *Degrowth*, Newcastle upon Tyne, Agenda.

Kallis, G., Kostakis, V., Lange, S., Muraca, B., Paulson, S., and Schmelzer, M. (2018) "Research on Degrowth," *Annual Review of Environment and Resources*, vol. 43 pp. 291–316.

Latouche, S. (2010) *Farewell to Growth*, Cambridge, Polity.

Muraca, B. (2013) "Décroissance: A project for radical social transformation," *Environmental Values,* vol. 22, pp. 147-169.

Muraca, B., Schmelzer, M. (2017) "Sustainable Degrowth: Historical Roots of the Search for Alternatives to Growth in Three Regions," in: Borowy, I., and Schmelzer, M., *History of the Future of Economic Growth. Historical Roots of Current Debates on Sustainable Degrowth,* London and New York, Routledge, pp. 174–97.

Schmelzer, M., and Vetter, A. (2019) *Degrowth/Postwachstum zur Einführung,* Hamburg, Junius Verlag.

Schmelzer, M., Dennis E., and Schmidt, G. (eds.) (2018) "Entwachstum – Utopie, Konturen und Spannungen des Degrowth-Spektrums, Special Issue," [on the degrowth movement], *Forschungsjournal Soziale Bewegungen,* vol. 31, no. 4.

Chapter 10

The montage shows: Left: The Open Architecture Network provides free architectural and design information to anyone interested and has helped hundreds of projects worldwide, including the design and construction of these seismic-proof houses in Pakistan. Middle: Front page of the pamphlet "I don't exchange anymore, I want my life back" published in 2015 in German. Right: The logo of the website "demonetize.it". (Image: Authors)

Demonetize: The Problem is Money

Andrea*s Exner, Justin Morgan, Franz Nahrada, Anitra Nelson, Christian Siefkes

Andrea*s is working on solidarity economies, commons, and resource and urban geographies from a perspective of social ecological transformation. Justin is a writer and linguist with interests in economics and social justice. Franz is studying specific transformation patterns in the area of knowledge communities linked to physical locations (global villages, virtual coops, demonetization by collaborative cycles). Anitra, an activist-scholar (Associate Professor at the Centre for Urban Research at RMIT University in Australia) has researched and written on non-monetary economies since completing her doctoral thesis published by Routledge as *Marx's Concept of Money: The God of Commodities* (1999). And Christian is a software engineer and author who explores the possibilities of commons-based peer production and a life after capitalism.

1. The Problem is Money

The key idea of demonetization is to free ourselves from monetary relations: the market, buying and selling, have to be considerably reduced, and eventually abolished, to create a better society. This is only possible through conscious and participatory forms of co-operation.

Demonetization's theoretical perspective is ultimately descended from that of Karl Marx, albeit with feminist and ecological modifications. A basic insight of the demonetization perspective is that money, exchange and value are historical social forms, creations of society that are not eternal, but only appear to be because they are deeply ingrained by our socialization as individuals and in our everyday lives. If we look beyond money, there is in fact a range of approaches to choose from for sharing resources, planning work, distributing products, and making decisions. Visions of a moneyless economy are diverse, and include concepts such as the commons, peer production, worker self-management, stigmergy (a type of "emergent self-organization")[1] and voluntary co-operation, as well as gift economies and the solidarity economy.

Though demonetization is narrowly defined, advocates diverge on its consequences, normative issues such as the understanding of freedom and happiness, the conception of an ethically just society, and what transitionary methods are legitimate, effective or feasible.

Demonetization implies going beyond the exchange of

so-called "equivalents" in general and the idea of a common standard of value. Arguments for demonetization share the basic proposition that money and exchange of equivalents (markets) limit the potential of society to satisfy the needs of all – contrary to many movements that see money as a neutral tool for free exchange. These arguments are the topic of the next section.

Markets, Money and Growth Cannot Be Separated

The potential to produce is driven by social needs and constrained by various factors, such as the availability of raw materials, technologies, knowledge and socio-political rules. But in a market economy, the extent of production, labor conditions and types of products created are governed by consumers' purchasing power and business owners' expectations of profit. Fulfilling concrete human needs is not the main aim or criterion for success. Hunger, lack of shelter, social exclusion, psychological frustration and other human suffering are compatible with monetized production. In many cases, the material and technological resources required to prevent such suffering are available – as with hunger and preventable diseases – but the market is unable to deploy those resources because the people who would benefit do not have enough money. Such suffering is an unavoidable outcome of a monetized economy, where those who invest decide exactly what is produced, how and for whom. Production takes place only *by* those with money, and only *for* those who have the money and desire to purchase – not on the basis of real needs.

Furthermore, the need to earn money, "make money," to spend money and balance our accounts become key to our feelings of self-worth and status as individuals. Competition is a necessary feature of a free market; agents do not create products according to social needs but rather become workers in private firms producing for sale with the aim of making profits. Monetary, economic and financial crises are intricately linked to the lack of coordination of production and distribution in a monetized economy: just because a product is made does not mean it will sell. Systematic overproduction leads to waste as well as unmet needs in market economies. At the same time, it leads to breakdowns, be it single enterprises, entire sectors or economies as a whole. So-called "disruptive" processes and "innovations" create invisible scars in the social fabric which are rarely healed and also destroy cultural traditions as well as society's overall ability to plan.

By monetarily accounting for the whole process of production, managers are most concerned with optimizing their own income and wealth despite the related ecological and social outcomes. Therefore, in a monetized economy, it is hard to conceive of degrowth as a conscious and socially legitimate reduction of economic throughput and activity, since this would entail a massive financial loss. Yet, currently, in advanced economies degrowth is a necessity for the sustainable use of the planet's limited resources.

It is important to note that these criticisms apply to any society based on a system on monetary exchange (that is, any market economy). In a market economy, all production depends upon capital. It makes no difference whether this capital is obtained on credit, with or without interest, whether it is managed by the state, by private firms or by co-operatives, or whether money is denominated in a local currency or a national or international one. Social needs would still be ignored, competition would still lead to overproduction and crisis, and degrowth would lead to a financial loss, which would threaten the whole process of production. Only a demonetized society is capable of degrowth.

Visions of a Moneyless Economy

The idea of abolishing money is not new. Certain tendencies in the Socialist, Marxist and Anarchist movements have promoted an economy without money or exchange, as has the Zeitgeist movement, but it is important to note that they do not use the "demonetization" label to describe themselves. Similarly, Free/Libre Open Source Software favors free sharing over exchange and monetary gain, without labeling itself "demonetarist." Those who do use the label "demonetization" aim to bring money and exchange back to the forefront of attention – for example, counteracting market socialism with non-market socialism, and by highlighting these existing demonetarist tendencies.

This also means that demonetarists do not offer a unified vision of a moneyless economy — what it could look like and how it could work — since demonetization is primarily a "discourse intervention" and not a vision of a future system. For example, anarcho-communists — basing their theory on the works of Peter Kropotkin, Errico Malatesta and Mikhail Bakunin — advocate replacing money with an agro-industrial federation, based on voluntary co-operation between producers to meet social needs. The ideas of workers' self-management and accountable systems of delegation are key to their approach. Meanwhile, the modern Open Source movement has no revolutionary vision but it is possible to extrapolate the tendencies we see in peer production. Commons-based peer production could be generalized to society as a whole, using for example the concept of stigmergy ("self-selection") to distribute labor. Yet another approach is the gift economy — an economic form well-attested in human societies of the past and present, which might be either the basis of a moneyless economic system, or an adjunct to it.

Most visions of demonetization reject coercive methods and propose solutions beyond the state. Nevertheless, there are differences of opinion about the balance between collective and individual freedoms in a demonetized society.

Regardless of the details, a demonetized economy is based on production for use rather than production for profit. This means that ecological factors can be taken into consideration when making production decisions. It means that overproduction is avoided, as producers cooperate with each other to meet demand based on people's needs. It also allows people's overall working time to be reduced, as they no longer have a constant need to earn as much money as they can to feel secure or better than others. In short, the growth imperative is structurally eliminated. These are the factors that would allow a demonetized economy to realize the goals of degrowth.

Demonetization: A Cross-Cutting Issue
Advocates have different reasons for demonetization. Attention is often called to gender relations and to what has been called "structural patriarchy," separating two spheres of society, one associated with the construct of woman and femininity (the non-monetary sector), the other one with man and masculinity (the monetary sector). Hence it is argued that the money economy is intricately linked to the gender binary. The money economy needs the household and care economies, which are forced upon biologically defined women and constructed as aspects of femininity. At the same time, household and care economies are dominated, exploited and devalued.

Alternatively, there may be a focus on the potential of human expression that is limited by a money economy, such as compulsion to commercialize inventions, rather than freely share our creativity, and desires for cooperation, conviviality, sensuality and enjoyment of life (not paid work). Others who advocate demonetization focus on environmental issues, which are related to the degrowth debate. Contemporary non-market socialists combine social and environmental limitations and inefficiencies of the market to argue for a society beyond money.

2. Practical and Academic

A community or society sharing resources and skills according to needs is the original vision of communism. This vision has a long historical record and dates back at least to the Middle Ages.

From the 20th century, demonetized practices appeared within the early Kibbutz movement that began in 1910 in Israel. During the Spanish Revolution of 1936–1939, money was abolished in many areas, and replaced either with free stores of goods or with various kinds of voucher or rationing systems.

Under the influence of Otto Neurath, who argued against a common standard of value and for a socialism based on a "natural economy," Soviet revolutionaries (1918–1921) seriously discussed the possibility of instituting a moneyless economy, some advocating for a unit of account based on labor time or energy (effort). Meanwhile Soviet accountants persisted in using the depreciating ruble as a unit of account and Lenin's New Economic Policy halted all talk of socialism without money. Money became a tool of state policy and structured the unequal power between workers and party elites.

Later, in the great economic debate (1963–1965) in Cuba, Che Guevara (supported by Ernest Mandel) argued against money, markets, and material incentives and for a new consciousness, voluntary labor and moral incentives. Guevara criticized the Soviet wage system and argued that, in as much as the state sector directly managed resources, labor and their product, no money or prices were necessary. However, in the transition, he suggested a temporary budgetary system in which money did feature, in its essential function, as a unit of account. Having lost the debate, he left Cuba but, later in 1967, Castro credited his position saying: "We want to demystify money, not to rehabilitate it. We even intend to abolish it completely."

More important for practical reasons are demonetized practices in recent periods of history, which were often linked to protest movements, those following the events of 1968 being a prominent example. For instance, as part of the hippie and counter-culture movement in San Francisco during the 1960s, the legendary anonymous group called the Diggers (referring to the historical Diggers movement from the English Civil War,

1642–1649) practiced free kitchens and medical care based on donations and voluntary labor. In the course of labor struggles in Italy in the 1970s, appropriation of goods and basic services such as shelter and electricity dispensed with the principle of exchange. More recently, visions of demonetization based on existing practices were mentioned in pamphlets like *The Coming Insurrection* or *Research and Destroy*.[2] Discussions and attempts at practicing demonetization also played a role in the context of Bolivarian Socialism in Venezuela.

Some movements propagating a demonetization approach refuse to be labeled as left-wing (or as right-wing), for example the Zeitgeist movement. Zeitgeist propagates the vision of a so-called "resource-based" post-scarcity economy where nobody is forced to work and there is enough for everyone. While this vision sounds nice enough, the specific ideas of the Zeitgeist movement are not without their problems. They seem to believe that the "right" use of computers and technology can bring plenty and harmony, but have little to say about whether such technological solutions wouldn't create their own problems and lead to new exclusions. They also seem somewhat blasé about the ecological effects of their vision, though they maintain that it would be sustainable. Zeitgeist has occasionally been accused of propagating structural anti-semitism, but it seems that such accusations are based more on prejudices than on facts. In this context, it's important to point out that the movement is unrelated to the first "Zeitgeist" movie made by the controversial filmmaker Peter Joseph – only Joseph's later sequels served as inspiration.[3]

To our knowledge, demonetization is mainly promoted as a radical way of thinking by white academics or members of the middle class not working at university. We suppose that they are mainly downwardly mobile advocates or supporters filling the ranks of precarious labor. As a set of social initiatives, the range of social agents involved in non-monetary practices is much broader, reaching from the poorest and most discriminated members of societies mainly in the Global South to the technologically most advanced and economically privileged milieus of the "creative class" centered in the Global North. On the theoretical side this implies an asymmetry in terms of race, but balance concerning gender in terms of the composition of respective milieus (but not necessarily the power relations between genders) on both the theoretical and practical sides. In Austria and Germany there are weak links to queer feminist currents in middle class milieus. Anecdotal evidence seems to show that younger generations are particularly interested in demonetization, as became obvious for instance at the Solidarity Economy congress in Vienna 2013.

3. Broad Alliances: Solidarity Economies, Commons and Subsistence Economies

In contributions to the degrowth debate, demonetization stresses the role of money, exchange and value in enabling, driving and forcing economic growth, which is coupled to growing resource use and many other social and ecological problems. This role is also reflected in social practices that promote degrowth. Against this backdrop, demonetization and degrowth seem appropriately positioned for mutual influence that may strengthen their respective agendas.

The demonetization perspective has to be distinguished from the seemingly similar, but very different approach centered on the critique of interest. The critique of interest, which was first and most prominently formulated by Pierre Joseph Proudhon and Silvio Gesell, locates the basic problem of the monetized economy not in money, exchange and value as such, but rather in interest charged on private loans or on the public creation of money. In this perspective, the problem is not competition as such, but crises caused by the inability to repay interest, thus resembling liberal and neoliberal approaches to economy and society. This leads to a vision of a market economy without interest. While some degrowth supporters controversially identify interest charged on loans as the basic problem and advocate its abolition, demonetization advocates argue that this does not go far enough and would not ensure a degrowth economy.

Three movements in particular are important for the demonetization perspective: solidarity economies, commons, and subsistence economies. These do not necessarily denote separate social practices, but rather refer to different theoretical discourses, political framings, and organizational approaches.

On the one hand, the broad variety of analytic, strategic and visionary approaches makes alliances with other social movements and theoretical currents easy, but entails the danger of weakening the prime goal of demonetization. On the other hand, the narrow definition of its ultimate goal keeps the central issue of demonetization clearly circumscribed and probably makes it hard to be co-opted by agents that stand in the way of emancipatory social change. While it seems that alliance building is the advantage of degrowth as a discourse, demonetization is a reminder of the need for radical social change, and of the possibility to start this change here and now.

4. Radicalizing the Message of Degrowth

We propose to sharpen the degrowth discourse through the lens of demonetization, in a way that may radicalize its core message or its way of raising questions. Unlike debates about the role of lifestyle or ethical consumerism and investment, or those who trust in political regulation or in the power of individual or small-scale behavioral change (in terms of frugality or sufficiency), demonetization proposes to lay the emphasis on debating the conditions and forces of harmful economic growth as they are related to money, exchange and value. Furthermore, demonetization may inspire degrowth debates due to its richness in utopian models.

Degrowth, on the other hand, may raise interest within demonetization debates and initiatives to make the ecological question more central.

5. A Unified Anti-Capitalist Movement?

A practical movement for social transformation may involve the creation of new "demonetized spaces" within the capitalist economy. The Free/Libre Open Source Software movement is often cited as an example of this, along with various other peer-to-peer technologies that put knowledge and creative works increasingly outside of the market economy, where free content licenses protect them (at least in theory) from commodification. Various other projects in the solidarity economy can also be mentioned. Those may include community supported agriculture, surplus food distribution, income-sharing housing communes and others. Yet these movements are very isolated from each other. The Open Source movement, for example, claims no association with anti-capitalism, much less a perspective like demonetization, even though it counts as an example of how moneyless economics can work.

To aim for radical social change, it would be necessary to link these kinds of projects together. Developing a serious anti-capitalist tendency would require that projects co-operate to gradually demonetize their operations to remove them from the market altogether. For example, free software and free content licenses can be used to prevent the commercialization of software and digital media, creating a digital commons. It's less clear how a similar process can be promoted for the physical world, to create a commons of land and housing, for example.

Being positioned against money and exchange, demonetization is necessarily an anti-capitalist perspective, and indeed, it draws much of its theoretical background and proponents from Marxism and Anarchism. Yet in the twenty-first century, despite the global economic crisis, the traditional labor movement is surprisingly weak, at least among the general population in Western countries. What we have now is far from the visions of an international and inclusive labor movement with the capacity to carry out a global, coordinated insurrection against the capitalist order, despite the globalized nature of the market economy. With such a diversity of approaches and perspectives it remains to be seen whether a unified anti-capitalist movement will re-emerge.

Endnotes

1 According to Wikipedia, "stigmergy is a mechanism of indirect coordination, through the environment, between agents or actions. The principle is that the trace left in the environment by an action stimulates the performance of a next action, by the same or a different agent. In that way, subsequent actions tend to reinforce and build on each other, leading to the spontaneous emergence of coherent, apparently systematic activity." en.wikipedia.org/wiki/Stigmergy (5 February 2019).

2 Invisible Committee, 2008; Research and Destroy, 2008.

3 The editors of *Degrowth in Movement(s)* regard the Zeitgeist-Movement as problematic for a variety of reasons. However, in the spirit of transparency and a culture of open debate, they have decided to not delete this reference.

Links

Acts of Sharing: welcome.actsofsharing.com

Searching for the new in the old: keimform.de

Demonetize it!: demonetize.it

Society after money — opening a dialog (in German): nach-dem-geld.de

EXIT! — Crisis and critique of the commodity society: exit-online.org

Crisis — critique of the commodity society: krisis.org

Mundraub — Platform for fruit in public spaces: mundraub.org
Streifzüge: streifzuege.org
World Socialist Movement: worldsocialism.org

Literature

Nelson, A. (2011) "Money versus Socialism," in Nelson, A, Timmerman, F. (eds.) *Life Without Money: Building. Fair and Sustainable Economies,* London, Pluto Press, pp. 23–44.

Nelson, A., Timmerman, F. (eds.) (2011) *Life Without Money: Building. Fair and Sustainable Economies,* London, Pluto Press.

Exner, A. (2014) "Degrowth and Demonetization: On the Limits of a Non-Capitalist Market Economy," *Capitalism Nature Socialism,* vol. 25, no. 3, pp. 9–27.

Research and Destroy (2009) *Communiqué from an Absent Future: On the Terminus of Student Life.* Available at theanarchistlibrary.org/library/research-and-destroy-communique-from-an-absent-future-the-terminus-of-student-life (Accessed 5 February 2019).

Vaughan, G. (1997) *For-Giving: A Feminist Criticism of Exchange,* Austin, Plain View Press.

The Invisible Committee (2008) *The Coming Insurrection.* Available at libcom.org/library/coming-insurrection-invisible-committee (Accessed 5 February 2019).

Chapter 11

Hard work and self-sufficiency: potato harvest in the ecovillage Sieben Linden in Germany. (Image: Freundeskreis Ökodorf e.V.)

Ecovillages: Living Degrowth as a Community

Christiane Kliemann

Christiane is a freelance journalist, degrowth activist and co-founder of the website degrowth.info. She lived in the ecovillage *Sieben Linden* from 2015 to 2016. In order to highlight the views of long-term ecovillage inhabitants and their networks, this article was written in close collaboration with Kariin Ottmar, Eva Stützel and Chironya Stanellè, who have all been active members of the ecovillage movement for many years.

1. Unity in diversity: putting collective and holistic sustainability into practice

Rob Hopkins, founder of the Transition Town movement that

spread from England over the world called transition towns a "practical manifestation of a post-growth society."[1] If this is true for the transition town movement it applies even more to the ecovillage movement, which for several decades has made concerted efforts to create small communities that are as socially just and environmentally sustainable as possible in all areas of life. In this sense, many ecovillages can be seen as potential models for a "good life" after growth, thereby representing interesting practical training fields for degrowth. It is no coincidence that the guidelines for many ecovillages are very similar to the vision for a future degrowth society.

The ecovillage movement arose as an attempt to be part of the solution instead of the problem; a solution that can best be developed in small, manageable contexts, where people can have a direct influence on social and ecological issues. In such a context it is possible to experience self-efficacy and to put holistic approaches into practice.

The Global Ecovillage Network (GEN) defines ecovillages as "intentional or traditional communities, which are consciously designed through locally-owned participatory processes to regenerate social and natural environments and to increase quality of life."[2] The movement is based on the core values of an open, democratic, humane and peaceful society that is shaped by all its members, working with equality and solidarity in partnership with one another. This includes the acceptance of different cultures, religions and spiritual beliefs, open-mindedness and a delight in sharing cultures as well as showing respect and mindfulness towards other people, life and nature. A holistic approach integrates the four dimensions of sustainability: ecology, economy, society and culture.

One of many possible paths towards social change

Far from promoting their way of life as the one and only solution for the whole world, ecovillages see themselves as one instrument among others—similar to a musical instrument in an orchestra. Ecovillages seek to take up people's ideas for change from various backgrounds and to demonstrate ideas and models for social-environmental change. In doing so, they try to combine environmental principles and technologies with grassroots democracy and socially innovative structures. Depending on their orientation and focus, they draw inspiration from ecological, socio-political or spiritual approaches. Although most ecovillages are situated —as the name suggests— in rural areas and primarily concentrate on demonstrating a different way of rural life and on revitalizing and reconnecting economically underdeveloped regions, the term "ecovillage" is not only limited to "villages" as such. The term also encompasses urban communes and housing and living projects, which strive to unite the four dimensions of sustainability and thus become model sites for research and training for society as a whole. Ecovillages are active in the following areas:

- regional development
- cooperative social economy
- community building and development
- grassroots democracy
- developing a new culture of communication and conflict management
- holistic education
- local organic food production and permaculture
- ecological construction
- renewable energy sources
- waste reduction and sorting
- establishing local economic and resource cycles
- global responsibility and environmental justice
- sufficiency
- subsistence

From individual back-to-nature projects to a global political network

Ecovillages and community projects first started positioning themselves as a visible political movement with the founding of the GEN network in 1995. Until then, there had only been loose networks of various projects. Founded in Findhorn, Scotland, one of the oldest ecovillages in Europe, GEN was set up by Hildur and Ross Jackson, founders of the Danish non-governmental organization Gaia Trust. Prior to that, the couple had been active documenting interesting projects and organizing meetings that brought together representatives from prominent pioneer projects from around the world —a process that ultimately led to the founding of GEN. Now, more than 20 years later, GEN has over a thousand members worldwide, as well as five continental and numerous national networks representing the political interests of the ecovillage movement.

Life in an ecovillage: countryside idyll or political statement?

One key characteristic of the ecovillage movement is that it developed as a positive alternative vision rather than a form of opposition to existing structures. This sometimes leads to criticism that the movement is too apolitical, and that its members are simply seeking to escape to a countryside idyll. The key question here (and the subject of intense debate) is whether life in an ecovillage – and thereby the practical implementation of alternatives – can be considered a political statement in itself. Those that say "yes" argue that ecovillagers withdraw from capitalist structures and help others to develop and set up concrete alternatives to capitalism. This creates an interesting parallel to the existing discourse about care work, which, if interpreted in the appropriate feminist context, can have far-reaching political implications. Accordingly, the overarching context of degrowth could be used as a framework in which the concept of living in ecovillages can be seen as highly political.

Ecovillages, communities and their networks very often adopt concrete political stances when it comes to specific issues. Furthermore, many ecovillagers actively engage in a wide range of political contexts, e.g. in local resistance groups against nuclear waste transport, coal mining or militarism. However, for others, the various practical aspects of self-organization related to life in an ecovillage can be so time-consuming that there is little room for involvement in other activities. A large part of the movement's explicitly political work is therefore delegated to the GEN network. True, the ecovillage movement has not developed an overall political, social or economic concept as an alternative to capitalism —but a world inspired by ecovillages would certainly consist of diverse and manifold social networks of support, solidarity and gift economy which would make it much easier to live sustainably and act in an environmentally and socially responsible manner. There would be more community gardens, regional self-sufficiency, community-supported, smallholder agriculture, grassroots democratic self-organization, a culture of sharing and an economic system with much less social disparity than today.

2. The Global Ecovillage Network: raising awareness for social-ecological change

In addition to the numerous ecovillages and community projects around the world, the Global Ecovillage Network is one of the key stakeholders active at a higher political level. It is made up of representatives from active member communities and is divided into five continental sub-networks (e.g. GEN Europe), which can, in turn, be broken down into smaller national networks. One of GEN International's core areas of focus is cooperation and reciprocal learning between projects from the Global North and the Global South.

In addition to projects still under development and intentional communities without an explicit eco-focus, the GEN project database lists approximately 300 established ecovillages, and features an interactive map with a good overview of the global distribution of member projects. However, GEN is not only a sharing platform for its members, but also develops its own projects beyond the scope of individual ecovillages. For example, it also seeks to raise awareness for the movement among key social and political actors. Furthermore, GEN hopes to strategically pass on the expertise that it has obtained from many years of development and educational work within these communities.

Help for refugees on Lesbos; lobby work in Brussels; and the cultivation of urban resilience: strategies for social-ecological change in Europe

GEN Europe focusses its activities on promoting widespread social-ecological change —at strategic points and in various fields— and reacting to current crises such as the disastrous refugee situation. "As ecovillages, we stand for social justice and a humane world, in which people are not prevented from exercising their right to asylum in the EU."[3] Thus, GEN Europe has been helping its members to become actively involved and provide practical aid, both working with refugees in their own regions and on the Greek island of Lesbos, for example, where huge numbers of refugees are stranded in inhumane conditions. The network works closely with other NGOs, local authorities and groups, and the local university to ensure that the help provided by GEN members and volunteers can be seamlessly integrated into other support structures.

At an EU level, GEN is also working towards ensuring that voices calling for social-ecological change are heard by decision-makers. GEN Europe was therefore instrumental in setting up *Ecolise*, a coalition of GEN Europe, various transition town initiatives and interested universities that seek to represent social-ecological change on a regional level in Brussels and help practical projects take advantage of existing EU structures.

Under the auspices of GEN Europe, and funded by the German Federal Environmental Agency, the Urban Resilience and New Communality project has been just one example of how GEN works to use the experiences of ecovillages and communities for urban planning work. Launched in May 2015, this research and dialogue project investigated the opportunities and limitations of the ecovillage approach for sustainable urban and regional development and sought to create an exchange between local stakeholders. In a dialogue process with stakeholders from politics, city councils and sustainable urban development groups, the project looked at "how the understanding of sustainability as it is cultivated in ecovillages and communities (. . .) can also help cities, neighborhoods and urban projects to strengthen their renewability and resilience."[4]

Ecovillagers: not only academics, but a wide range of individuals committed to emancipatory values

Just as in the degrowth movement, many of those involved in ecovillages —and especially in the GEN network— are academics and/or members of the educated middle classes. However, due to their practical nature, ecovillages also attract skilled craftspeople and a range of other individuals who choose to "opt out" of conventional society, thus bringing a different perspective into the group.

Also like the degrowth movement, GEN clearly distances itself from nationalist and undemocratic projects. The following types of project are excluded from membership:[5]

- projects with a racial or nationalist program;
- projects which discriminate against or exclude people based on their heritage, appearance, religion, ideology, gender, sexual identity or orientation;
- projects that restrict people's freedom of expression or

freedom of movement, or that make it difficult to leave the community;

- projects in which any kind of financial or sexual exploitation or abuse of group members or children is carried out;
- projects which inhibit children's access to education, medical care and other family members outside of the community;
- projects where personality cults or hierarchies and power structures are in place, which the members have not created in a free, joint agreement and which they cannot change;
- projects in which people are physically or psychologically coerced into accepting dogmas, a "correct" doctrine or majority opinions.

3. Ecovillages as fields of experience and allies for degrowth and other related movements

With their commitment to a more regionalized society, a value and solidarity-based understanding of prosperity, and the principle of direct participation in decision-making processes, ecovillages have values that are quite close to degrowth, both in theory and practice, and can even be seen as its practical manifestation and testing ground. However, it must be noted that degrowth emerged primarily as a theoretical concept for society and the economy as a whole from which a distinct degrowth practice has yet to be developed. For their part, ecovillages emerged from practice and move towards the vision of a more sustainable, just and supportive society.

What unites the ecovillage and degrowth movements is that they both follow a broad and holistic approach – degrowth in theory and at a higher societal and political level; ecovillages in practice and at a local level. In this context, ecovillages represent the diversity and the wider social pursuit that degrowth also stands for.

This holistic, practical approach makes ecovillage projects an ideal testing ground for exploring what life in a degrowth-based society might actually look and feel like —not just in selected areas, but on a day-to-day basis in all areas of life and over years or even decades. In this sense, many other social movements concentrating on specific aspects of the much needed transformation of society could act as useful allies for both movements.

When looking at ecovillage and community projects in terms of the extent to which their often radical theoretical demands can actually be sustained in a holistic practice on a long-term basis, one thing quickly becomes clear. Anyone who wants to create long-lasting, future-proof alternatives has to find the right balance between long-term goals, and the surprisingly persistent mental infrastructures of a capitalist, growth-driven society and the resulting habits and patterns. Otherwise, idealistic projects can fail very quickly when faced with harsh reality. In order to slowly keep moving in the chosen direction, successful ecovillage projects therefore seek to establish conditions that will help recognize obstructive mental infrastructures and change them without making unrealistically high demands. In this regard, certain spiritual practices that are often frowned upon in left-wing circles can also be of help. Techniques for group work and self-reflection borrowed from spiritual practice play an important role in many of these projects.

Such fields of experience seem to be indispensable for the continuing development of the degrowth approach. In their analysis of the degrowth movement, Matthias Schmelzer and Dennis Eversberg characterize degrowth's "transformational practice" as one

> that starts out from the everyday, opening up experimental spaces for acting differently (in squats, urban gardens, repair cafés, or climate camps), and aspiring to 'become something

> different' in the process, to experimentally turn oneself into a different subject emancipated from the imperatives of growth.[6]

The already existing holistic niches or precursors of a potential post-growth society can thus be considered a valuable field of experience for degrowth, as well as a field for conducting research into functioning transitional strategies and the practical viability of theoretical degrowth approaches. The ecovillages movement could be a valuable partner for the degrowth movement, thanks to its experience in forming alliances with stakeholders from the Global South. Conversely, the degrowth movement can offer orientation to ecovillages, helping them to see concrete practical decisions in a wider social context, i.e. providing perspectives that are easily overlooked in a practical, local context.

Becoming visible as pioneers of change – in diversity and cooperation

The common values that guide the ecovillage movement not only resonate significantly with degrowth, but also with other social movements represented in this book. There is already close cooperation with the transition town movement, for example, and looser ties have been established with other movements as well. Many ecovillagers are also active in citizen-led energy cooperatives, the commons movement and community-supported agriculture, among others.

The ecovillage perspective on cooperation between degrowth and other movements highlights the importance of making these various pioneers of change visible as a diverse and multi-faceted collective movement, thereby increasing their effectiveness and political momentum. This means bringing the numerous alternatives that have been developed in social niches into the public eye. In this sense, the ecovillage movement hopes for stronger networks and closer collaboration in the years to come, in order to better amplify the voices of all those who advocate social-ecological change.

4. Putting degrowth to the test: learning arenas and potential pitfalls

From the ecovillage movement's point of view, degrowth is still too theoretical. It could thus profit from the experiences of ecovillages, which show what happens when theoretical ideals are put into practice and how this can succeed: Which social changes occur and what are the necessary prerequisites? What is it like to embrace something completely new and different and let it permanently influence all areas of life?

The core competence of the ecovillage movement: community building and communication

The long years of experience from older ecovillage projects have shown that very active and engaged members are especially prone to burning out over time. For these individuals, a certain fatigue can start to set in, leading to the risk of falling into a routine and following old patterns. It was this tension between political demands, daily reality and the very tangible personal needs and idiosyncrasies of those involved that led to the development of the strong social focus of the ecovillage movement.

Project members learned that taking care of each other and establishing a culture of constructive communication is key for achieving long-term success. The core competence of the ecovillage movement thus lies in community building and communication. This expertise could also be helpful for other social movements and political groups, as interpersonal issues often stand in the way of long-term success whenever people come together for a common goal. Community building techniques such as non-violent communication or deep ecology can be used to facilitate a different type of human encounter, which can in turn foster a genuine connection and a sense of mutual understanding. In the course of their long-term development, ecovillages and community projects were able to build up a wealth of experience with these and other techniques.

Aspiration and reality: Does the ecovillage movement really live out its ideals? Are degrowth concepts too naive?

Even in many ecovillages and community projects that have a much more practical approach than degrowth, there are often discrepancies between theoretical aspirations and reality. The wide range of expectations of those involved can make reaching concrete agreements difficult, and many people feel frustrated by the fact that so much time is taken up by communication and decision-making processes. (An additional problem is that there aren't always enough people in the first place to carry out the practical tasks that the project depends on and also assume long-term responsibility.) However, these processes are a requirement for the project to work as a whole. The time and energy demanded by social processes is thus often underestimated, which in turn leads to a lack of time for the practical matters that are supposed to be the real issue.

Based on this experience, the ecovillage movement also seeks to relativize certain expectations of a degrowth-compatible lifestyle that can be perceived as too naive. Achieving a comparatively high degree of regional, collective self-sufficiency means a lot of hard work, something that is often underestimated from a theoretical perspective.

How much radicalism is possible? How much adaptation to the mainstream is necessary?

Like the degrowth movement, the ecovillage movement is also actively promoting its aims and values within society, inspiring it and thus also increasing its political impact. Based on their experience, ecovillages have learnt that this is only possible if their claims are not too radical, so that people are not put off.

Otherwise, the projects will remain within a niche and have little widespread influence. Similarly, the difficult experiences resulting from extremely radical approaches over the long term have brought ecovillages a little closer to the mainstream, allowing them to become more attractive for it. Although this allows them to have a greater impact on the general public, it also means that they attract a different clientele, which increases the risk that the orientation and aims of the projects can become too watered down.

This experience raises questions that the ecovillage movement has yet to answer but that are also relevant for degrowth: How much radicalism is possible? To what extent is it necessary to adapt to wider society in order to mobilize as many people as possible for one's own goals?

5. A broad social movement as a social-ecological alternative to right-wing populism

From an ecovillages perspective, it is important that the various movements are not seen as separate from each other, but rather as part of a single, broad, emancipatory movement that already exists —even if it is not yet visible as such. With right-wing populism on the rise throughout Europe, it is absolutely essential to achieve greater political momentum in order to offer real and humane alternatives to right-wing pseudo-alternatives. When traditional parties seem to suffer from a complete lack of imagination in facing the multiple crises of capitalism, the so-called "center of society" should have more choices than the status quo on the one hand and right-wing populism on the other. For an emancipatory alternative to have even the slightest chance of being perceived as a realistic option, these movements urgently need to get together under one roof where all members feel represented.

In setting up a common program for such a diverse and multi-faceted alternative, the ecovillage movement can help to place the focus on commonalities instead of differences – an approach that is already put into practice in many ecovillage communities. The potential in our diversity thus lies in seeing ourselves as different instruments in the same orchestra, all playing the same piece of music. This would give us the strength to change the world. We're already on our way.

Translation: Santiago Killing-Stringer

Endnotes

1 Hopkins, 2014.

2 GEN, 2014.

3 GEN Europe, no year.

4 GEN Germany, 2015.

5 From an internal communication sent to members of GEN Germany.

6 Schmelzer and Eversberg, 2017, p. 352.

Links

Global Ecovillage Network (GEN-International): ecovillage.org

GEN-Europe: gen-europe.org

GEN-Germany: gen-deutschland.de

Sieben Linden, ecovillage in Germany: siebenlinden.de

Literature

GEN (2014) *What is an Ecovillage?*, available at gen.ecovillage.org/de/article/what-ecovillage (Accessed 30 January 2019).

GEN-Europe e. V. (2014.) *Ökodörfer als Modelle gelebter Nachhaltigkeit*, available at gen-europe.org/fileadmin/_migrated/content_uploads/Broschuere-Oekodoerfer-als-Modelle-gelebter-Nachhaltigkeit.pdf (Accessed 30 January 2019).

GEN Europe (2015) *refuGEN – GEN Takes Action regarding the Refugee Crisis on the Island of Lesvos*, available at http://gen-europe.org/activities/news/news-detail/artikel/refugen/

index.htm (Accessed 6 March 2016).

Hopkins, R. (2014) *Rob Hopkins: Transition Town is the practical manifestation of a postgrowth society* (Video), available at degrowth.de/en/2014/07/rob-hopkins-transition-town-is-the-practical-manifestation-of-a-postgrowth-society (Accessed 30 January 2019).

Joubert, K., and Dregger, L. (eds.) (2015) *Ecovillage: 1001 Ways to Heal the Planet.* Axminster, Triarchy Press.

Miller, F., (ed.) (2018), *Ecovillages around the World: 20 Regenerative Designs for Sustainable Communities,* Rochester, Findhorn Press.

Schmelzer, M., and Eversberg, E. (2017) "Beyond Growth, Capitalism, and Industrialism? Consensus, Divisions and Currents within the Emerging Movement for Sustainable Degrowth," *Interface: A Journal for and about Social Movements,* vol. 9, no. 1, pp. 327–56, available at interfacejournal.net/wordpress/wp-content/uploads/2017/07/Interface-9-1-Schmelzer-and-Eversberg.pdf (Accessed 30 January 2019).

Chapter 12

Activists of the Nyéléni movement protest against food speculation on the occasion of the meeting of the finance ministers of the G20. (Image: Anna Korzenszky)

Food Sovereignty: Fighting for Good Food for All

Irmi Salzer and Julianna Fehlinger

Irmi and Julianna are part of the movement for food sovereignty and write from the perspective of Via Campesina Austria (Organisation of Austrian small scale and mountain farmers, ÖBV) (Irmi) and the agro-political group Agrar Attac (Julianna). Both are mainly active in Austrian networks and participate in the Nyéléni movement for food sovereignty. But they are also involved in the European Nyéléni process and are thus connected to partners throughout Europe. Irmi is an organic farmer in Burgenland and Julianna is sometimes a community farmer and sometimes an alpine farmer.

1. Food sovereignty: The right of all people to democratically decide how food is produced, distributed and consumed

Food sovereignty as a concept was first presented in 1996 at the World Food Summit of the Food and Agriculture Organisation of the United Nations (FAO) by La Via Campesina (literally "the peasants' way"), a global organization of peasant farmers, rural workers, fishing communities, and landless and indigenous peoples. Since then, food sovereignty has evolved into the political *leitmotif* of a growing number of social actors from the widest possible range of societal groups fighting for the transformation of a global food and agricultural system dominated by industrial interests and focused solely on profit.

At the beginning of the 1990s, small farmers' movements (at first mainly in Latin America and Europe, then in the rest of the world) realized that, in light of the globalization of agricultural markets and the increasing political power of institutions such as the WTO in the agriculture sector, it was necessary to form a globally active alliance of farmers. By founding La Via Campesina they sought to oppose through a strong transnational movement the neoliberal tendencies that were restricting the lives and survival chances of millions of small farmers and worsening the situation of hungry people all over the globe. As an answer to the technical term "food security" that was coined by the FAO and that fails to address a number of questions, the young movement developed the concept of "food sovereignty." Food sovereignty addresses the power structures in which our food system is embedded; it addresses the conditions of food production and distribution; it asks about the consequences of our production methods for future generations; and it places the people who produce and consume food products at center stage.

The principles of food sovereignty

Food sovereignty can be understood as a framework that must continuously be put into practice through concrete, local activities and struggles. Food sovereignty cannot be defined from the top down and for all time, but can only be shaped through a collective process of dialogue. Throughout the Nyéléni process (Nyéléni is the name of the bottom-up exchange process by the global food sovereignty movement; see below), the attempt has been made to define the main principles of food sovereignty based on the wide range of realities of both the farmers and the "eaters." Such principles include valuing food producers, the primary importance of feeding the population (instead of producing for export), the establishment of local production systems and the strengthening of local control over food, the development of knowledge and skills, and, last but not least, working with nature instead of against it.

Food sovereignty encompasses the rights of individuals, communities and institutions (including states), as well as a responsible relationship with nature, animals and other human beings. In the prevailing agricultural and food system, a majority of producers are denied their right to democratically participate in all political areas contingent to the production, processing and distribution of food products. International trade agreements, agricultural policies, GMO legislation, hygiene regulations, directives regarding access to markets, production regulations, etc. are on the whole adopted without the people directly affected having any right to participate in the process. The right to democratically choose and monitor agricultural, food, fishing, social, trade or energy policies is a necessary first step in order to enforce other rights such as the right to food, education and access to resources.

Only when these rights are enforced is it possible for producers to fulfill their responsibility regarding natural resources such as the soil, and biodiversity and the climate, so that future generations are also able to produce high-quality foods.

Food sovereignty means that we must act in solidarity. Transnational solidarity, networking and mutual support are necessary to fight against exploitation and domination mechanisms. Local resistance and local alternatives must be completed through a global perspective.

2. From the peasants to the eaters – defining food sovereignty together and uniting social and ecological struggles in the South and North

Food sovereignty has been developed since the 1990s as an alternative for the Global North *and* South. At the beginning, the debate around food sovereignty was mainly led by La Via Campesina. However, La Via Campesina recognized early on that a profound change and democratization of agriculture and food systems can only be achieved if the movement sought to form alliances beyond those with producers, and to forge ties with other movements. Thus, the first International Forum for Food Sovereignty, the Nyéléni Forum, took place in Mali in 2007. Together with initiatives and organizations connected with environmental rights, human rights, consumer, women's, and also urban movements, the principles of food sovereignty were developed, and common goals, opponents and demands were identified. Since then, both regional and national forums have been held. Based on the common principles of democratization, solidarity, local control, and greater care for the environment, movements for food sovereignty are continuously seeking to both create and advance alternative practices.

With regard to production models, adaptable (resilient) agro-ecological production methods are tested that, for example, use open-pollinated, non-GMO seeds, reduce agricultural dependence on fossil fuels and are based on natural cycles.

In the area of food supply, producer-consumer networks are constructed, e.g. by replacing traditional markets with relationships based on solidarity (Community Supported Agriculture - CSA), or by ensuring that producers earn a living wage through collective buying. Participatory Guarantee Systems (PGS) are trust-based certification systems that replace state control and supervision, and alternative education networks that enable knowledge sharing on an equal footing, creating a collective space for all those involved in the agricultural and food system.

In order to stop the competition for land and soil and allow access to land for everybody who wants to farm it, models are being developed that remove land from the capitalist cycle of exploitation and promote the use of land as a commons.

The food sovereignty movement demands global social rights and dignified work conditions for all people – irrespective of their social origins or gender – throughout the agriculture and food system. Through emancipatory processes, citizens should be empowered to participate actively and equally in shaping the political framework of the agriculture and food system. In this respect, the actors in the Global South and North face both similar and dissimilar political and social problems. The diversity of the groups coming together under the "big tent" of food sovereignty is a strength, but also a challenge for the global food sovereignty movement.[1]

Democratization and the right to have rights

In order to enforce the right to democratic participation in the agriculture and food system, it is necessary to create conditions that do not arise of their own accord in our societies marked by exclusion and domination. Low-income people, migrants and women are often particularly shut out from participation. The food sovereignty movement is therefore fighting for conditions that enable all people to demand and enforce their social, economic and cultural rights and their right to participate in decision-making processes.

3. Working together against false alternatives and for social-ecological transformation

Degrowth and food sovereignty are closely related, being often supported by the same activists (especially in German speaking countries) and similar initiatives (such as Community Supported Agriculture, urban gardening, ecological agriculture, food co-ops, the occupation of fields) or are based on the same approaches for alternative paths (e.g. subsistence, unconditional basic income, commons, environmental and climate justice). All these approaches and initiatives are areas of experimentation for both food sovereignty and degrowth. In both movements, the combination —mainly non-institutional— of science, social movements and practical (collective) experience plays an important role.

Both food sovereignty and degrowth envision a new type of prosperity and well-being, one that includes social-ecological forms of production on the one hand, and a comprehensive democratization of society (and the economy) on the other. In both cases the aim is to create new values that enable a good life for all based on solidarity and ecological living. Both movements should only be thought of in global terms and not just from a national perspective.

The concept of food sovereignty has a history of more than 20 years and is constantly being reformulated through concrete struggles in both the Global South and the Global North. The degrowth discourse (as a widely debated concept) is younger and more clearly shaped by academic currents from the Global North. It has been taken up by many activist groups and grassroots initiatives and has developed a huge mobilization potential in recent times.

In the following section we would like to establish certain criteria for analyzing the possibility of bringing together degrowth and food sovereignty.

Analyzing power and domination structures

We consider that the fruitful currents of the degrowth movement are those that clearly label the profiteers of the capitalist model of accumulation and study the growth imperative of capitalist market economics. The concept of food sovereignty only has a limited capacity to expose the forces behind this growth imperative and to understand the social consequences that would result from overcoming it. Food sovereignty's main focus of fundamental criticism is the profit mentality that fails to take human needs into account or that creates needs in order to increase demand and consumption. The market is thus revealed as being a poor mechanism of allocation and distribution (the most current example being the crisis in the milk market). In order to advance the food sovereignty movement, the degrowth debate should be capable of showing why the economy has to grow under capitalism, which type of growth must be reduced and which domination structures are directly embedded in the growth imperative. It is therefore important to understand power not only in terms of possession but also as a social force, as a relationship of power.

A joint study of social and ecological crises

In the degrowth movement, there is both a social and an ecological current of growth criticism. Only when it is possible to bring together the questions and points of criticism of both currents and to translate these into common perspectives and demands, i.e. when degrowth seeks to achieve a social *and* ecological —a social-ecological— transformation, will degrowth be able to enrich the food sovereignty movement. The food sovereignty movement itself is constantly seeking to maintain a balance between these two transformation strategies.

The world is not a commodity – positioning ourselves against capitalist enclosure

Current capitalist dynamics seek to turn increasing areas of society into marketable commodities. In addition to labor, which became a commodity at the beginning of capitalism, and certain aspects of processed nature (such as food products), other aspects of nature (such as greenhouse gases) and of society (especially care work) are increasingly being turned into commodities. Positioning ourselves clearly against these processes and seeking to achieve the organization of such areas as commons is an important step for a joint path of degrowth and food sovereignty.

Together against false alternatives

The main arguments of both degrowth and food sovereignty are already firmly anchored in the general world views of many critical citizens – and both movements can take advantage of this situation. Most of these individuals would agree with the sentence: "We live on a finite planet on which there cannot be infinite growth" and also with criticism of industrial agriculture and factory farming systems. The essence of both degrowth and food sovereignty, however, is that they seek to politicize people and to show clearly that supermarkets selling organic products contribute as little to saving the world as so-called "green growth." To this purpose, it is necessary to escalate the economic and sociopolitical perspectives of progressive sectors of society towards questions of wealth distribution and not let them stagnate in moralizing anti-consumerism. This is the only way to leave behind false alternatives (such as the "green economy," critical consumption and organic certifications) and approaches, which are too deeply rooted in pragmatic politics. Instead we need to work on utopias, such as degrowth and food sovereignty.

4. Focusing the criticism of growth on production and addressing dominance relations in the use of resources

Weder Wachsen noch Weichen! (roughly "We won't grow and won't yield either!") is one of the main slogans of the European farmers' movement. It is a criticism of the change in agricultural structures that exerts massive pressure on small farms and has been causing farm abandonment for decades. This structural change is intrinsically tied up with the liberalization of agricultural markets and the industrialization of agriculture. The slogan refers to the farms themselves, which – in order to continue enabling a farm-based agricultural system – should neither grow (in terms of area farmed) nor cease to exist. In this sense, growth does not refer directly to the concept of gross domestic product (GDP) growth, criticized by the degrowth movement when placed at the heart of economics and politics. However, both types of growth are closely related. For its part, the type of growth alluded to in the slogan opposed by the farmers' movement, refers to increasing efficiency per man hour —not per surface area— on the farms. According to the agro-industry, the whole of agricultural production must and will grow and become more efficient thanks to the structural change in the agricultural industry, supposedly in order to "feed the world's hungry." However, the AASTD[2] Report has clearly shown that in terms of surface area and units of energy invested, smaller, agro-ecological farming systems are much more efficient than industrial-economic agriculture based on monocultures and factory farming. In addition, small farms are more capable of adapting to the needs of people and thus ensuring a sufficient food supply for all.

Currently, due to the elimination of the milk quota in the European Union in April 2015 and the crisis in prices for agricultural products (especially milk, but also pork), the above-mentioned slogan is once again being increasingly heard. We see this as an opportunity to carry out a debate that is critical of growth and that addresses the production side of the problem and not, as is usually the case, only consumption. Food sovereignty has a wealth of experience in the area of direct involvement with agricultural and food politics, and this can be of value for the degrowth movement.

Within the food sovereignty movement, there is often insufficient systematic thought given to the concept of growth. The movement mainly addresses the negative consequences of these policies for agriculture and food in general, but questions such as why economic growth is absolutely necessary in capitalism and its importance as a tool for keeping society content (a growing pie makes it easier to solve problems of distribution . . .) are barely touched upon. Yet such a debate would significantly increase the movement's capacity for action.

Subsistence, social romanticism and resource quotas

Subsistence or self-sufficiency is recognized by segments of the food sovereignty movement as a positive concept when it refers to the regionalization of food production. However, it is not seen as an end in itself. Especially in the Global South, subsistence and semi-subsistence agriculture are often insufficient to provide food producers with a good life. Thus, the main focus of the movement for food sovereignty is on the creation and strengthening of local and regional production and distribution systems and on recuperating community control over such systems —and individualistically abandoning society is seen as a form of depolitizisation. The movement is based on collective action and solidarity, and no demands are made for (individual) self-restraint and frugality. In addition, the movement does not content itself with the creation of anti-civilizational parallel alternative projects. At the Nyéléni Europe Forum in Krems in 2011, the Nyéléni movement set forth the following strategy of action: Resist! Transform! Build alternatives! Significantly, these three strategies are applied simultaneously and with the same degree of priority. In our opinion, degrowth's sufficiency-oriented current and focus (at least in certain segments) on individual changes in behavior could especially benefit from such a politicization.

A return to former ways of living, often preached about in moralistic undertones by segments of the degrowth movement, is not a vision shared by the movement for food sovereignty. Ambitions of this nature filter out historical dominance relations and reduce the question of ecologically and socially just economics to measurable indicators (such as the ecological footprint) or otherwise tend to be unrealistically romantic. Although peasant agriculture of the past centuries in most of Europe generally followed the principles of a circular economy, it was also highly hierarchical and patriarchal in its organization. In addition, advances in communications technology have opened up historical opportunities for transnational solidarity movements. A fruitful connection between the innovations of modernity, on the one hand, and traditional cultural technologies as well as social forms of organization (e.g. commons), on the other, must be the goal of any emancipatory movement.

The demand for a system of quotas for resource use, often heard in the context of post-growth movements, is considered especially problematic in the food sovereignty movement. Anybody studying the finite nature and protection of resources such as water and land must always take into account the associated power relations, mechanisms of exclusion, and questions of distribution. For example, what does the obligation to reduce CO2 emissions mean for the one billion people on this planet who don't have access to electricity? Individual – and in the worst case marketable – resource quotas are authoritarian and technocratic pseudo-solutions that fail to address relations of power and do not help us achieve a social-ecological transformation. They are based on a monetary view of nature and life, and only further their commodification.

5. "A good life for all!" – Through solidarity and mutual learning among social and ecological movements

The starting point for common emancipatory movements must be solidarity between the struggles involved and the realization that future successes will be founded on a complementary relationship between the movements. We must therefore be open to learning from each other and sharing experiences. In addition, this requires a continuing debate on the dominant nature of capitalist growth (see also Chapter 1 of this volume). Production and consumption - economic growth - must be analyzed as capitalist, patriarchal, racified and post-colonial social relations, as argued by Ulrich Brand und Markus Wissen, in order to create the foundations for a social-ecological transformation based on solidarity.[3]

The goal of fighting for a good life for all seems to us to be the most important common message of the emancipatory movements. The definition of a good life is developed on a daily basis in the complementary social movements and their struggles.

Once again, the so-called "liberation from excess" (so the book title of a widely-read German book on postgrowth) cannot be the goal of emancipatory movements.[4] To date, this has only been possible through the postcolonial exploitation of the countries in the Global South and especially of the lower social classes of the Global North and South. The most important social struggle in our capitalist society is the one between poor and rich; and the homogenizing question of how all our societies can free themselves from excess is, in our eyes, a cynical one. Now that so many people are waiting at the gates of Europe to participate in some of the excess, it is made especially and brutally clear that hardly anybody in Europe is prepared to give anything up, or is able to do so: On the one hand, most people are benefiting less and less from excess due to the reductions in real wages; on the other hand we see a clear case of protection of acquired possessions. To not admit this openly, those fleeing from other countries are simply treated as criminals. The fact that this strategy is even possible is in our opinion due to the enormous social inequality advanced by global neoliberal politics. Those who should really be collectively liberated from their excess are not targeted.

In addition to a relationship based on solidarity between different social and ecological movements, we would also like to speak out in favor of the simultaneous application of diverse political strategies. As mentioned above, the movement for food sovereignty seeks to enable a transformation through three different but complementary and reciprocal strategies: Resist! Transform! Build alternatives!

Although, in light of neoliberal-capitalist land grabbing, the destruction of the foundations of life, and the violent exclusion of more and more people, it is urgently necessary to develop common strategies and build up common alternatives, and it is probably unrealistic and from our point of view not even desirable to join energies into a single, unified movement. Social movements need to take each other into account and complement each other in a context of solidarity. But each movement must fight its own battles.

Translation: Santiago Killing-Stringer

Endnotes

1 Patel, 2009.

2 International Assessment of Agricultural Knowledge, Science and Technology for Development (United Nations Organization).

3 Brand and Wissen, 2018.

4 Peach, 2012.

Links

FIAN International – Organization for the Right to Food: fian.

org

Hands on the Land for Food Sovereignty – Campaign against landgrabbing: handsontheland.net

La Via Campesina International: viacampesina.org

Nyéléni Europe: eurovia.org/campaign/nyeleni

Uniterre – Swiss farmer union (in French): uniterre.ch/fr

Podcast "The Secret Ingredient": thesecretingredient.org

Literature

Brand, U., and Wissen, M. (2018) *Limits to Capitalist Nature: Theorizing and Overcoming the Imperial Mode of Living*, London, Rowman & Littlefield.

ETC Group (2017) *Who will feed us? The Industrial Food Chain vs. The Peasant Food Web*, 3rd Edition, ETC Group. available at etcgroup.org/sites/www.etcgroup.org/files/files/etc-who willfeedus-english-webshare.pdf (Accessed 30 January 2019).

Nyéléni Forum (2007) *Declaration of Nyéléni*, Nyéléni Forum: Sélingué/Mali. Available at nyeleni.org/spip.php?article290 (Accessed 30 January 2019).

Paech, N. (2012) *Liberation from Excess: The Road to a Post-Growth Economy*, München, oekom.

Patel, R. (ed.) (2009), *Food Sovereignty*, Special Issue, *The Journal of Peasant Studies*, vol. 36, no. 3, pp. 663-706. Available at tandfonline.com/doi/pdf/10.1080/03066150903143079 (Accessed 30 January 2019).

Patel, R. (2007) *The Stuffed and the Starved. The Hidden Battle for the World Food System*, London, Portobello Books.

Patel, R. (2009) *Food Sovereignty – A Brief Introduction,* available at rajpatel.org/2009/11/02/food-sovereignty-a-brief-introduction (Accessed 30 January 2019).

Patel, R. and Moore, J. (2017) *A History of the World in Seven Cheap Things. A Guide to Capitalism, Nature, and the Future of the Planet*, Oakland, University of California Press.

Chapter 13

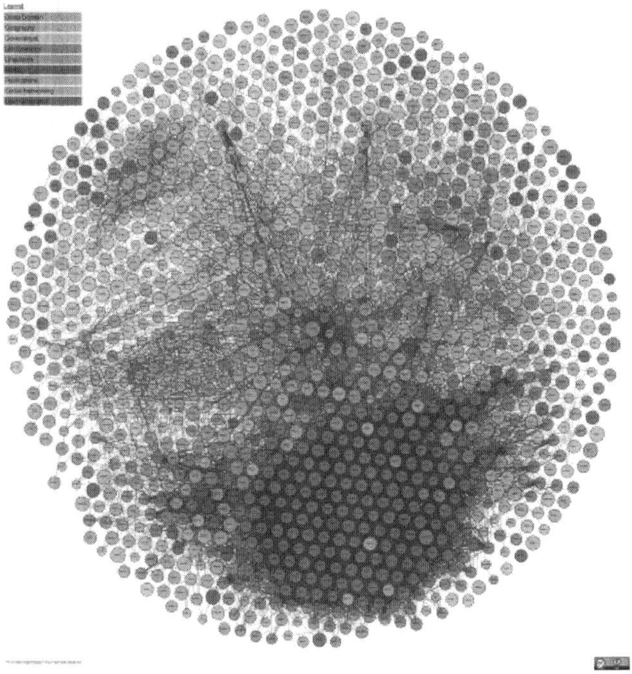

The Cross-Domain Linked Open Data Cloud as of January 2019.
(Image: CC BY, lod-cloud.net)

Free-Software: Re-decentralizing the Internet and Developing Commons

Gualter Barbas Baptista

This text has been written from a perspective of people who are part of the Free-Software Movement and initiatives for decentralized internet aggregated around the *librehosters network*. Those who have been involved in writing this text are personally involved in the design of infrastructures, platforms and services as digital commons.[1]

1. Free, not just for free: running, checking, changing and redistributing software

The key idea behind the free software movement is to give the ability to the users of software – which is present in basically any electronic device we use today – to have the freedom to run, study and change the software, and to redistribute it in any way. The free software movement appears officially in the 1980s, as a reaction to the increasing dominance of proprietary software. This dominance emerged in the late 60s, with the increasing production costs of ever more complex software.

In contrast to proprietary software, which maps to an industrial competition environment protected by patent systems, the philosophy of free software focuses on removing any restrictions from the use and modifications of software, which are an obstacle to cooperation between peers. It aims in that way at promoting the progress of technology with the goal "to liberate everyone in cyberspace."[2]

At this point, an important clarification and distinction between the terms open source and free software should be made. Although they are often used interchangeably and to a large extent overlapping, open source software licenses may put restrictions on the (re)use of software. On "free" or "libre" software, such restrictions should not be present ("free" is here not meant in the sense of "free beer," but rather in the sense of "free speech"). In order to overcome the debate, the term free/libre open source software (FLOSS) has been proposed. Nevertheless, it is the free software movement which appears as strongly politicized and therefore closer to degrowth. As a contributor at the *Chaos Communications Congress* (the biggest hackers congress in Europe happening yearly in Germany) argued, the concept of open source was pushed forward in order to include the emerging expansion of free software "into the neo-liberal ideology and the capitalist economy."[3]

The development of the free software movement is historically bound with the vision of a world wide web (www, short web) as it was conceived by its founder Tim-Berners Lee. The core of his philosophy is that the internet as a platform provides freedom and agency to its users. Up to 1996, the Internet was mostly indeed a place for sharing knowledge and establishing communication, away from commercial interests - its commercial use was in fact forbidden. Nowadays it is difficult to avoid the commercial Internet: Google, Dropbox or Facebook are just a few examples of corporations making business out of our data, documents and relationships in the Internet. This delegation of agency (and often ownership) to corporate "data silos" on the cloud is one of the main threats to the movements' vision of a free web.

At the same time, we are observing the emergence of new patterns of production and consumption of technology. Social-technological innovations, rather than pure technological innovations, seem to be the dominant pattern of innovation. Code development and recombination "factories," such as the famous GitHub, have become social networks for a global sharing of digital production. The Sharing Economy brings new forms of relationships between producers and consumers, by establishing a peer-to-peer mode of access to resources.

These developments do not pass without critique also from within the free-software movement: GitHub is also a centralized commercial platform, and the Sharing Economy has been to a large extent cooptated by the for-profit interests and the controversial model of billion-worth start-ups, such as AirBnb or Uber. This led several organizations standing behind the idea of the Sharing Economy, such as *OuiShare*, to propose the alternate concept of Collaborative Economy to distinguish initiatives based on horizontal networks and participation of a community.

At the hardware level, FabLabs, Repair Cafés or Open Source Ecology are engaged in a worldwide knowledge sharing: people involved share their accumulated experiences while they engage in production and learn with their local communities (of practice). Furthermore, there are initiatives such as the fairphone or the fair mouse, which attempt to achieve more ecological and fair means of production. In doing so they are revealing how difficult it is, within the current political ecology of resource extractivism to actually achieve a fair and ecological production of technological artefacts.

2. From software activists to technology creators: user and hacker communities interconnected in global networks

It is difficult to describe who is part of a movement that is so diffuse and embedded at different levels across other movements. A few key figures and institutions are nevertheless worth mentioning.

Richard Stallman, the *GNU* Project and the *Free Software Foundation (FSF)* are probably some of the most important actors in the genesis of free software as a movement. The *GNU* project was founded by Stallman in 1983 at the Massachusetts Institute of Technology (MIT), with the aim of developing tools and eventually building an operating system consisting exclusively of free software. In 1992, the only missing part in the operating system was the kernel[4]. The release of the Linux kernel under a GNU Public License (GPL) in 1992 provided the missing piece to the operating system. The Linux kernel is an amazingly successful example of a convergence of global efforts: the 10,239 lines of code of the Linux Kernel, originally released by the Finnish student Linus Torvalds in 1991, has expanded to over 18 million lines of source code protected as a commons by the GPL. Its success has been immense: most of the internet as it is today, as well as a huge number of consumer devices - from smartphones running with Android to TomTom-GPS in cars - are built on top of the Linux Kernel. Because of the GPL constraints, any piece of software built with or from it must also make its source code available. As a consequence, all activity around GPL source code, be it non-profit or for profit, brings a contribution back to the global commons of source code and algorithms.

The membership-based institution *World Wide Web Consortium (W3C)* is defining standards for the web, while also promoting convergence of visions on what the web should look like. It is structured into multiple working groups, which are generally open for contributors to join. The *W3C* aims at developing common protocols that promote the evolution of the world wide web and at the same time at improving the conditions for collaboration of different actors.

Community networks, often supported by wireless (open source) technology (such as the *Freifunk* initiative in Germany) contribute to the development of "mesh networks" at the grassroots level. The low costs of a Raspberry Pi (a single-board computer) help to run a DIY cloud service (e.g. Nextcloud) on its own server, while costing as little as 30 €, consuming around 10 Watts of power and fitting into the palm of the hand.

A growing number of collectives are recombining and further developing existing free software into stacks that provide a more democratic access to services, shaped to needs and uses of the target communities. As an example, the *Librehosters network* encourages decentralization through federation and distributed platforms, based on values like transparency, fairness, privacy and contributions to the commons. More and more protocols and software are able to federate between instances, i.e. to allow the exchange between users connected to different nodes. Some examples include the Matrix (a communications protocol providing a very nice alternative to Slack via the Riot application), Mastodon (a Twitter-alternative) or Tim Berners-Lee's Social Linked Data (Solid).

Even at the higher institutional level of the EU, concerns about the continuous trend of concentration of information into services hosted by corporations overseas and the global surveillance backdoors, exposed by citizenfour Edward Snowden, have prompted action. In recent years hundreds of millions of Euros have been released under the Horizon 2020 research and innovation program to support "collective awareness platforms for sustainability and social innovation." The fund specifically recognizes the contribution of hacker communities and grassroots movements and looks favorably on consortia that include actors from these communities.

3. Questioning technology by commonly owning it

Within the degrowth movement, technology, and especially digital technology, is often taken as something to be reduced or removed as much as possible from life and society. While demanding this, it ignores the fact that we live in the age of digital communication, where digital technology - even when not directly used - is already part of the life of nearly every citizen in the world.

In this sense, not engaging and helping to shape the development of the digital infrastructure simply means that someone else will do it for you, with or without consent. Derrida's "paradox of hospitality" points to an interesting aspect here: the first violence a foreigner faces is the obligation to ask for hospitality in the language of the host – which is in contradiction to the idea of hospitality. This metaphor has been applied to technology by Claudio Ciborra: if the host is to absorb the technology successfully, he must learn to speak in its language and adopt the culture of the tool where appropriate. In other words, if you don't develop your own technology, you will need to adapt to the language and patterns of the technology someone else developed - maybe in contradiction to your cultural values.

The complexity of the industrial-technological complex is today supported by large institutions and corporations. These progressively distance their users from the technological choices and agency, from the infrastructure that hosts it, the processes of technological production, and of the resource extraction necessary for its maintenance. Increasing centralization prohibits digital and analogue networks. Media theorist Douglas Rushkoff shows that the century we are living in is no longer shaped by the mechanical, huge, 19th century factory, but rather by brands, titans of the digital world, which establish their monopolies with socially networked platforms. These he understands as a spike of a late or new capitalism. Massive amounts of venture capitals are injected into ideas emerging into the digital society, with the objective of capturing as many users and data as possible, and eventually establishing a monopoly and universality in the service provision: no one should get a ride if not on Uber, no one should find friends if not on Facebook, no one should find a date if not on Tinder. Still Rushkoff, and along with him a few other intellectuals, hackers and activists in the collaborative economy, free software and commons movement, sees the internet as having a distributive power without precedent in the history of Humanity.

Nevertheless, the Internet is being increasingly reduced to the usage of a few platforms, which most often act as isolated silos of information. This is blocking the core of the decentralized web: the hyperlink. The famous Iranian blogger Derakshan writes how he, after spending a few years in prison (2008-2015), was confronted with the dominance of the social networks and feared how these would make the hyperlink obsolete:

> The hyperlink was my currency six years ago. Stemming from the idea of the hypertext, the hyperlink provided a diversity and decentralization that the real world lacked. The hyperlink represented the open, interconnected spirit of the world wide web – a vision that started with its inventor, Tim Berners-Lee. The hyperlink was a way to abandon centralization - all the links, lines and hierarchies - and replace them with something

more distributed, a system of nodes and networks.[5]

The web with the hyperlink, represents in a way a tool in the digital world to build an autonomous society as described by the Greco-French theoretician Cornelius Castoriadis. The current threats that the hyperlink faces are therefore also threats to the emergence of degrowth utopias.

Networks of learning

It is possible to draw parallels to Ivan Illich's concept of the "learning webs."[6] In *Deschooling Society*, Illich argues that a good education system should follow three purposes: to provide all that want to learn with access to resources at any time in their lives; to make it possible for all who want to share knowledge to find those who want to learn it from them; and to create opportunities for those who want to present an issue to the public to make their arguments known. Illich develops an example of a decentralized scheme of learning: a network of tapes. People would be provided with tape recorders and empty tapes, which "would provide opportunity for free expression: literate and illiterate alike could record, preserve, disseminate, and repeat their opinions." Reference services and other mechanisms for bringing peers in exchange would facilitate access to the resources the student is looking for. Illich's network of tapes as well as the Internet of hyperlinks replaces the radical monopoly over the hegemonic discourse with a multiverse of narratives.

Up to now, research and praxis on degrowth has unfortunately brought too little contribution in building up a coherent, critical vision on different innovations and movements that are emerging on the digital technology scene. While in the last years more and more publications on the topics of technology and degrowth appeared in academic journals, there is nevertheless often a distancing of the actors of degrowth from taking active part in the technological and cultural developments of the digital age -

as if diving in and getting busy with it would be in contradiction with a meaning of life rooted on voluntary simplicity and harmony with nature.

4. Degrowth debates can help to critically guide social and technological development

The main historical contributions of the free software movement have probably been on the production of digital commons: source code, data, information, algorithms, knowledge. In addition to it, a whole culture of collaboration based on the ideas of freedom and autonomy developed, as seen in the previously mentioned global collective efforts such as Wikipedia or the Linux Kernel.

The developments and new modes of production and consumption being pushed by the so-called "Sharing Economy" also provide interesting insights into the degrowth debate. Rather than completely dismissing the patterns of exchange of the sharing economy because of their current institutional framing, Maurie Cohen argues that "reciprocal relationships, producer-consumer cooperatives could bring the intentions of production and consumption into closer alignment."[7] The challenge would be to develop a "more efficacious sharing economy" capable of constraining the "expansion of mediated micro-entrepreneurship and serialized rental in favor of modes consistent with communitarian provisioning." Cohen calls for Platform Cooperativism as an alternative institutional setting for enabling these new patterns of reciprocal relationships. Research on institutions and democratic practices as present in the degrowth movement can give valuable insights on how the Sharing Economy could be (re)designed.

This blurring of roles between producers and consumers, enabled by technology, is at the core of the praxis of the Sharing Economy, and a broad range of social businesses. It leads to the emergence of a new type of economical agent, which the futurist Alvin Toffler called "prosumers." Critics have expressed concern that this dynamic may contribute to the generation of new forms of capitalist exploitation by generating unpaid labor, while keeping power and decision structures untouched.[8] Bauwens as well as Benkler and Nissenbaum argue, however, that production which follows the distributed logic of peer-to-peer and commons-based peer-production may operate independently of a market logic or existing power structures.[9] Also, here the degrowth movement could critically engage in the debate and contribute to a systemic understanding of these emerging production and consumption patterns.

Another ongoing debate is on the optimal architecture for the infrastructure and services being provided: should we have fully distributed (peer-to-peer) or decentralized, federated and autonomously controlled networks? Technologies that enable the construction of divided networks (such as Blockchain) recently make headlines. A debate discussing social and political questions which are arising with such new networks are, on the other hand, largely missing. Approaches for a global distributed system will necessarily need a global algorithm, which defines criteria for allowed transactions or which creates a basis of trust between crypto-anonymized users. But is it possible to reach a "global consensus" for an automatized judgment of trust? Who decides about the technology to be used? How is privacy assured? How can trust between people be built if there is no institution or place where it can be attached other than the algorithms placed in machines that take care of their transactions?

Supporters of decentralization, such as the federated approach practiced by initiatives such as *Indieweb* or *Librehosters*, argue for distributed processes, rather than consensus. They trust in the creative powers of the people involved, rather than in the automation of all transactions. Local or thematically bound communities can localize, control and determine such processes. On a technical level it then only needs minimal standards of cooperation (interoperability) such as with the hyperlink.

These new processes and roles will beyond doubt have a great influence on institutional settings – on a social as well as a technological level. Debates within the degrowth movement around democracy, autonomy, institutions and technology can help to shape the still to be built networks and platforms and the relations between them. The Ecobytes association has been collaborating with international networks on degrowth and community-supported agriculture, combining community building and agile management practices, both online and with events such as mapping jams or hackathons. The aim is to conduct a socio-technical process able to develop a technological stack adapted to the specific needs and values of these initiatives rather than the profit-driven stance of most IT corporations and startups.

5. Individual and collective freedom

An alliance between the free software movement and the degrowth movement is not only possible, but has the potential to be a melting pot for the emergence of new visions and utopias.

Earlier in this chapter, reference was made to important degrowth sources, in particular to the visions of Illich and Castoriadis. We saw how Illich presents the learning webs as a proposal to overcome the radical monopolies on education; or how Castoriadis's autonomism materializes in the philosophy and praxis of the web. To take the words of the latter, "a free society is a society in which power is actually exercised by the collectivity, but a collectivity in which all effectively participate in equality. And this equality of effective participation, as goal to attain, must not remain a purely formal rule; it must be insured, as much as possible, by actual institutions."[10]

The dimensions of democracy and justice have been equally subjected to strong focus and debate among some of the main references of the free software movement: these converge on the importance of not only having access to technology, but also on the capacity to understand and use the technology autonomously. Richard Stallman, speaking at the 2015 *Chaos Communication Congress*, synthesizes the concern and awareness of the movement on the radical monopolies forming around digital technology: "teaching children to use proprietary software is like teaching them to smoke." Collective ownership of technical infrastructures and data, interoperability, linked open data (LOD), and the semantic web with its vocabularies and ontologies are some words that are expected to appear more and more in the discourses engaged in building up postgrowth futures.

It is hard to imagine that Ivan Illich would not feel excited about the convivial, deschooling and deinstitutionalization potential of the world wide web and an underlying commons infrastructure. Making research projects to accumulate even more knowledge on how things work or should work is really not the interesting thing to do today. We rather need more convivial research in the field, capable of bringing scientists - also non-technical ones - to the collaborative development of platforms, ontologies and vocabularies for data openness and interoperability. Supporting events such as hackathons, or using (and supporting) commons server infrastructure and free software services are examples of actions that support the transformations and resistances happening in the field of technology and the digital commons.

Stallman, Rushkoff, Cohen, and most free software activists and hackers would probably not consider themselves as part of the degrowth movement. But we see a pattern emerging, which brings together (some) social businesses, the do-it-yourself culture, the capitalist-critical grassroots, the commons and free software movements. They converge on the will to (re) appropriate and decommercialize technology. They organize and often collaborate in building up Illich's "learning webs."

The web in fact enables us to come a step further in overcoming the institutional boundaries and centralization of the learning process, of which Illich is so critical. The vision for a web that provides freedom and agency to its users - and which is currently under threat - is part of the core and philosophy of the world wide web. And this freedom of individuals is the central piece for building up the utopian autonomous society that Castoriadis envisions on his Project of Individual and Collective Autonomy:

> An autonomous society implies autonomous individuals – and vice versa. Autonomous society, autonomous individuals: free society, free individuals. Freedom – But what is freedom? And what freedom? What is at issue is not inner freedom, but effective, social, concrete freedom, namely, to mention one primary feature, the largest possible space for movement and activity the institution of society can ensure for the individual. This freedom can exist only as dimension and mode of the institution of society.[11]

The struggle for free software and the free web is also a struggle of the degrowth movement.

Endnotes

1 This text has been written collectively on github: github.com/gandhiano/technology-degrowth (Accessed 31 January 2019).

2 Stallman, 2006.

3 Prug, 2007.

4 The kernel (also called nucleus) is a computer program that constitutes the central core of a computer's operating system. It has complete control over everything that occurs in the system: en.wikipedia.org/wiki/Kernel (operating_system) (Accessed 30 January 2019).

5 Derakshan, 2015.

6 Illich, 1970.

7 Cohen, 2015.
8 Ritzer and Jurgenson, 2010.
9 Bauwens, 2005; Benkler and Nissenbaum, 2006.
10 Castoriadis, 1993, pp. 317-18.
11 Ibid.

Links

Citizenfour – documentary: thoughtmaybe.com/citizenfour/

Ecobytes – list of librehoster: github.com/ecobytes/awesome-librehosters

Steal this Film – documentary: youtube.com/watch?v=Ijo98_nUhrk

The Internet's Own Boy – documentary: youtube.com/watch?v=7ZBe1VFy0gc

The Pirate Bay: Away from Keyboard – documentary: youtube.com/watch?v=eTOKXCEwo_8

Literature

Bauwens, M. (2005) "The Political Economy of Peer Production," *CTheory*, vol. 1. Available at https://journals.uvic.ca/index.php/ctheory/article/view/14464/5306 (Accessed 30 January 2019).

Benkler, Y., Nissenbaum, H. (2006) "Commons Based Peer Production and Virtue," *Journal of Political Philosophy*, vol. 4, pp. 394-419.

Castoriadis, C. (1993) *Political and Social Writings* (Vol. 3), Minneapolis/London: University of Minnesota Press.

Cohen, M. (2015) *How Platform Cooperativism Can Accelerate Sustainable Consumption*, available at shareable.net/blog/how-platform-cooperativism-can-accelerate-sustainable-consumption (Accessed 30 January 2019).

Derakshan, H. (2015) *The Web We Have to Save*, available at medium.com/matter/the-web-we-have-to-save-2eb1fe15a426 (Accessed 30 January 2019).

Illich, I. (1971) *Deschooling Society*, New York: Harper & Row.

Prug, T. (2007) *Hacking Ideologies, Part 2: Open Source, a Capitalist Movement*, available at events.ccc.de/congress/2007/Fahrplan/attachments/967_24c3.HackingIdeologies.OpenSource.a.capitalist.movement.pdf (Accessed 30 January 2019).

Ritzer, G.; Jurgenson, N. (2010) "Production, Consumption, Prosumption. The Nature of Capitalism in the Age of the Digital *Journal of Consumer Culture*, vol. 1, pp. 13-36.

Stallman, R. (2006) *Stallman interviewed by Sean Daly*, available at groklaw.net/article.php?story=20060625001523547 (Accessed 30 January 2019).

Chapter 14

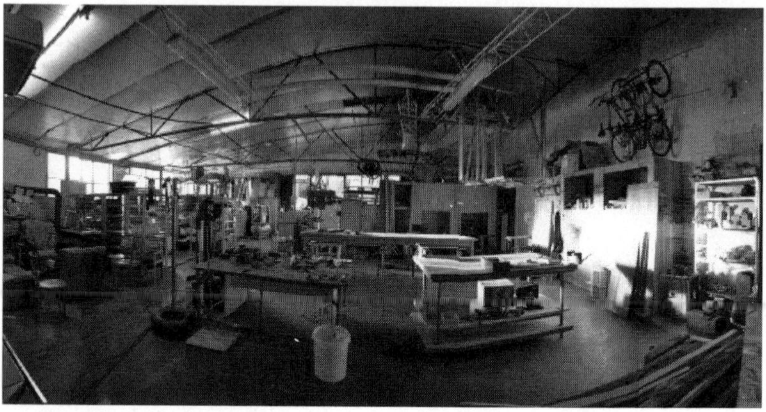

The open workshop WerkBox3 in Munich offers countless possibilities for DIY and DIT. (Image: Stephanie Schmitz)

Open Workshops: Collectively Creating and Using Infrastructure

Tom Hansing

Open workshops have been Tom's main area of interest for years: first when he was one of the initiators of the open serigraphy workshop SDW-Neukölln, then as a founding member of the German Federation of Open Workshops (Verbund Offener Werkstätten) and since 2010 as a scientific collaborator of the anstiftung foundation, which advises, researches and networks do-it-yourself (DIY) initiatives and spaces. This text represents his personal views.

1. Doing things together instead of consuming alone: open workshops create commons-based free spaces for productive do-it-yourself and do-it-together cultures

The main goal of the open workshop mentality is to create and maintain easily accessible spaces containing a productive infrastructure. These spaces can have many names: "DIY houses," "thing factories," "DIY workshops," "open labs," "co-making spaces" or "wood shops" and can represent different concepts, philosophies, proposals and types of equipment. However, they are all united by the idea of sharing know-how, tools and machines, technology, and materials in a space for common action.

These spaces are independent of external commercial interests and are open to anybody who wants to work manually, technically or artistically with a DIY philosophy. They are independent open spaces for independent work and initiatives —for young and old, amateurs and (semi-)professionals, artists and handicrafts producers, artisans and nerds, individuals and groups. Instead of replicating asymmetrical teacher-student structures, open workshops foster a free exchange of knowledge and a mutual teaching-learning process on equal footing. You could say that the ideal workshop project brings together the productive capabilities of a factory with the educational offer of a university and the comfort and social integration of a café or community center.

(Re)cultivating DIY open spaces as a common good

In the ultra-commercialized life of modern society, the idea of working with one's hands and using different materials, technologies, tools and types of equipment to do so has all but disappeared. In schools and public education institutions, the use of workshops is generally linked to specific course contents and, additionally, to the individual user's status as either school student, college student or apprentice. In other words, it is limited to a specific temporal context and is not an end in itself. The workshops of educational institutions respond to their intrinsic systemic goals, not to those of their users. For their part, most commercial workshops exist to produce or repair commodities, and are therefore organized according to market-based notions of efficiency, are in private hands, and are not openly accessible, either. Then there are certain collaborative workshops offered as a leisure activity that tend to focus on specific products, i.e. on a temporary use in predefined and guided courses, and are rarely made openly accessible beyond this.

In our densely populated urban areas, space is a rare commodity. At the same time DIY is dependent on space, especially when it is seen in broader terms as social and self-empowerment on the basis of technical, mechanical, artistic and artisanal methods, techniques and processes – not just as tinkering (alone) in one's garage.

Open workshops take DIY out of basements and garages and create self-organized spaces for working together with others. DIY is a conscious act and open workshops create the open space for it. Here, the users can renegotiate what individuals can, should and are allowed to do as consumers. Those involved create ad hoc structures for the appropriation of education without external control, to test out new abilities, to realize the individual projects of its users and give rise to peer-organized commons. One of the main results is the creation of open spaces for exchange, mutual inspiration and support. Instead of commercial models, these spaces seek to test out social and economic "operating systems" that have the potential to replace monetary exchange in the long term with a system of contributions and communal responsibility. The goal of achieving the economic feasibility of an individual project through solidarity is thus more important than making a profit: added value for many, instead of profit for the few.

Doing things together and changing the world

Can "open workshops" be called a movement? Yes and no. "Open workshop" is not a uniform concept, but rather an umbrella term with many different subcategories, and a phenomenon that manifests in extremely diverse ways: from informally organized groups to non-profit organizations and even commercial businesses. The one thing that can be said is that these new forms of sharing, exchanging, using and DIY can have system-changing potential, and open workshops are a part of this wave. Authors such as Jeremy Rifkin believe that the new game rules of so-called collaborative or share economies will replace the mechanisms of old-school capitalism in the middle to long-term. The authors of a recently published study on the potentials of the sharing economy in Berlin argue that the collaborative economy does not only change our lifestyles, but also the way we think, act and live together, our values.[1] Use instead of property and access instead of status: These ideas of collaborative action are continuously spreading to new areas of our globalized and connected society.

Some open workshop groups see themselves more readily than others as a movement or as part of a movement. It is clear, however, that especially younger generations of do-it-together practitioners are increasingly less willing to accept predetermined spaces and commercialized concepts. In addition, they not only demand the right to co-determination regardless of social or cultural background, but put this idea into practice in very concrete terms. They seek to foster self-sufficiency and innovation by creating spaces that are both playgrounds and laboratories of ideas – both a social experiment and proof that it is always possible to achieve more together than alone. In this sense, for the creators and users of open workshops, collective DIY and the open sharing of production expertise and means is more than just a leisure activity. It is an important building block in the foundation of a new (global) society based on the common good, on the principles of participation and solidarity, and on respect for our limited planetary resources. One of the core ideas is doubtlessly the common use of the material and immaterial means of production, and possibly even the democratization of production in the sense of self-empowerment.

Fab labs: From elite universities to grassroots practices

In addition to infrastructure for traditional forms of DIY, a very specific form of open workshop has become increasingly common in recent years: the fab lab (fabrication laboratory). The first fab lab was founded in 2001 as the result of a lecture series of the physicist Neil Gershenfeld of the Center for Bits and Atoms of the Massachusetts Institute of Technology. Under the slogan "How to make (almost) anything," his goal was to find out which machines and tools are necessary to manufacture all those things that can and cannot be bought, and thus design a set of equipment that is not made for mass production but for personal (digital) production, i.e. the production of things according to one's own ideas and needs. The basic equipment of the fab lab includes machines that normally belong in an industrial context, such as laser cutters, CNC machines (e.g. milling machines) and 3-D printers, which all work with digital templates. This concept created at an elite university has since grown into a global movement and is applied by a wide range of grassroots initiatives. The sharing of skills for working with computers and design and control software, as well as the operation of the machines themselves are all part of the basic educational concept of the labs. The Fab Charter[2] states the goal of giving individuals access to modern production means and processes in order to produce personalized single pieces or prototypes as a community resource. Currently, the platform of the international fab lab movement fablabs.io lists 1,325 facilities worldwide. At the 2018 version of the yearly international Fab Lab Conference the decision was made to set down common goals for the European region, increase networking, and strengthen collaboration beyond national borders and ideological differences.[3] One of the goals identified was to increase the chances of obtaining EU funding for non-academic grassroots initiatives.

2. Open workshops provide infrastructure for DIY from low to high tech, in the city and the country, and with easy access for all ages, educational backgrounds and social groups

The workshops listed on the platform of the Federation of Open Workshops (Verbund Offener Werkstätten e. V.) are a representative sample of all the different manifestations of the open workshop idea. Engineers and mechanical enthusiasts of every age, software developers, environmental technicians, artists, artisans, nerds, geeks and DIYers of all varieties see in open workshops a place of action that they then open up to a wide range of users, organizing and offering workshops and courses and advising and assisting others with their projects. Most workshops are individual initiatives, but some are a part of cultural, citizens' or youth centers or high schools or businesses. Some have been active for decades, others are just starting out. Some identify themselves with specific communities or concepts, such as the aforementioned fab labs, or have a thematic or technical focus with specific equipment, e.g. woodworking, bicycle repairs, metalworking, silkscreen printing, ceramics or the building of specific objects (such as cargo bikes). Some are multifunctional spaces that bring together different areas and types of equipment. These places enable diverse types of work with a wide range of materials and objects, including the development and building of complex machines and devices. It is interesting to note that, for most people, their participation in workshop projects does not (yet) replace traditional paid work. It is seen as a complement to or an expansion of their lives in ways not offered by their daily lives, jobs or formal education institutions. Thus, those spaces for action and experience that are independent of the market and the city and made possible through shared values in the community support the practical realization of more sustainable lifestyles: through making instead of buying, repairing instead of throwing away, open-source instead of patents. Here we see potential cornerstones for new forms of economy.

Locally organized and (generally speaking) open

An open workshop is always an actual physical place. Its initiators are therefore locally active, managing schedules for open, restricted and supervised use, as well as the different courses, workshops and projects involved. Some projects follow the principle of "restricted openness," meaning that they are targeted at specific interest groups. Hackerspaces are an example of this, where those involved create infrastructure mainly for others like them, organizing exchange and meeting places for all types of IT fans dedicated to free software or Internet politics, or finding creative and unexpected approaches to hardware. We all know the stereotype of the nerd who is only able to or only wants to communicate with those "in the know." However, there has already been criticism, even from inside these groups themselves, of the fact that hackerspaces are only open to "compatible" people.

The participants: social competencies are crucial

Those involved in the different areas and currents where open workshops play a role share the vision that productive infrastructure should be made available as a common good and that access should not be determined by educational background, the size of a person's wallet or any cultural, religious or social factors.

A person's participation is not dependent on their level as an expert or beginner, or on their age, background or gender. The decisive factors are rather social competencies and the ability to work well in (heterogeneous) groups. Of course, in general the type of workshop determines its user to an extent, and so repair projects tend to bring together the generation of over 50s, whereas fab labs are usually a place for the young, well-educated and tech-savvy. You won't necessarily find a unified political worldview shared by all, but then again that's nobody's goal. The glue that brings all these diverse initiatives together is common action and the search for openness.

Most of these projects don't take place within a structure of commercial services or paid work. Because of this, it is not always possible to make a clean split between organizers on the one side and users on the other. Most participants have multiple roles. (As in many community projects, around 80 percent of the common work is actually carried around by 20 percent of the people.) Open workshops are used as meeting places and places of action by a wide range of groups. Precisely because it is not a clearly defined concept, but rather a hands-on approach to implementing practical knowledge and manual skills in a new socio-spatial and material way, many of the aspects of open workshops can also be found in other currents, such as transition towns or urban gardening.

3. A lack of mutual awareness, commoning as a unifying element and common open spaces as a chance for the future

At present, degrowth debates and open workshop scenarios have hardly been brought together into a common vision of sustainable development pathways. More joint action could thus be effective in making core ideas and shared values visible. Commonalities will not manifest on their own. Local projects must know and be aware of each other in order to create a synergy effect. The magic word "networking" could, especially in the case of open workshops, lead to a more intensive and diverse use and therefore to a strengthening of a solidarity-based culture of contributions. This, in turn, promotes mutual inspiration and local support.

The inclusion of a wide range of movements in the project *Degrowth in Movement(s)* and their placement in the degrowth context allows community resources to shine in a new light. It would be ideal for these different, isolated movements to bring together their common values and convictions. To do this we need common goals. The open workshops movement has the goal of promoting the existence of common infrastructure in concrete places.

Commoning as a unifying element

The experiences of those involved in the creation, operation and maintenance of open workshops are a valuable contribution to the development of stable structures for a peer and commons-based society. Collectivization, self-organization, and the focus on regional and local economic cycles —which are also a part of other currents and initiatives in the degrowth context – can all be found here, not as blueprints, but rather as practical examples of grassroots, open-source infrastructures. What is decisive for those involved is access, not the underlying relations of property: commoning as a lifestyle could be seen as a unifying example in the concrete places where participants of degrowth and open workshops are active.

Creating common, open spaces and infrastructure with the highest possible degree of plurality

Generally speaking, a local group of a movement will always try to create open, physical spaces to carry out community activities. This leads to the question: What would cities, towns and communities look like if multifunctional community spaces were a natural part of the landscape? And we are not talking about private property kindly made available to a specific group, but self-managed, self-organized collective property managed by a community of "users" that is as diverse as possible. In order to get close to achieving the maximum degree of plurality possible, without endangering cohesion,[4] it is necessary to have an open discussion regarding the commonalities, differences, sources of conflict and existing and possible alliances between the different movements. In the second place, groups should dare more often to experiment with the creation of common, community-based infrastructure in real places. This should be done by groups that still don't realize that they can work together synergistically because of their (supposedly?) different approaches. In other words, the idea would be to create common open space irrespective of shared concepts in order to approach this ideal of maximum plurality and openness and to create realistic ad hoc structures for different groups to come into contact.

4. Open workshops as living labs? Instead of focusing on differences, we can turn to ideology-free spaces as a source of commons

Workshops follow an inherent logic and order that is more important than the individual interests of those that use them. A workshop is not an arbitrary space, but a specific arrangement of equipment and spatial functions. You have to *engage* with the workshop and throw out any ballast so as to develop individual sources of potential together with others in the space. Opinions, judgments and convictions are secondary when it comes to making the most out of such a productive setting. In this sense, workshops can be seen as spaces that provide "freedom from ideology."

The wide range of approaches brought together under the degrowth umbrella has given rise to struggles for the moral high ground that are not necessarily helpful when it comes to discovering deeper commonalities and shared concerns. Which is the right path? The fact that fab labs are gleefully used by some to produce plastic "toys" with 3-D printers, or blinking, beeping gadgets out of minicomputers, is for others a source of criticism: Who needs that? Whom does it help? Isn't this the opposite of degrowth? Isn't this another way for capitalism to subsume yet another movement because those involved just naively "play along," instead of fulfilling their potential to create new rules for the big game?

Open-source everything

Seen through a different lens, this supposedly naive "messing around," this new desire to deconstruct, understand and appropriate technology, is a sign that the preconditions for self-empowerment are changing. Today, affordable electronic parts, open-source software and hardware, readily available, comprehensive knowledge on any topic imaginable, as well as networking and exchange possibilities allow many to implement complex projects that would have been unthinkable a few years ago. Every day we use a significant number of products and services without understanding in the least how they work. To change something, you have to understand it first. The open-source paradigm (hardware, design) seeks to put an end to these black boxes and closed loops, and create openness. Now, it is possible to find freely available blueprints, designs and self-sufficiency concepts for all important areas of life, such as food, water treatment, energy, housing and mobility. High and low tech approaches thus come together time and time again in the search for developing "appropriate technologies."[5]

Together, different political currents could fertilize, "cultivate" and create awareness in the open-workshop culture, because "doing it yourself" doesn't necessarily mean producing in a sustainable or future-oriented way.[6] In other words, certain values and ideas from degrowth concepts could provide guidance to certain "doers," expanding their horizons and helping them find a context for their own action. In addition, open workshops are themselves living labs that can help find an economic system beyond the concept of growth. When people that normally don't have anything to do with each other "come together" in a productive exchange, things always start to get interesting. My suggestion is therefore that we dare to go into the "other camp" and —instead of arguing about ethical questions or defending our personal truths— simply do something together and solve a (small) concrete problem through our own work. To put it broadly: therapy instead of diagnosis, concrete instead of abstract, doing instead of (only) talking.

5. Using existing infrastructure as a building block for a plural movement

Instead of always having to invest money, time and energy into equipping new spaces, existing infrastructure could be gradually made available for an open and self-organized use. (Free) space and equipment are essential resources for a strong, emancipatory movement. There is actually more than enough room and equipment to go around: there is a surplus, not a shortage. Schools are a good example. A large number of the existing schools in Germany have workshops, but they are only for internal use. There is no way to use them outside of courses and curricular programs without supervision or a set schedule. Thus, these workshops are often unused and empty, especially in the afternoon and evening. What if, in accordance with a broader vision of workshops, schools were to become a new place of (self) education in order to meet the need for self-organization and collaboration?

So why not make existing infrastructure, such as school workshops, available to independently organized workshop groups when they are not used? These rooms with equipment could be rented out with a series of rights and obligations, opening up a new space of opportunities without significant material investments.

It is still unclear how all this could be turned into commons-based infrastructure in the long run. To do so, it might be necessary to tackle the "holy cow" of private property and replace profit with social added value. The resulting, socially worked out set of rules for a solidarity-based approach to abundance—brought about through small, organized local groups in a responsible social practice grounded in daily life— could perhaps be called a "pluriversalist system." This "vision" of using existing infrastructure differently without a "system reboot" and making this a reality through a convincing practical approach is in itself close to the degrowth vision. I refer to "degrowth approaches" here as a heterogeneous "melting pot" of different groups that makes it possible to implement this practice regardless of ideological differences – like a "real utopia."[7]

In order for the open workshops vision to truly release its society-changing potential, two criteria must be fulfilled:

- DIY – in its forms that highlight the idea of commons and the economic transformation of the system – will become increasingly important for a society that practices resilient and sustainable ways of living, and "doing things oneself" will stop being a niche and become part of the mainstream.
- These new peer and common-based operating systems will be flexibly adapted by each group to the local conditions and they will operate stably. In other words, there will be a comprehensive and reliable material and social responsibility for goods (such as spaces and equipment) that will be assumed by the collective, in a general environment of mutual respect and appreciation between all different enablers and commons practitioners.

In order for this to be successful, it is not only necessary to have alternative places of action but also a new understanding of what can be commons-based infrastructure and what these new forms of use could look like.

Translation: Santiago Killing-Stringer

Endnotes

1 Leisman et al., 2012.

2 Available at fab.cba.mit.edu/about/charter (Accessed 30 January 2019).

3 Memorandum of understanding, available at sites.google.com/view/europa-makes-network/home (Accessed 30 January 2019).

4 Alain Caillé uses the term "pluriversalism". See also greeneuropeanjournal.eu/the-convivialist-manifesto (Accessed 30 January 2019).

5 A definition by the Kollektiv für angepasste Technik (Collective for Appropriate Technology): kante.info/uber-uns/angepasste-technik (Accessed 30 January 2019).

6 Petschow, 2014.

7 Wright, 2010.

Links

Open source Hardware Association: oshwa.org

Repair initiatives in Germany: reparatur-initiativen.de

Verbund Offener Werkstätten, association of open workshops: offene-werkstaetten.org

Fab City – locally productive, globally connected cities: fab.city

Online social network of the international Fab Lab community: fablabs.io/labs/map

List of Hacker Spaces: wiki.hackerspaces.org/List_of_Hacker_Spaces

Map to find Maker Spaces: thisishardware.org/maker_spaces

Literature

Anderson, C. (2012) *Makers: The New Industrial Revolution*, New York, Crown Business.

Baier, A., Müller, C., Werner, K. (eds.) (2013) *Stadt der Commonisten – Neue urbane Räume des Do it yourself*, Bielefeld, transript.

Baier, A., Hansing, T., Müller, C., and Werner, K. (eds.)

(2016) *Die Welt reparieren. Selbermachen und Open Source als postkapitalistische Praxis*, Bielefeld, transcript.

Bollier, D., and Helfrich, S. (eds.) (2013) *The Wealth of the Commons: A World Beyond Market & State*, Amherst, Levellers Press.

Leismann, K., Schmitt, M., Rohn, H., and Baedeke, C. (2012) *Nutzen statt Besitzen – Auf dem Weg zu einer ressourcenschonenden Konsumkultur*, Berlin, Heinrich-Böll-Stiftung. Available at boell.de/sites/default/files/Endf_NutzenStattBesitzen_web.pdf (Accessed 28 January 2019).

Petschow, U., Ferdinand, J.-P., Dickel, S., Flämig, H., Steinfeldt, M., and Worobei, A. (2014) *Dezentrale Produktion, 3D-Druck und Nachhaltigkeit*. Berlin, Institut für ökologische Wirtschaftsforschung. Available at ioew.de/fileadmin/_migrated/tx_ukioewdb/IOEW_SR_206_Dezentrale_Produktion_3D-Druck_und_Nachhaltigkeit.pdf (Accessed 28 January 2019).

Rifkin, J. (2014) *The Zero Marginal Cost Society: The Internet of Things, the Collaborative Commons, and the Eclipse of Capitalism*, New York, Macmillan.

Siefkes, C. (2007) *From Exchange to Contributions: Generalizing Peer Production into the Physical World*, Berlin, Siefkes Verlag.

Chapter 15

Working-group on economics, 1996 in Roberto Barrios/Chiapas (Image: Bärbel Högner)

Peoples Global Action: (Truly) Global Grassroots Resistance

Friederike Habermann

Friederike travelled to the 1996 Intercontinental Gathering of the Zapatistas in Mexico, and from then on was involved in the development of the alter-globalization movement. She served as the press coordinator in the initially crucial network *Peoples Global Action*, a now defunct worldwide network of grassroots movements. Today, the historian and economist works as an independent academic. In her work, she explores social movements, different economic models, and the intersectionality of power structures. She lives in a commons-based project near Berlin.

1. After the end of *history* is being made: Without capitalism, without dominance

We have reached the "end of history," announced political

scientist Francis Fukuyama after the collapse of the Soviet Union, when what passed for socialism was once again replaced by capitalism. On 1 January 1994, the date that the North American Free Trade Agreement (NAFTA) came into effect, acceptance of neoliberalism was at its peak. On this date, a small, barely armed rebel movement from the jungles of the Mexican state of Chiapas mounted a rebellion: the *Zapatista Army of National Liberation EZLN* (*Ejército Zapatista de Liberación Nacional*). Before long their spokesperson, Subcomandante Marcos, proclaimed that it was not about seizing power, but about recreating the world. In their autonomous zones, the Zapatistas began the process of building freedom, democracy and justice. In fact, it was actually the women of the *EZLN* who had begun this process during an internal rebellion a year earlier. And this is no trivial matter: the Zapatistas support the abolition of *all* relationships of dominance.

Through their *Intercontinental Gatherings for Humanity and Against Neoliberalism* in 1996 and 1997, the Zapatistas brought together movements characterized by a similar understanding of politics on a global scale for the first time. Inspired by their Second Declaration of La Realidad and their call for a network of resistance, representatives from (predominantly grassroots) movements in over seventy countries came together and founded the worldwide network, *Peoples Global Action* (*PGA*). Yes: *peoples,* not *people's* – which is what most of the people who only *heard* the name thought – because indigenous peoples were involved from the outset, guiding the way: whether they were Adivasis from India, Maoris from Aotearoa aka New Zealand, or the Ecuadorian *CONAIE* alliance.

The fact that I write *Peoples Global Action* incorrectly by omitting the apostrophe (the correct spelling would be: *Peoples'*), opens up the possibility of it also being read as *People's* – i.e. Global Action Network of People. I began writing the name this way when I was acting as press coordinator for the *PGA*, a role that I had occupied since the protests against the World Trade Organization (WTO) in Geneva in May 1998. Though, while the protests were a success, our attempt to spread the news wasn't. Despite the fact that, after days and days of demonstrations and riots, Geneva's police chief was talking of a new 1968, and although coordinated campaigns were taking place worldwide —including 40,000 homeless and landless Brazilians marching on the national capital for a week, and the *Global Street Party*, which took place simultaneously on all continents— this new form of protest did not penetrate the consciousness of the global public.

When not a single news article appeared in the Western media after 200,000 farmers had demonstrated in India, the same farmers decided to send a few more emissaries to Europe at their earliest opportunity. In the spring of 1999, on the occasion of the EU and G8 double summit in Cologne, nearly 500 people from the Global South travelled in buses through eleven countries for five weeks, campaigning and meeting local activists. From the *Global Street Parties*, the *Global Action Days* were born: simultaneously coordinated worldwide actions. However, "this wall of silence that we are encountering," as M.D. Nanjundaswamy of Indian peasant movement *KRRS* expressed it in Geneva in 1998, was not even dented. When, in 1999 in Cologne, hundreds of *KRRS* members, dressed in white robes and green scarves, tried to take over public transport to go and laugh at the powers that be, they were rounded up and taken to a prison outside the city; the only newspaper that reported the event the next day published the headline: "300 autonomists occupy tram."

At the Seattle protests against the WTO Conference in the autumn of the same year, this silence was partially broken: the successful blockade on the first day, which also contributed to the failure of the negotiations, combined with the euphoric mood of the 50,000 protesters who remained for days on end, electrified a global audience. *Peoples Global Action (PGA)* was insofar a driving force behind this, as the American *Direct Action Network* – organizing the blockades in Seattle and leading to the strategic success of preventing the first day of the conference – had adopted *PGA's* fundamental principles. *PGA* was present as an international networking force solely through its five-week mini-caravan tour across the USA – although through this, we did contribute to the broad mobilization of 50,000 demonstrators in Seattle.

When the alter-globalization movement returned to Europe to protest against the International Monetary Fund (IMF) and the World Bank in Prague in September 2000, this time it was again *PGA* structures which directly initiated the process. Although the atmosphere was perhaps not as euphoric, these days of campaigning were also successful, and the protests ultimately led to a social movement: After this, *PGA* had nothing to do with organizing the demonstrations against the EU summit in Nice in December of the same year. And in the following months, it seemed that not even a meeting between trade ministers could take place without local blockades being planned.

But many grassroots movements from the Global South were unhappy with the concept of "summit hopping." To them, this form of action seemed too short-lived, and they were also often unable to participate due to problems with visas and plane tickets; individuals from the Global North, however, could afford the travel more easily, and were granted visas. For this reason, *Peoples Global Action* decided to hold a meeting of delegates at the same time as the Prague protests. Thus, at the very moment that the alter-globalization movement became a real force, *PGA* decided to focus on longer-term campaigns, the first being against Plan Colombia.[1] While the "movement of movements" continued to grow, *PGA*'s relevance faded in the wake of its departure from the summit protests.[2]

The alter-globalization movement experienced a massive setback at the G8 summit in Genoa in 2001, where members were faced with repressive tactics. In events later referred to as the "Chilean night," activists were pulled out of demonstrations or attacked in their sleep. Many of them were detained in police stations for days and beaten. To cap it all, just a month and a half later, 9/11 happened. A week later, the third major *Peoples Global Action* international conference took place, this time in Cochabamba, Bolivia.[3] Arriving delegates and organizers were subjected to massive legal repression. For the first time, topics included the commons, and alternatives to the dominant economic system. It was also the last time, as no further conferences followed. This enormous strength, that had made it possible to carry out major events almost out of nowhere, did not repeat itself.

Many individual activists (from the north) were also suffering burnout as a result of their intense commitment, or were no longer able to devote themselves so intensively to *PGA*; many movements (from the south) had their hands full with their own local struggles. Simply put, *PGA's* decentralized structure hampered its continuity. It is also likely that the foundation of the World Social Forum in 2001 contributed to the *PGA's* loss of protagonism; from then on, the forum provided an annual opportunity for tens of thousands to well over one hundred thousand people to meet and discuss alternatives.

2. "If you have only come to help me . . ."

To date, the prevailing belief is still, wrongly, that the protests against the exponents of neoliberalism (the World Trade Organization, the World Bank, and the International Monetary Fund) were essentially initiated by organizations from the Global North. *Attac* is regarded by many as being synonymous with "the alter-globalization movement." In reality, the impetus came fundamentally from the Zapatistas, Indian farmers, and various indigenous movements, and thus from those who are truly marginalized in the globalized world.

In *PGA* nobody spoke of being "globalization-critical" like *Attac*, or of an "anti-globalization movement"; it was not a question of "improving the design" of neoliberal globalization or of national solutions, but of coordinating grassroots resistance globally, and through it an emancipatory form of globalization. In order to avoid the entrenched hierarchies which can accompany the easy access to funding of those in the Global North, no continuous funding system was set up. Instead, donations were collected for each campaign. Instead of a board of directors, one movement in each world region (Western and Eastern Europe, North, Central and South America, the Middle East, South-Eastern Pacific, etc.) functioned as a "conveners' group." This group was responsible for ensuring that the process continued. Every time there was an international conference, the conveners changed. From the outset, attention was paid to ensuring gender equality between speakers at the conferences, as well as to equitable North-South representation.

PGA's five fundamental principles or hallmarks are:

1. A very clear rejection of capitalism, imperialism and feudalism; all trade agreements, institutions and governments that promote destructive globalization.

2. We reject all forms and systems of domination and discrimination including, but not limited to, patriarchy, racism and religious fundamentalism of all creeds. We embrace the full dignity of all human beings.

3. A confrontational attitude, since we do not think that lobbying can have a major impact in such biased and undemocratic organizations, in which transnational capital is the only real policy-maker;

4. A call to direct action and civil disobedience, support for social movements' struggles, advocating forms of resistance which maximize respect for life and oppressed peoples' rights, as well as the construction of local alternatives to global capitalism.

5. An organizational philosophy based on decentralization

and autonomy.

At meetings of the World Social Forum and at climate protests, many former *PGA* activists, specifically those representing grassroots movements from the Global South, express regret that a network similar to *Peoples Global Action* no longer exists. What is missing is a network which gives voice to the "subaltern," as postcolonial theorists refer to the most marginalized population groups in the world: including, for example, textile workers from Bangladesh, fishermen from Sri Lanka and the Philippines, and domestic workers from Bolivia, in addition to the indigenous movements or the black communities of Colombia.[4] Not as flagship attractions for non-governmental organizations from the Global North, but hand in hand with, for example, autonomous movements from Europe or the Canadian postal workers. While the *PGA* manifesto was never completed, and never gained greater importance, the above quote from "an Australian Aboriginal woman" was crucial: "If you have only come to help me, then you can go back home. But if you consider my struggle as part of your struggle for survival, then maybe we can work together."[5]

3. Peoples Global Action was creating commons

At degrowth events these days, it is not uncommon for me to hear the question from people coming across the idea for the first time: "How can we spread these insights in the Global South?" The concept of post-development, that is to say, the rejection of the growth path imposed on us by worldwide economic institutions, was being discussed as early as the 1980s – and was largely shaped in the south. It is thanks to Wolfgang Sachs in particular, that these ideas were disseminated throughout Germany in the 1990s, thus laying a significant foundation for post-growth in the country.

Post-development is an enigmatic term which includes a variety of very different approaches. Degrowth is another such catch-all definition; it includes not only Niko Paech's concept of the post-growth economy, but also non-capitalist economies right through to the economy of contribution, or demonetization (see the chapter on demonetization) or, using my term, ecommony. The "movement of movements" born from the protests in Seattle was, and is, equally diverse. What all these currents have in common is that we are, in various ways, searching for an alternative to the dominant economic system. Whereas post-development had a predominantly theoretical base, and *PGA* was a network for action, degrowth has the potential to drive both: theory and practice.

In this respect, today it comes as no surprise that former *PGA* activists, and consistently dissident grassroots movements from the Global South – for example, against the Narmada Valley dam in India, or the Kuna of Panama movement – have established contact with or are part of conceptually similar parts of the degrowth movement.

In addition to the question of substantive agreement, the type of organization is crucial – and here we come to the commons as a concept which was self-evidently practiced in *PGA,* and which plays a decisive theoretical role in the degrowth movement today. *PGA* was organized as a gift economy: money was at most available in the form of pocket money – for example, one hundred German marks per month for non-stop campaigning in the weeks leading up to an event, if dumpster diving wasn't enough. Accommodation, computers; everything was organized as a gift economy, that is to say, provided voluntarily by various individuals, often simply by third parties who had been asked to provide support. A conscious decision was made to have no paid staff, no office structures, and no financial resources beyond those required for the events themselves. Prior to such events, money was "collected" – today we would probably call it crowdfunding.

Therefore, it is no coincidence that former *PGA* activists can now be found in the commons movement. This is true of Massimo de Angelis, whom I first came across in an economics working group in the Chiapas jungle in 1996. At the beginning of the new millennium, he founded the web journal *The Commoner*, the first platform for transnational debate on commons. What I myself had not realized at the time had struck him: While the struggles falling under the *PGA* umbrella initially appeared very different, the majority in fact involved commons, that is to say, land or resources belonging to and/or affecting the whole community. For example, the Narmada Valley in India was a commons which allowed people to live well, instead of vegetating in a slum in the nearest big city. The struggles in Cochabamba focused on water as a commons.

As stressed by de Angelis, commons often arise in the first place out of struggles against their negation:[6] struggles against land grabs raise the question of land for those who cultivate it; struggles against intellectual property rights lead to the question of the knowledge commons; struggles against environmental degradation draw attention to the question of the natural commons; struggles against the privatization of water, education and health lead to demands for water, education and health as commons.

There are many approaches and struggles around commons with which the degrowth movement should also show solidarity. Since capitalism is impossible without growth, it requires a radically different form of economic organization. According to de Angelis, freedom from the restrictions of ownership would cause cooperation, inventiveness and social innovations to be driven by needs and desires.[7] This enables the development of diverse "powers-to," which then seek to rid themselves of the "powers-over." This also results in links to today's degrowth movement: from a common negation of the existing economic model and the associated power structures, to a world in which the power of the many is able to develop creatively. It should not simply be about defensive battles, or disputes about how to design the economy, but about every struggle against every relationship of power that restricts people's freedom to develop.

4. It takes us all to save the world

My suggestions for the degrowth movement are derived from the above-mentioned points: if activists from the Global North remain surrounded by their own kind, the consequence is the threat of climate colonialism and environmental racism. An example would be the "Keep it up!" slogan propagated in the name of green growth. This type of green growth is made possible by switching to renewable energy also based on energy plants in the Global South. This phenomenon now represents a major cause of land grabbing; not uncommonly of land that was being used as a commons. Also known by movements in the south as "greed economy" (a pun on "green economy"), the fact that this alignment is rejected by the degrowth movement shows that it provides an essential point of connection between north and south. In general, saving the world is not possible from the perspective of the "omnipotent white eye," to use the phrasing of postcolonial theorist Stuart Hall.[8] Hall used this term to refer to the colonial mentality of knowing better about everything, because the Europeans always believed that they were "further on." This attitude is still widespread today, obviously not least in economic and environmental issues.

Thus, what we need is global networking. Selectively inviting specific intellectuals to events or to write articles is not enough. It's about being in exchange with the "subalterns," the most marginalized groups, without reproducing hegemonies within these interactions. The World Social Forum has often been criticized for the latter, as the majority of those exchanging their views in the forum, even if they come from the Global South, are academics, male, and *white*. But if it goes beyond the level of face-saving events, the north and south can learn a lot from each other.

Perhaps, through the struggles in the Global South, the degrowth movement may begin to understand that post-growth does not have to be accompanied by sacrifice. When the Indian Adivasi fight for their right to live in the jungle instead of becoming IT experts – as per the explicit wishes of one government official – this takes ideas about what constitutes wealth and what constitutes sacrifice, and turns them upside down. And as far as political mobilization goes, there is another important lesson to be learned: it's not about money. For those who believe that the early stages of any movement necessarily involves a request for finance, this can be a crucial insight.

5. Together!

For decades, the movements of the Global South which remained, and remain, dissident, were those where a partially autonomous economic base secured the living conditions, yet also allowed for another way of living, and a different way of understanding the world. From this dynamic, spaces of another nature, "peninsulas against the current," are formed.[9] Communities of this type enable potential alternatives to capitalism to be seen more clearly, as they can be tested through day-to-day living. Occasional Saturday demo supporters who otherwise live within a capitalist understanding of the world quickly forget how to think beyond this viewpoint. That is why it is important to create similar peninsulas in the north. These do not have to be stand-alone projects; they can be other ways of living and coexisting in the city, links to other people at work, or simply freecycling networks on the Internet.

Although *Peoples Global Action* rejected lobbying, the struggle for political achievements on the legislative level might be useful. However, it will only become possible through a change in our common understanding. To this end, our efforts should not focus on demands, but on what David Graeber (who was active in *PGA* offshoots) defines as direct action: living in the here and now, the way we think is right.

My vision? A degrowth or post-development or buen-vivir or whatever-you-wanna-call-it movement, and an alter-globalization or climate or whatever-you-wanna-call-it movement unite in the spirit of *Peoples Global Action* to create a new movement of movements which places both resistance and the reorganization of day-to-day life at its heart. The caravans, the convergence centers (centers of activity) during the summit storms, the camps set up by *Occupy* and other such insurgent movements since 2010, and the current climate camps were, and are, examples of this. Without such subcultural "peninsulas against the current," we cannot develop a broad-based movement. For this reason, it is vitally important, not least for degrowth protagonists, to create areas of resistance where different experiences can be lived.

Translation: Kate Bell

Endnotes

1 In the summer of 2000, the US Congress granted a financial injection of $ 1.3 billion to the Colombian regime. Allegedly this was to fund the fight against the drugs mafia, but the real reason was to secure control of this geopolitically and strategically important region, and to ensure the implementation of a neoliberal development agenda.

2 Klein, 2003.

3 The second international conference had taken place in Bangalore, India, in August 1999.

4 Spivak, 1988.

5 The original quote, by the way, is somewhat different: "If you have only come to help me, then you're wasting your time. But if you come because your liberation is bound up with mine, then let's work together." The quote comes from a woman who has made quite a name for herself: Lilla

Watson, an (educational) activist from Brisbane. However, she herself points out that attributing the quote to her is not the full story, as it was born out of the collective process of a group of Aboriginal activists. But isn't it always the case that insights are attributed to individuals, even though new ideas only emerge when we are together?

6 De Angelis, 2002.

7 Ibid.

8 Hall, 1981.

9 Habermann, 2009.

Links

Peoples Global Action (PGA; Acción Global de los Pueblos): agp.org

Video on PGA: degrowth.info/en/dim/degrowth-in-movements/peoples-global-action

Literature

De Angelis, M. (2003) "Reflections on Alternatives, Commons and Communities. Or: Building a New World from the Bottom Up," *The Commoner*, vol. 6. Available at www.commoner.org.uk/deangelis06.pdf (Accessed 30 January 2019).

Hall, S. (1981) "The Whites of Their Eyes: Racist ideologies and the media," in: Bridges, G. and Brunt, R. (eds.), *Silver Linings: Some strategies for the eighties*, London, Lawrence and Wishart, pp. 28-52.

Klein, N. (2002), *Fences and Windows: Dispatches from the Front Lines of the Globalization Debate*, London, Picador.

Notes from Nowhere (2003) *We are Everywhere. The Irresistible Rise of Global Anticapitalism*, London/New York, Verso.

Spivak, G. C. (1988) *Can the Subaltern Speak?*, Basingstoke, Macmillan.

Chapter 16

Landcover, forest clearance and plantation development in PT Megakarya Jaya Raya (PT MJR) palm oil concession (Image: ©Ulet Ifansasti/Greenpeace

Post-Extractivism: Against the Exploitation of Natural Resources

Ulrich Brand

Ulrich is a Professor of International Politics at the University of Vienna, where he teaches and researches. He is a co-editor of the Blätter für deutsche und internationale Politik (*Journal for German and International Politics*) and a member of the scientific advisory board of Attac Deutschland. He was a scientific member of the committee of inquiry Wachstum, Wohlstand, Lebensqualität (Growth, Prosperity, Quality of Life) of the German Bundestag (2011–2013). He writes this text from the position of an "activist scholar" and as a *white* man who has worked his way up from a non-academic family background (why – in his own words – he tends to be "overzealous"). He has been working for many years on the analysis of hegemonic developments in Europe and Latin America, as well as on the alternatives that have arisen there.

1. Criticism of neo-extractivism and use of post-extractivism as a new term and condition for a good life

For the past two decades there has been an intense debate in Latin America regarding possible alternatives to neoliberal capitalism. At first glance, these concepts – which have been referenced in different countries by social movements and established left-wing and left-liberal parties in search of fundamental alternatives – are very different from the degrowth perspective. However, and this is my main argument, the degrowth movement can learn from these ideas. To explain this I will refer to the discussion surrounding post-extractivism (a term I will define later on), sometimes also referred to as neo-extractivism, which in essence is a critical discussion on the currently dominant development model in Latin America.[1]

Critics of the neo-extractivist model in Latin America fear that the region will become increasingly dependent on the global market due to an excessive focus on mining, agro-industrial monocultures, and the extraction of fossil fuels such as coal, oil and gas. They warn that this economic model will increasingly lead to the destruction of the ecological bases of life, the shifting of costs and negative consequences onto others, high social and ecological costs, and an increasing ignorance on the part of political decision-makers regarding social and political (minority) rights. The different practices of resource extraction are thus linked to territorial transformation processes that result in a rearrangement of landscapes, social and labor relations, and a fragmentation of common space. These processes are characterized by: the creation of new borders and divisions, the emergence of enclave economies, the granting of exclusive exploitation rights, an undemocratic use of nature, and widespread ecological destruction.

Neo-extractivism is a development and social model fundamentally based on the exploitation of raw materials and the appropriation of the income generated by said extraction through local elites, the state, and national or transnational companies. The continuation of a resource-intensive life, consumption and production style in the Global North and South (a phenomenon which degrowth also considers highly problematic) could boost neo-extractivism even more, as the demand for raw materials continues to rise.

It is thus more important than ever to create a dialogue between the degrowth and post-extractivism perspectives. The achievement of the goals of degrowth and of the alternatives to resource extractivism require more than anything a change in *international* political, socio-economic and cultural relations. The continuation of an imperialistic production model and lifestyle that is largely established in the Global North and is becoming increasingly so in many countries of the Global South – with its implications for power and political dominance, the structure of society and the global market – is a fundamental obstacle to any alternative.

What are the key elements of the term "post-extractivism"?

The criticism of modern capitalism and post-colonialism: At a fundamental level, it is not only about criticizing the exploitation of raw materials and the resulting socio-economic, political and ecological problems. Rather, the term post-extractivism refers to the fact that these processes are a part of a comprehensive development model and understanding of the world. The targets of criticism are the unwavering Western belief in modern progress, the corresponding growth paradigm, the vision of nature as a resource to be exploited, the authoritarian and vertical political dominance models, and the asymmetric integration into the global market. It is not a total rejection of any form of societal extraction and use of raw materials. The aim is rather to expose and reject the way in which this hegemonic appropriation for the global capitalist market destroys nature and society.

On this basis, the Latin American debate distinguishes between three forms of extractivism: "predatory" extractivism, which is the currently dominant form; "sensible" extractivism, which would be carried out according to certain ecological and social standards; and "indispensable" extractivism, i.e. that which is necessary for social development (of course, what constitutes "indispensable extractivism" must be negotiated by all of society). In actual fact, the third option should not be considered extractivism as a development model, but rather a judicious form of resource extraction and use based on a social and political consensus.

This perspective is accompanied by demands for a decolonization of knowledge and knowledge systems, in a context of criticism and rejection of European instrumental and imperialist logic.

Diagnosing the crisis: The post-extractivism debate is generally based on the premise that there is currently a widespread civilizational crisis. This extends far beyond the diagnosis of individual economic, financial or other crises.

Experience of social mobilization: In contrast to Europe, countries such as Bolivia and Ecuador have seen radical movements leading to left-wing governments and constitutional reforms. The past 15 years have therefore shown that it is possible for social mobilizations to lead to fundamental changes. To an extent, this also applies to Venezuela, Argentina and Brazil. In all of these cases, the stated goal is not to "go back" or to romanticize indigenous, community-based forms of life, but to recognize the existence of multiple forms of knowledge and experiences of the world.

Territory: The term "giro eco-territorial" coined by Maristella

Svampa (one possible translation could be "eco-territorial reorientation of the struggle") expresses the fact that the main struggles in Latin America right now are over land and territories, accompanied by struggles for greater autonomy and self-determination, and against social exclusion, ecological destruction and the commodification of human beings and nature. The main demands are for moratoriums on large-scale projects and the direct involvement of those affected in the said projects.

Goals of a new societal model: A transition to a post-extractivist society would involve overcoming *predatory* extractivism in a first stage and replacing it with *sensible* extractivism, through the introduction of social and ecological standards, more advanced technology, compensation payments to affected communities and a range of other measures. This would reduce economic dependency on foreign countries and allow these states greater freedom in the search for alternative economic policies. The second phase would be the transition to an economic model in which the exploitation of natural resources is reduced to a minimum. This would be accompanied by a recognition of a plural economy, with agrarian reforms, adapted technologies, a restructuring of the existing system of taxes and subsidies, a fundamental restructuring of the generally authoritarian systems and concepts of education, a deeper level of cooperation between Latin American countries and, especially in Andean countries, the development of plurinational states.

Connecting economic, social and ecological questions: Like the degrowth perspective, post-extractivism also aims at a widespread societal change. For its part, degrowth has a clearer focus on the ecological debate and on people, i.e. it is more anthropocentric. In both discussions, however, the term "environmental justice" plays an important role. In my opinion, the post-extractivist perspective —in accordance with the experiences in Latin America – provides a clearer overview of the general conditions and forms of social reproduction beyond market economics and paid work ("social" is used in a broad sense here and also includes economic and natural relations). In this regard, its closest equivalent would be the feminist perspective in the degrowth debate.

Vision of nature, relation with nature, and the rights of nature: Especially in one area, the Latin American perspective goes beyond most degrowth positions. There is a more radical questioning of the modern capitalistic juxtaposition of society and nature, and the generally accepted model of subjugation and (over)use of the latter, often resulting in its destruction. This "óptica mercantilista" or "mercantile lens" that only sees nature as a commodity and disregards the specific conditions of nature and its reproduction is criticized as being a Eurocentric perspective. Nature cannot be separated from society; it is not something to be manipulated and taken apart. Human beings should be seen as a part of nature and non-human nature should be given its own intrinsic value.

Cultural identities: The most recent cycle of social mobilizations in Latin America cannot be understood without taking into account the years 1992 (500 years after the beginning of colonization) and 1994 (rebellion of the Zapatistas in Mexico). After centuries of post-colonial exploitation, racism and patriarchal structures, questions of cultural identity are seen as crucial. The Andean countries in particular have seen the development of discussions on interculturalism driven by widespread indigenous protests and mobilizations.

Power and dominance structures: A review of the literature on post-extractivism, the alternatives to the existing development model and a "good life" reveals a greater focus on power and hegemony than in the degrowth debate. This is due to concrete historical reasons. In Latin America, explicit and structural violence, exclusion and humiliation and the asymmetry in power structures are much more visible and a part of daily life than in many parts of Europe.

The question that must then be asked is: To what extent can these concepts largely rooted in indigenous life experiences and territorial conflicts achieve resonance in Europe where urbanization is much more advanced and many people have lost touch with rural life?

2. Post-extractivism as a new term and as a condition for a good life

In Latin America, many terms are used to describe fundamental alternatives to the current situation. These do not include the terms "degrowth" or "post-growth." In the Andean countries, one concept that is currently of particular importance is that of "a good life" (in Spanish, "*buen vivir*" or "*buenos convivires*"; in Ecuadorian Quechua, "*sumak kawsay*"; in Bolivian Aymara, "*suma quamaña*"). The election of left-wing presidents in Bolivia (2005) and Ecuador (2006) led to the drafting of new constitutions in which these countries, among other things, defined themselves as plurinational states that recognized and expanded the autonomy of indigenous peoples and set down the rights of nature. In fact, the achievement of a good life is now explicitly stated as a national goal in both constitutions. However, in other countries such as Brazil these terms do not play an important role. Here, the term that could most closely be used to describe the multiple alternatives and forms of resistance is "environmental justice." This encompasses myriad concrete struggles to achieve food sovereignty, the right to the city, citizenship and other goals — all of which are increasingly seen as being part of the concept of a good life.

One way to link the two together could be the concept of post-extractivism. It has its origins in the successful mobilizations against neoliberal policies, economic models and power structures on the one hand, and a critique of neo-extractivism on the other. The quest to outline and strengthen the concepts of post-extractivism can be seen as an attempt to create the preconditions necessary for implementing the concepts of a good life and, in addition, to contribute directly to the struggle for a good life from a radical perspective.

However, it is first necessary to specify what is contained in "a good life," because it is the subject of intense political and scientific debate. Ecuador's national development plan, for example, is also referred to as the *"Plan del Buen Vivir"* (plan for a good life) and states the goal of moving away from neo-extractivism, but it fails to achieve this in practice. On the other hand, it is unclear whether or not the current proposals of *buen vivir* can accommodate the degrowth perspectives of dematerialization, decommodification and decentralization.

Criticism of and resistance to the neo-extractivist model is ubiquitous. The first group to resist is the local population that directly suffers the negative consequences of the neo-extractivist economic activities. When mining companies shovel away whole mountains and use up huge amounts of drinking water, e.g. to extract gold, and the excavated soil is then taken to other regions and dumped there, this leads to the political activation and possible organization of the local population. These processes are often supported by critical NGOs and scientists, who provide knowledge about the economic, social and ecological consequences of large-scale mining activities and disprove the false promises of investors who claim they will bring jobs and prosperity. This support often leads to a degree of media coverage.

One important development in recent years has been the growing coordination between different resistance movements in regional and national forums, in order to have an exchange, forge common strategies and work on alternatives. This also leads to a greater visibility of resistance movements on a regional, national and even international level.

This criticism seeks to expose the struggles and costs that

result from the current development model. The term post-extractivism seeks to unite and strengthen this wide range of criticisms, resistance movements and alternatives through their commonalities. This is made even more important by the fact that, outside the affected regions and on a national level, the negative consequences of mining, fossil fuel extraction, and agro-industrial activities have long been ignored or suppressed, a situation which continues until now.

3. Degrowth and post-extractivism: together against a neoliberal capitalist system that is increasingly based on the commodification of social relations and nature

For both degrowth and post-extractivism, the deeply rooted views and practices that surround the ideas of progress and growth are a central problem. Both provide a combined analysis of different elements of the crisis and axes of conflict and develop a general social perspective for the future. Social inequality and ecological problems are in both cases a main focus of criticism. There is also consensus on the fact that a large portion of the known fossil fuel reserves should remain in the ground.

Both perspectives are mainly used by progressive (politically left-wing and academically critical) forces to challenge the existing development and growth models, including varieties such as so-called "green growth" and "sustainable development." The emphasis on issues of distribution and equality, among others, shows that both positions seek to politicize the issue of distribution and thus present alternatives to the often very limited progressive economic and socio-political debate. In this sense, they are both positions against false alternatives, against positions too deeply rooted in realpolitik. If one is not able to *imagine* farther reaching possibilities and their realization, then it will not be possible to bring about change.

Both perspectives require social forces that are willing to imagine and seek to achieve far-reaching changes. At the same time, there is no master plan or uniform strategy: strategies, initiatives and alliances should be developed – or should arise out of practical necessity – and implemented according to each context.

In general, these movements place little trust in existing social and political institutions such as the state, the market or the general public, although their importance for the transformative process is not denied. Especially the state, which in other progressive approaches is considered the central motor of change, is seen here as being embedded in a development model that is problematic per se (more on this below).

Both degrowth and post-extractivism are based on an alternative understanding of prosperity, which encompasses political action, a socially and ecologically adequate production system, and an attractive life for people. It is necessary to change the destabilizing forms of capitalist growth and the interests that drive it. This would make it possible to consider social conditions under which people can develop as individuals and live in a solidarity-based, social environment, itself a precondition for unrestricted personal development.

Despite the differences between them (see below), both perspectives are ultimately very critical of dominant knowledge structures (post-extractivism) and of dominant scientific structures (degrowth; especially regarding neoclassicism and neoclassical environmental economics, but also regarding Keynesianism).

4. Learning from post-extractivism and its fundamentally critical understanding of capitalism as a hegemonic system

In my view, the post-extractivist perspective places a clearer emphasis than degrowth on the hegemonic and destructive mechanisms of a post-colonial, patriarchal and hierarchizing capitalist system. In the former, experiences with the global market and imperialist policies, as well as the dynamics of commodification and submission are very present. Likewise, in the Latin American discussion, the wide range of existing problems due to inequality are presented more clearly in relation to the dominant capitalist production system and lifestyle. The post-extractivist perspective understands that it is not only a production and consumption system, but also a system of power and dominance – over people and, ultimately, over nature. Degrowth could learn from this more fundamental understanding of capitalism.

In other areas, the perspectives can also enrich each other: the degrowth perspective aims at achieving a voluntary, frictionless and just transition to a regime with less production and consumption, and often proposes concrete alternatives and niche activities. Post-extractivism, in the light of Latin American experiences, would counter that this notion of a voluntary and frictionless transition in all likelihood underestimates the underlying social relations of power, deeply rooted mentalities, materialized structures and conflicting interests. In Latin America, these conflicts are much clearer and are therefore treated in a much more explicit manner.

Criticism of neo-extractivism is closely related to a criticism of the social power and dominance structures through which certain forms of appropriation and submission of nature are achieved. For example, the debate "Alternatives to Development" formulates a profound critique of the concept of development and its associated practices.[2] This debate originates in the Global South and can therefore provide the unique perspective of the South on these problems. Of course, the degrowth perspective also deals de facto with social and political dominance structures, but this is rarely made explicit and would have to be expressed more clearly.

My suggestion for degrowth would be to deliver a critique of the Western, rationalistic and dichotomizing understanding of nature and the resulting relationship with nature. In the European context such a perspective would not be new, but in degrowth it is barely present. A discussion on the rights of nature can and should have greater prominence in the context of degrowth.

5. Post-extractivism as an attempt to create the conditions for a good life and to contribute to the struggle from a radical position

Post-extractivism is a *glocal* undertaking, i.e. it goes from the local, through the national and regional, to the global, and back again.

For the degrowth perspective and for an eventual movement that could arise under this banner, it is essential to clearly show how what is happening in other regions of the globe is inexorably entwined with the imperialist production system and lifestyle that are dominant in Europe. If not, degrowth might succumb to navel-gazing and fail to recognize the destructive basis of its own alternatives. The Portuguese legal and social scholar Boaventura de Sousa Santos refers to the "Epistemologies of the South," which – like colonialism and the flow of natural resources from the Global South – are denied in the knowledge and practices of the Global North.[3]

Any alternative perspective in Europe, and this includes degrowth, should recognize the emancipatory struggles and alternatives in other parts of the world and seek to understand the relationship between them and its own approach. Ultimately, the goal all over the world is to picture and realize alternative forms of prosperity and good living – against the impositions of the capitalist growth imperative, the associated humiliation and exploitation, its racist, patriarchal and imperialist structures and the ubiquitous exploitation of nature. To create ways of producing and living that are based on solidarity and ecological sustainability, that is the goal that unites the myriad struggles around the world of which degrowth is an important part.

Translation: Santiago Killing-Stringer

Endnotes

1 This text is based on a more comprehensive analysis published in: Brand 2015. I would like to thank Johannes Apel, Nina Treu, Dennis Eversberg and Matthias Schmelzer for their valuable advice.

2 Lang and Mokrani, 2013.

3 Santos, 2008.

Links

Alternatives to Development – Permanent Working Group or Rosa Luxemburg Foundation: rosalux.org.ec/grupo

Literature

Acosta, A. (2017) "Living Well: ideas for reinventing the future," *Third World Quaterly*, vol. 38, no. 12, pp. 2600-2616.

Acosta, A., and Brand, U. (2017) *Salidas del laberinto capitalista. Decrecimiento y Postextractivismo,* Barcelona, Icaria Publisher.

Brand, U., Dietz, K., and Lang, M. (2016) "Neo-Extractivism in Latin America – one side of a new phase of global capitalist dynamics," *Revista de Ciencia Política*, vol. 11, no. 21, pp. 125-159.

Brand, U., and Wissen, M. (2018) *The Limits to Capitalist Nature: Theorizing and Overcoming the Imperial Mode of Living*, London and New York, Rowman & Littlefield.

Fatheuer, T. (2012) *Buen Vivir: a brief introduction to Latin America's new concepts for the good life and the rights of nature,* Berlin, Heinrich Böll Foundation.

Gudynas, E. (2016) "Beyond varieties of development: disputes and alternatives," *Third World Quarterly*, vol. 37, no. 4, pp. 721-732.

Lang, M., Mokrani, D. (eds.) (2013) Beyond Development.

Alternative Visions from Latin America, Amsterdam/Quito, Transnational Institute/Rosa Luxemburg Foundation.

De Sousa Santos, B. (2014) *Epistemologies of the South. Justice against Epistemicide*, Boulder, Paradigm Publishers.

Svampa, M. (2016) *Debates Latinoamericanos. Indianismo, desarrollo, dependencia, populismo*, Buenos Aires, Edhasa.

Chapter 17

Community Radio mobiliser of the Deccan Development Society in Telangana (Image: Author)

Radical Ecological Democracy: Reflections from the South on Degrowth

Ashish Kothari

Ashish is a member of *Kalpavriksh*, which has been active on environment and development issues in India since 1979. He has been on the steering committee of the ICCA Consortium, a global network of working in territories and areas conserved by indigenous peoples and local communities; has been on the boards of *Greenpeace International* and *Greenpeace India*; and is a member of *Beyond Development*, a global working group set up by the *Rosa Luxemburg Stiftung*. *Kalpavriksh* currently coordinates the *Vikalp Sangam* (Alternatives Confluence) process in India, under which principles and values related to ecoswaraj are being evolved. It also manages the RED e-list and website, and has helped initiate the Global Tapestry of Alternatives. Ashish was also co-coordinator of a global activist-academic research project on environmental justice, ACKnowl-EJ.

1. Ecoswaraj as a response to the social and ecological bankruptcy of the currently dominant development and governance system

The multiple crises that humanity is facing are becoming increasingly visible: in the form of disasters related to ecological damage, the stark inequalities between a tiny minority of ultra-rich and the vast numbers of desperately poor, the health epidemics related to both deprivation and affluence, mass refugee migrations in many parts of the world, and the scarcity of several once-abundant resources. Countries like China and India are fast joining the already-industrialized nations in putting even more stress on the planet, or in colonizing less powerful regions of the earth. In such a situation, there is an urgent quest for alternative pathways for well-being that are sustainable, equitable and just.

There is no doubt that as a species we have to downsize if we are to respect the limits; not only for ourselves but —just as importantly— for the millions of other species that co-inhabit the earth with us. It is timely, therefore, to talk of degrowth in the context of humanity as a whole, and most certainly in the context of the Global North which is overconsuming and overdumping.

But is degrowth, or the reduction of material and energy uses for human use, a valid and viable strategy for the Global South, i.e. countries and populations (including some in industrialized countries) that have not reached an excessive or even acceptable level of prosperity? Perhaps not. What is needed is for these regions and peoples to find their own home-grown visions and pathways of change. I will talk here of one such example: *ecoswaraj* or *radical ecological democracy* (*RED*), which is emerging from practical and conceptual processes in India.

India currently sees itself as entering into the elite league of economic superpowers. Along with China, it has enjoyed the world's highest growth rates in the last couple of decades. But this has come at a horrendous cost to the environment, and to hundreds of millions of people who are directly dependent on the environment.[1] It has also created an increasing schism between the rich and poor, so that 1% of the population now owns nearly 70% of the country's wealth, while at least two-thirds of its people remain deprived of basic needs, and employment scarcity is staring at a hundred million young people who have recently joined the workforce.

The problem lies partly in the growth fetish. An economic policy that assumes that growth will magically translate into the poor rising above the poverty line and everyone getting productive jobs is fundamentally flawed. It ignores the fact that many of the gains of growth could be cornered by the already rich, that mechanization may offset any new job generation, and that inflation may make things even worse for much of the population. This is compounded by the increasing withdrawal of the state from basic services (the trend being to privatize them) and the serious inefficiencies and corruption in whatever service delivery that still exists. All of this is built on top of a deeply hierarchical society, with unthinkable oppression and exploitation of "lower" castes, women, and the landless.

Ecological suicide is as much a part of the history of "development" as are deprivation and inequalities. The global story of humanity crossing several planetary boundaries is mirrored in India. Two reports, not from environmental activists but from the very institutions that otherwise champion unbridled growth, have admitted as much. The *Chamber of Indian Industries* (along with the *Global Footprint Network*) said in 2008 that India is already consuming twice as much as its natural resources can sustain. The *World Bank* reported in 2013 that environmental damage (based on a few parameters such as impact on people's health) is knocking 5.7% off of GDP growth. If all impacts of such damage were to be accounted for, even using the limited methodology of environmental economics, we would possibly be in a negative growth phase.

Communities and citizens in India are, however, not taking all of this lying down. At any given moment in the last couple of decades, there have been several hundred resistance movements, from a few families refusing to part with their land for the industry, to thousands of people protesting a mega-hydro project; from *dalit* (so-called "untouchables," the lowest in the caste hierarchy) and women's demands for basic human rights, to students protesting the decline in public support for educational institutions. Simultaneously, people are also coming up with innovative, positive transformations in their lives, on their own or with support from civil society organizations and occasionally even governments. It is from both the resistance and the reconstruction (*sangharsh* and *nirman*) initiatives that the idea of ecoswaraj or radical ecological democracy (RED) has emerged.

The term *swaraj* can be loosely translated as "self-rule" — though it is much more than just a governance concept— and refers to a combination of individual and collective autonomy, mutual responsibility, rights, and responsibilities. Although older than him, the concept was popularized by Gandhi as part of India's freedom struggle against British colonial power, and is referred to in his seminal book *Hind Swaraj* as a civilizational ethos comprising the elements mentioned above. I have added "eco" to more explicitly integrate the principle of ecological wisdom and resilience into this political and cultural ethos (though it is already implicit in Gandhi's formulation). Ecoswaraj or RED envisions a society in which all people and communities are empowered to be part of decisions affecting their lives (radical or direct democracy) in ways that are ecologically sensitive and socially equitable. Below I will further explain this concept and refer to its various key elements.

2. Ecoswaraj or RED is an emerging framework for communities and organizations exploring alternative visions and pathways

In the drylands of Andhra Pradesh and Telangana in southern India, small farmers — including *dalit* women[2] – of the *Deccan Development Society* have transformed their lives by reviving organic farming using their own seeds, achieving full food sovereignty, collectivizing resources and labor, securing basic rights, forming cooperatives or companies to negotiate better returns, forming community-run media (films, radio), and throwing off the traditional social stigmas associated with them. In the forested landscapes of Maharashtra in central India, several communities in Gadchiroli & Chandrapur districts have taken back control over their surrounding forests, initiated sustainable harvesting of bamboo and other forest produce, converted the earnings into enhanced energy, livelihoods, and food security, and in at least one village (Mendha-Lekha), turned all private lands back into the commons. City-level or national associations in Pune, Bangalore, Delhi and elsewhere are fighting for the right of hawkers, rickshaw-pullers, waste pickers, and other marginalized sections to spaces and services of the city, and enhanced conditions for livelihood and living. Learning and educational institutions such as the *Adivasi Academy* in the indigenous regions of the west Indian state of Gujarat, and *SECMOL* in the high-altitude region of Ladakh, provide opportunities that – unlike mainstream education – enable students to remain connected with their cultural and ecological roots while also learning modern subjects and skills.

These are just a very few examples of communities, government agencies, businesses and individuals showing ecologically sensitive, socially equitable pathways to food and water security, enhanced livelihoods and jobs, nature and natural resource conservation, manufacturing and services, social (including gender) justice, and other sectors of economy and society. For these purposes, a range of alternative media, arts, and other aspects of human creativity are being pressed into service. And it is not only those in desperate situations or crises that are acting. Increasingly, the middle classes in some cities are also asserting their desire to live more responsibly, e.g. by mobilizing to revive urban wetlands, moving towards full recycling of their waste and decentralized water harvesting and by asserting their right to be a part of city planning through participatory budgeting.

There is not the space to describe any of the above in detail, and I and others have done so in several publications elsewhere.[3] Of course, these initiatives are not perfect (for instance, equity for traditionally unprivileged groups is weak in many), there are huge gaps in coverage, and for the most part they are small and scattered. But they increasingly show the potential of alternatives, and several have demonstrated larger spread by influencing policy changes and networking. For instance, over a dozen Indian states now have policies or programs to support organic farming (even the central government included it in its 2016 budget for the first time), undoubtedly influenced by the examples demonstrated by farmers and by the increasing urban demand for healthy food. Similarly, grassroots successes in renewable energy have prompted governments to significantly enhance financial support for it, though often in flawed ways (e.g. letting them be controlled by large corporations).

Having visited, documented, or supported several such initiatives, and having been a part of resistance movements in the last 40 years, I believe that the most important task is to learn the essence of these initiatives, and to see if the values and principles emerging from them can suggest a cohesive framework for challenging the currently dominant mindset and practice of growth-centerd "developmentality."

In a series of dialogues and confluences starting in 2014, called *Vikalp Sangam* (Alternatives Confluence), several hundred practitioners and thinkers (not exclusive categories, of course!) have discussed such a framework and agreed on the following crucial elements or pillars of a transformation[4]:

1. *Ecological sustainability and wisdom,* including the conservation of nature (ecosystems, species, functions, cycles) and its resilience, ensuring that human activities are based on environmental ethics and are within planetary limits.

2. *Social well-being and justice,* including lives that are physically, socially, culturally, and spiritually fulfilling, where there is equity (including gender equity) in socio-economic and political entitlements, benefits, rights and responsibilities, and where cultural diversity is celebrated and promoted. Attempts to bring back ancient Indian beliefs in "enoughness," voluntary simplicity or austerity, without falling into the trap of bigoted religiosity, are part of this.

3. *Direct democracy,* where decision-making starts at the smallest unit of human settlement, in which every human has the right, capacity and opportunity to take part; envisaging larger levels of representative or delegated governance that are downwardly accountable, defined on the basis of ecological and cultural contiguity and linkages ("ecoregions" or "biocultural" regions).

4. *Economic democracy,* in which local communities have control over the means of production, distribution, exchange, and markets; where localization is a key principle and larger trade and exchange are built on it. This is the basis of several initiatives at producer companies and cooperatives, and producer-consumer linkages in fields such as food and crafts. The re-invention of non-monetized exchanges (barter and other forms) and local bazaars, infused with equity principles that may have been weak in the past, has to be part of this process.

5. *Knowledge commons and cultural diversity,* where the

generation, conservation, transmission and use of knowledge (including traditional and modern forms) are collective processes, not confined to formal sector "experts" or to state or corporate run institutions; and where the diversity of cultures is celebrated and sustained.

It is important to note that the above does not fit into any prevalent political or economic ideology. We use *ecoswaraj* because the Gandhian concept of *swaraj* (and the Gandhian economist Kumarappa's "economics of permanence") has many aspects that are relevant, but learnings and struggles based on Marxist ideas, those of the *dalit* leader BR Ambedkar, those of Rabindranath Tagore ("City and Village"), or MN Roy and others are also essential parts of the heritage of these initiatives. Crucially, though, indigenous peoples and local communities and others base their actions and thoughts on their own diverse situations, and what emerges is a set of common values that transcends any particular established ideology. Such values include: collective working and solidarity, respect for diversity and pluralism, the dignity of labor, empathy and respect for the rest of nature, simplicity, equity and justice, rights with responsibilities, self-reliance, autonomy and freedom, and others.

3. The principles of ecoswaraj and degrowth resonate, and there is potential for further cooperation

From what limited understanding I have of the concept and practice of "degrowth," I believe that in many of the above ways, RED resonates well with it. But there may also be crucial differences, given that a blanket proposal for degrowth is unlikely to be appropriate or acceptable within the Global South for whom deprivations of basic needs is a reality. It is therefore a crucial agenda for all of us to look at both commonalities and differences of alternative approaches including ecoswaraj, degrowth, *buen vivir,* ecofeminism, *ubuntu,* solidarity economies, and others (for nearly 100 such approaches, see the compilation in Kothari et al 2019). A beginning was made as a civil society initiative towards *Peoples' Sustainability Treaties* in relation to the Rio+20 conference, but much greater networking and collective work will be required in the coming years.

Some of the crucial questions that could be posed as part of such work include: What are the historical factors that are common to the experiences of the Global North and South (e.g. colonialism and capitalism), and what are the crucial differences (e.g. spiritual traditions, cosmovisions)? What are the principles of process that underlie initiatives striving for an alternative to currently dominant systems? Which of these are common to the Global North and South (e.g. those of solidarity and collective action), and which are different (e.g. the environmentalism of the marginalized oriented towards survival and basic needs vs. that of the relatively well-off oriented towards reducing unsustainability). What are the commonalities and differences in ethical values? These questions should be posed and answered based on an understanding of practical initiatives grounded in different settings.

This kind of collaboration is also important for us to collectively advocate fundamental alternatives to the "green economy," "green growth" and even "sustainable development" agendas that are being promoted globally (and which through the Sustainable Development Goals received "official" sanction at the highest UN level in late 2015), showing that there are other viable pathways that challenge capitalism, statism, patriarchy, racism, etc.[5]

For this it is necessary to work more closely together, pro-actively understanding each other's contexts and initiatives. It would be fascinating for joint teams of practitioner/activist researchers to move around looking at a range of grassroots initiatives and address the kinds of questions I've mentioned above. Some of this has been part of a new project called Academi-

Activist Co-generation of Knowledge on Environmental Justice co-coordinated by the *Institute for Environmental Science and Technology at Universitat Autónoma de Barcelona,* Spain and *Kalpavriksh,* India. One part of this project is to examine and have a dialogue of alternative frameworks and worldviews emerging from environmental and social justice movements in different parts of the world. Another proposal under discussion is for a Global Alternatives Confluence, learning from the confluences taking place in India – a project was launched in mid-2019 as the Global Tapestry of Alternatives.

4. The diverse set of locally embedded frameworks can inspire each other

Each alternative worldview or framework arises within a particular socio-cultural, ecological, economic and political context, and cannot be replicated or applied as it is to another context. I do believe, however, that broad principles and values, and learnings about process, can be fruitfully applied. The emphasis of the degrowth "movement" on the need to scale down, for instance, can be useful in the context of classes within the South that are over-consuming, or overall for economies in the South (such as China and India) that may already be unsustainable in some aspects. Similarly, the North may have much to learn from those indigenous peoples and other local communities in the Global South that continue to show ways of living *within* nature, where some aspects of simple living still survive, or where holistic knowledge systems combining experiential, spiritual, and scientific elements are still strong.

The deepest meanings of *swaraj,* with its complex integration of freedom, collective responsibility, self-reliance and autonomy, could be something many Northern democracies and human rights regimes could learn from. This would be particularly important in order to find alternatives to the extreme individualism and social alienation from which the Global

North suffers and which even lead to superficial solutions like recycling without questioning over-consumption.

Conversely, there is much in the solidarity economy models emerging in Europe and elsewhere that we in the Global South could gainfully absorb. In particular, initiatives like digital commons, cafes and non-profit shops run cooperatively by urban youth, and social enterprises,[6] and others that are in the "modern" sector may be of interest to youth in the south that are looking for gainful sources of employment in urban contexts. And of course, there is plenty of exciting scope for southern worldviews to engage with each other; imagine the power of *buen vivir* and *sumac kawsay* and *swaraj* and *ubuntu* and myriad other such worldviews collectively presenting something attractive enough to engage people currently mesmerized by the consumertopia?

5. We do have opportunities to move this agenda forward

It is not easy to envision ideal futures in any detail (beyond the generic wish list of sustainability, equity, justice, peace, etc.). But envision them we must if we are to keep hope alive, find our bearings, and guide grassroots practice. However, the even harder task is to figure out specific and workable pathways to reach such a future, for these have to contend with the complex web of problems we are currently enmeshed in. Most challenging is the powerful resistance to fundamental change by those who occupy positions of power, not only within governments but also in the private sector, and within the dominant sections of society (which in the Indian context is uniquely characterized by caste as much as class, gender, and other forms of inequity and discrimination).

As high as these hurdles are, the growing number and reach of peoples' initiatives to resist the system and create alternatives are a source of hope. Peoples' movements and civil society organizations (including progressive workers' unions) will have to be the primary agents of change. At times, sections and individuals within government, political parties, and academic institutions have taken the lead or assisted communities and civil society organizations, and we must continue to push the limits of such institutions. Over time, as communities self-mobilize or are empowered through decentralization, political parties will feel greater pressure from their constituencies to reorient their focus towards issues of well-being based on sustainability and equity. But we cannot rely on political parties alone, for they are part of the DNA of representative democracy that itself needs to be transformed into radical, more direct forms of decision-making.

One great opportunity provided to our generations is the historical conjunction between the local and the global. At one level are the localization movements mentioned above. At the other is the growing mobilization around global issues, such as climate change, the global financial system, the industrial monopolies on food and agriculture, and the hegemony of multinational corporations. The conditions of the contemporary world are fostering mutually-reinforcing local and global mindsets. More than ever before, we are members both of immediate communities and also of the community of humanity, or – more broadly – the community of life, just as local ecosystems are part of one global ecological system. Greater awareness of our interdependence comes with each new global crisis, and with it the possibility of greater common cause. If the emerging movements around the world, based on multiple but overlapping worldviews (old and new) and transcending orthodox ideological standpoints, can come together, then there is much hope that pathways to a saner future will be forged, and walked.

Endnotes

1 Shrivastava and Kothari, 2012.

2 India's most oppressed group, so-called "untouchables" or *harijans,* struggling to overcome centuries' old marginalization. In this sense, *dalit* women are doubly disadvantaged as gender hierarchies too remain strongly entrenched.

3 Shrivastava and Kothari, 2012; Kothari, 2014; Kalpavriksh, 2015; Kalpavriksh, 2017; see also the links below.

4 These are embedded in a framework of elements, values, strategies, and other aspects of a holistic alternative vision evolving in the Vikalp Sangam process, pl. see kalpavriksh.org/our-work/alternatives (Accessed 31 January 2019). This builds on the Peoples' Sustainability Treaty on Radical Ecological Democracy, at radicalecologicaldemocracy.org. It should be noted that the initiatives on which such a vision is based do not necessarily use the term ecoswaraj or RED themselves. This term originated in our work, and though it is gaining acceptance, it is not meant to impose a uniform label on the diverse ways in which people articulate principles or worldviews themselves.

5 Kothari et al., 2015.

6 I've been privileged to visit some in Greece, Spain and Czech Republic.

Links

Alternatives India – Vikalp Sangam, website documenting the networking process of alternatives confluence since 2014: alternativesindia.org

Global Tapestry of Alternatives: www.globaltapestryofalternatives.org

Radical Ecological Democracy, initiative of the India based Kalpavriksh Environmental Action Group: radicalecologicaldemocracy.org

Academic-Activist Co-Produced Knowledge for Environmental Justice: acknowlej.org

ICCA Consortium: iccaconsortium.org

Podcast for *Degrowth in Movement(s)* and RED: soundcloud.com/degrowth-webportal/dib_radikale-oekologische-demokratie (first 40 seconds in German, thereafter English)

Literature

Kalpavriksh (2015) *Vikalp Sangam: In search of alternatives,* Poster exhibition available in book form at drive.google.com/file/d/0B-fW5lp3Tj9YMTg0NkdHcTVyZms/view?pref=2&pli=1 (Accessed 31 January 2019).

Kalpavriksh (2017) *The Search for Radical Alternatives: Key elements and principles,* Pune/Delhi, Kalpavriksh.

Kothari, A. (2014) "Radical Ecological Democracy: A path forward for India and beyond," *Development,* vol. 57, no. 1, pp. 36–45.

Kothari, A., Demaria, F., and Acosta, A. (2015) "Buen Vivir, Degrowth and Ecological Swaraj: Alternatives to sustainable development and the Green Economy," *Development,* vol. 57, no. 3–4, pp. 362–375.

Kothari, A., Salleh, A., Escobar, A., Demaria, F., and Acosta, A. (2019) *Pluriverse: A Post-Development Dictionary,* Delhi, Tulika and Authors UpFront..

Tagore, R. (1928) *City and Village.* Available at tagoreanworld.co.uk/?page_id=68 (Accessed 31 January 2019).

Shrivastava, A., and Kothari, A. (2012) *Churning the Earth: The Making of Global India,* Delhi, Viking/Penguin India.

Chapter 18

Demonstration at the Malian-Mauritanian border (at the southern border of the Sahara), whereto until the end of 2010 (and in some cases still) people migrating by boat are deported. Bamako-Dakar-caravan, 2011 (Image: afrique-europe-interact)

Refugee Movement: Struggling with Migration and Escape

Olaf Bernau

"We're here because you are destroying our countries" – this slogan coined by refugee self-organizations pointedly interlinks migration and escape with the complex dynamics of global exploitation and destruction. Against this backdrop, together with his local group, NoLager Bremen (Germany), Olaf has been actively involved in the Afrique-Europe-Interact network, an organizational process between African and European grass-roots initiatives that has been ongoing since 2009. Olaf has written this piece on his own, although he referenced many debates and organizational experiences, whether related to people who have fled to Germany, deported people in Togo or peasant activists in Mali. The history of Europe can hardly be told without immigration and emigration movements. And yet the stories in the respective countries are very different - with all the parallels that exist as well. For the events reported in this chapter (if they concern the situation in Europe itself), this means that not all, but quite a bit, can be transferred, especially to countries such as France, England, Belgium or the Netherlands.

1. The daily resistance faced by migrants and refugees is at the heart of the battle for global freedom of movement and equal rights

When several thousand people started heading for Austria on foot from Budapest's main train station on 4 September 2015, it not only dawned on Angela Merkel but on the European public as a whole: It was not activists who were prepared to literally unhinge the European border regime in those days. Crucially, it was the basic right to freedom of movement acquired en masse by very normal people – young and old, men, women and children, believers and non-believers, those who were healthy and those who were in wheelchairs. This simple yet basic assessment refers to the fact that it is the migrants and refugees who themselves are changing Germany from within Europe – and not just since the summer of migration in 2015, which has been misleadingly labelled by the political mainstream as a "refugee crisis."

The phrase "Germany is not an immigration country" was stated in the government's coalition agreement at the beginning of the Helmut Kohl era in 1982. In his wonderful book *Die Bleibenden* (The Remaining), journalist Christian Jakob cuttingly states that "the migration policy was a migration-obstructionist policy."[1] However, migrants and refugees have not accepted the notion that Germany did not want to be an immigration country.

Instead, according to Jakob, they have "defied this dogma, won access to Germany and have changed society in doing so" – this can be seen in cities such as Düsseldorf, Munich and Frankfurt, where 35-45% of the population are people with a migration background.

The understanding of migration and escape outlined here is based on the consideration that the term "social movement" should not be shortened from a social science perspective, but should instead be complemented by a dimension of daily resistance that is often already taking place. It should therefore be recognized that the dogged everyday struggles, or better put, survival strategies used by migrants and refugees, are acts of resistance. In other words, they are highly effective attempts to break down the borders of citizenship, to open up new transnational areas of freedom and equality, and to demand and make use of a right to mobility.

And yet: Even if the actual epicenter of the battle for freedom of movement and equal rights centers around the movements of migrants and refugees that are largely enabled by migrant community networks, these survival strategies have – strictly speaking – also always overlapped with interventions from political stakeholders. This refers to (diaspora) organizations and associations for migrants and refugees, as well as anti-racism groups, advisory services and NGOs, whereby the relevant transitions are not in any way selective. Just as politically organized migrants and refugees are mostly integrated in their migrant communities, similarly anti-racist activists have close personal and political ties with migrants and refugees. As a whole, the stakeholders and activists in question are as old and diverse as the immigration events of the past fifty years, as illustrated by certain key moments.[2]

Struggling with migration and escape since the 1960s

In the 1960s, students from African countries within the German

Socialist Student Union (SDS) were becoming ever more active against racism, deportations and African dictators – perhaps the most famous example being the successful demonstrations in 1964 against the racist film *Africa Addio* that glorified colonialism. In the 1970s, migrants from the guest-worker generation carried out numerous protests, including in Frankfurt, against overpriced rent and a lack of Kindergarten places. The situation reached a head in August 1973 when the Ford plant in Cologne was occupied after 500 Turkish workers were dismissed after returning late from their annual leave. An ineffable alliance between the police, plant management, the works council and German steel union IG-Metall members ended the unauthorized strike one week later. As a consequence, 100 workers were deported, some ended up in prison and 600 lost their jobs.

In the 1980s, refugees in the state of Baden-Württemberg were continuously demonstrating against camps established by the Minister President at the time Lothar Späth (Späth quote: "The African bush drums should already be clear: Don't come to Baden-Württemberg, you'll be forced into a camp there."). Furthermore, not only was the Pro Asyl pro-immigration advocacy organization founded in 1986 —for their part, the militant Revolutionary Cells *(Revolutionäre Zellen, RZ)* wrote during their refugee campaigns, which were more or less welcomed on the quiet in many places, that "migration movements [. . .] were only the billows of smoke from a volcano" and the anti-imperialist left was therefore invited to support the "will and determination of refugees."

In the course of reunification in the 1990s, there was a truly racist wall of hate directed at migrants and refugees. In 1992 alone, Nazis killed 34 people in Germany. The right of asylum was also de facto abolished in 1992, which – together with the Asylum Seekers Benefits Act introduced in 1993 and deportation figures that increased tenfold between 1988 and 1993 – resulted in refugees' living and residence situation intensifying extremely.

Correspondingly, not only were migrant Antifa groups founded at this time, but also more self-organized refugee organizations, including The Voice Refugee Forum, the Brandenburg Refugee Initiative and the Caravan for the Rights of Refugees and Migrants.[3]

In the 2000s, kanak attak – a network in which mainly second and third-generation migrants were active – took to the stage[4]; and the struggles which had begun in the 1990s became more distinct. And all this continued under a predominantly repressive federal migration policy.

By the 2010s at the very latest, as a consequence of the expansion of the EU border regime, the situation on the EU's outer edges or indeed in transit countries such as Ukraine, Libya and Morocco became ever more dramatic. In response to this, since 2009, there have been numerous mixed networks – those comprising refugees and non-refugees – such as Welcome to Europe or Afrique-Europe-Interact, whose program also aims to offer practical intervention on the transit routes heading for (western and northern) Europe; one particular example is the WatchTheMed Alarm Phone, an emergency number for refugees who find themselves in an emergency at sea. Finally, 2012 must be highlighted since this year saw the beginning of a cycle of political protests by refugees that continued until 2014, and which found support among the German public like never before —with the consequence that refugee solidarity "has not only become a dominating social movement and a booming industry, but also a pop-cultural hype," as Christian Jakob writes in his aforementioned book.

The right to have rights as the programmatic essence

With all the diversity among themes and debates, the connection to rights has emerged as the lowest common denominator from the very beginning, and was paradigmatically formulated in the manifesto of the "Kein Mensch ist illegal" (No person is illegal) network that sprung into being in 1997 at the documenta X exhibition:

> Every person has the right to decide for themselves where and how they want to live. The regulation of migration and the systematic denial of rights conflicts with the demand for equality in all social and political respects, based on the notion of respecting every person's human rights, regardless of their origin and papers.

More specifically: Until now, the normative point of reference for the battles outlined above is what was formerly postulated by the philosopher, Hannah Arendt, as the "right to have rights." However, it was always indisputable that rights are not guaranteed by anything or anyone in reality —particularly not by the state. Rather, in reference to the motto of escape and migrant battles, they must be eked out step-by-step: From their initial formulation and recognition as part of general conventions (such as at UN conventions, for example) through to becoming entrenched as a positive, i.e. valid and therefore enforceable, right.[5]

Escape and migrant debate currents

Not only are refugee self-organizations unhappy with the focus on local conditions; mixed networks such as Afrique-Europe-Interact are equally unhappy. Rather, they are including the backgrounds of escape and migration, for which the fulminant position paper, "On Colonial Injustice and Ongoing Barbarism," published in 2009 by The Voice Refugee Forum is cited as an example:

> [t]he human story will one day remember the 'Western Civilization' as the most cruel, destructive and ostracizing power that has ever existed. Will we ever know how many

> billions of people lost their lives directly or indirectly as a result?

These contextualizations were, however, disputed for a long time. More specifically, it means that within the environment of kanak attak, such an approach runs the risk of degrading people as playthings in objective pressure situations: It would play into the hands of a humanistic discussion, which considers refugees and migrants merely to be helpless victims, even accepting their situation, but not seeing them as social stakeholders who (offensively) demand and use their rights. However, this debate has now calmed down. Due to time constraints, many groups only focus on the local situation but do not (or no longer) question the necessity to also systematically consider the causes of escape and migration in principle.

A similar approach applies to a second debate current, which also arose at the beginning of the 2000s under the heading "Re-economizing anti-racism." The starting point was a thesis arguing that fortress Europe not only seeks isolation, but may also be interested in systematic illegalization in order to foster a giant pool of low-paid workers who are easy to blackmail – whether it is for the construction industry, agriculture or household service sectors. At that time, nobody questioned the factual effects of this kind of action (whether intended or not) that accompanied the EU border regime. However, groups such as The Voice Refugee Forum feared that focusing too closely on exploitative racist situations within the job market could detract from refugee-policy battles, particularly against camps, deportations and other discriminating measures.

2. Between networking and conflict: The escape and migrant movement as a giant mosaic

If we take the thesis formulated at the beginning seriously, which suggests that escape and migration events are at the heart of escape and migrant battles, it should be understandable why a precise description of the social composition of this movement landscape is hardly achievable, at least not quickly. Particularly since this setting comprises different people and generations – each with different education, work and immigration histories, not to mention differing political views.

Nevertheless, in recent decades there have always been attempts to bring together these various stakeholders in Germany, such as in 1998 when the Caravan for the Rights of Refugees and Migrants first went on tour, or since 2005 as part of the Young People Without Borders initiative calling for a right of residence, or at three NoBorder conferences in Frankfurt between 2010 and 2014. It may have worked occasionally, but in principle, it must first be recognized that real differences cannot be conquered or leveled out without further ado. To be more specific: Third-generation activists, who were born and have grown up in Germany, do not automatically have the same interests and priorities as irregularly employed nursing staff from Ukraine or refugees from Togo who are directly threatened by deportation.

Trans-identitary organization processes

In the meantime, the conduct of many German activists was mostly determined by ignorance, dominance and paternalism. As an example, when at the International Refugee Congress in Jena in 2000, attended by around 600 people from forty countries, the campaign against residence requirements came to life,[6] the left-radical mainstream at the time reacted ignorantly, or even contentiously. The project was labeled as "humanitarian" and therefore "limited to refugee policies"; furthermore, due to its persistence, The Voice Refugee Forum was accused of "piggy-backing" on the guilty conscience of European activists, simply with the aim of recruiting "campaign soldiers." Those scolded in this way were critical that this negative attitude was an expression of *white* ignorance with respect to a racist special regulation, which represented a permeating experience of humiliation, isolation and intimidation throughout the daily lives of refugees, and is therefore largely responsible for the fact that many refugees would hardly appreciate their right to political action or organization.

Taking these and other similar conflicts that have occurred into account, particularly as part of the Anti-racist border camps (1998-2003), a new approach was sought within the NoLager network (2002-2007): Activists with and without escape and migration experience reached an agreement to work on a trans-identity "We" project as part of an intensified cooperation. The aim was to create a political stakeholder that takes the different starting positions seriously but uses this as a basis to formulate common perspectives, interests and demands, therefore breaking down the polarizing us-and-them position arising from the racist social structure, at least on an anti-racist field.

The operational framework is based on the motto famously created by the (Australian) Murri activist Lilla Watson and printed on t-shirts by the Brandenburg Refugee Initiative in 2003: "If you have come here to help me, you are wasting your time. But if you have come because your liberation is bound up with mine, then let us work together." As a practical maxim, the concept of accountability that originated from critical-whiteness discussions among others was used (without this being theoretically discussed, however); i.e. the self-commitment of *white* activists to make themselves allies of refugees, migrants and people of color – along with systematically sharing their willingness, money, time, linguistic competency and other privileges.[7]

3. Growth-related causes of escape and migration as the lowest common denominator

Relations between degrowth and certain intervention currents of the escape and migrant movement are literally obvious. Because numerous reasons for escape directly or indirectly result from a capitalist growth imperative: It does not matter if we talk about market openings, privatization, investment facilitation, land grabbing, access to resources or resource wars, we are always referring to growth, often coupled with brutal economic competition —in other words, we are referring to increased sales opportunities, profitable investments, cheaper production locations and the appropriation of raw materials that are necessary to keep the capitalist high-performing economy running. Furthermore, there are also indirect connections: climate change further aggravates the continuously precarious situation of small farming households; or the fact that working together with corrupt regimes is almost unavoidable in order to implement imperial interests. In this respect, it cannot have been purely coincidental that the early degrowth debate (which admittedly operated under different names) predominantly subsided in the early 1980s, while countries in the South fell into ruin under the auspices of neoliberal structural adjustment programs from the IMF and World Bank in the name of growth.

Yet contradictions and gray areas abound since growth is not at all seen as a negative development by many migrants and refugees. They would rather see their money transfers (which account for more than double of the foreign aid figure) contribute to raising the living standards of their families and local communities. In principle, this is to be welcomed with open arms since it is primarily about meeting basic needs such as access to food, water, education and health services (either through increased consumption or small-business investments). At the same time, it can also result in materialistic actions for profit. In this case, migrants and refugees are financing status symbols such as large houses and cars with some of the money they are earning in Europe. But this is also far from objectionable, at least if we consider that the lifestyle enjoyed by most people in rich industrial countries continues to generate a significantly larger CO_2 footprint than in the Global South. Rather, this materialistic excess is problematic because it acts as a kind of promotional event for the capitalist consumerism model in each of these countries, and therefore the search for ecologically and socially acceptable developmental alternatives are regularly undermined.

One final thing to consider: The degrowth summer schools which took place in German mining areas in the summers from 2015 to 2018 were real highlights from a social and atmospheric point of view. There was a clear display of solidarity, with an extremely friendly atmosphere, and it was brilliantly organized. At the same time, the social composition was somewhat unsettling: predominantly *white*, young and academically qualified. To put it another way: There was no need to wrestle for understanding despite different starting conditions – which almost defines the character of migration and refugee-policy battles – in the context of these summer schools. Instead, a certain monoculturality prevailed, and while it did not prevent exciting debates, it was more of a paradoxical stance towards the discursive openness relating to complex problem areas around the globe – a contradiction to which I will return immediately.

4. What degrowth can learn from transnational organization processes

One of the central challenges faced by social movements in Africa is to start a conversation with the general population about alternative self-sufficient developmental opportunities. All key economic data supports the notion that, for the foreseeable future, most African countries do not stand the slightest chance of freeing themselves from their subordinate status on the global market as mere suppliers of raw materials (this focus on African countries is a result of the work carried out by Afrique-Europe-Interact, but other similar questions also apply to other regions of the world). In light of this, the degrowth movement could certainly be a valuable counterpart for social movements in the Global South, particularly when seeking answers to those questions that appear to be from macrosocial transition perspectives. In doing so, however, it is important to remember that people who find themselves with their backs to the economic wall are predominantly interested in tangible suggested solutions, not debates on the basic principles.

And this is exactly where degrowth could learn from transnational networks, such as Afrique-Europe-Interact. Thanks to its intensive work in mixed configurations – whether it is here or in an African-European context – Afrique-Europe-Interact has gained a wealth of experience as to how it is possible to not only build trust resources step-by-step, but also shared prospects of action, despite considerable economic, social, cultural and religious differences. In practice, transnational forms of organization tend to be highly contradictory on a political, social and personal level. For example, in Afrique-Europe-Interact in 2012 a transnational debate erupted due to the demands of many of the activists in Mali that, in order to enforce their right to self-defense (particularly against Islamic terrorist groups), the relatively small Mali army with its 12,000 soldiers be provided with adequate equipment, as well as training support from the German army. Of course, many European activists were literally sweating buckets while hearing this. On a social level, on the other hand, contradictions are often exemplified by questions about organization: In every village in Mali, you will find a village chief. Upon closer inspection, however, it becomes clear that a village chief is only respected as long as he adequately represents the will of the village, which in turn presupposes a democracy-based opinion-forming process. And to conclude, the personal angle: The fact is that transnational networking would not be possible without mutual support, particularly in relation to action processes that can sometimes be nerve-racking. Nevertheless, it would be absurd to want to seek out your own alter ego in a transnational organization of all places. In this regard, a fundamental challenge lies in repeatedly letting things stand or go uncommented (this applies to both sides), even if they shake the very foundations of your own political or personal self-image – such as when political difficulties are explained through supernatural phenomena, or e.g. regarding differing notions of gender.[8]

5. Get down from your observation towers and debate podiums, and join the common struggle!

This text is the result of an extremely friendly degrowth communication campaign. However, I cannot stop myself from shouting the local degrowth movement down – with respect – from their discourse-overgrown observation tower and debate podium. The balance of social power only changes in practical conflicts, such as those that should have been made clear by the depiction of escape and migrant battles.

At the same time, the gap in resources and violence that many movements experience has also been raised in these stories. From a contextual and political viewpoint, I would therefore rather see the degrowth movement participate more in battles relating to the causes of escape —no matter which way. Furthermore, battles fought by refugees in this country are consistently reliant on low-threshold support. Both should occur in the context of power sharing, because only those movements that share and redistribute their material, time and intellectual resources will be successful in the end.

Translation: Ellen Worrell

Endnotes

1 Jakob, 2016.

2 Interface, 2005.

3 Jakob, 2016.

4 Kanak Attak was founded in 1998, but has not been active since about 2005. The name plays with the racist attribution "Kanacke," which is still used in Germany today as a derogatory term for people with migration biographies. Accordingly, Kanak Attak rejects any form of identity politics, as it says in its founding appeal: "Kanak Attak does not ask for the passport or the origin, but turns against the question of the passport and the origin." The manifesto can be found online: kanak-attak.de/ka/about/manif_eng.html (Accessed 31 January 2019).

5 Bernau, 2006.

6 The so-called "Residenzpflicht" (residence obligation) is a regulation according to which certain refugees and migrants may leave their place of residence only with the permission of the local immigration authorities.

7 For the (border camp) conflicts mentioned here, as well as the fundamentals of the critical-whiteness concept, see Bernau (2012) and transact (2014).

8 Bernau, 2015.

Links

Afrique-Europe-Interact: afrique-europe-interact.net

Caravan for the rights of refugees and migrants: thecaravan.org/taxonomy/term/1

Kompass – monthly Antira newsletter: kompass.antira.info/en

Watch The Med Alarm Phone – Hotline for boatpeople in distress. No rescue, but Alarm: alarmphone.org/en

Welome to Europe - information with, about and for refugees in Greece: infomobile.w2eu.net

Degrowth in movement(s) video of the Refugee Movement: vimeo.com/175153015

Literature

Bernau, O. (alias Gregor Samsa) (2006) "Globale Rechte –

Hype oder kommunistisches Szenario? Globale Rechte im Spannunsfeld von Utopie, sozialen Kämpfen und positivem Recht", *analyse & kritik (ak) – Zeitung für linke Debatte und Praxis,* vol. 508. Available at akweb.de/ak_s/ak508/18.htm (Accessed 31 January 2019).

Bernau, O. (2012) "In der Autoritäts- und Identitätsfalle. Stichworte zur Debatte um criticalwhiteness anlässlich des diesjährigen Nobordercamps in Köln," *Phase 2,* vol. 44. Available at phase-zwei.org/hefte/artikel/in-der-autoritaets-und-identitaetsfalle-233 (Accessed 31 January 2019).

Bernau, O. (2015) "Im Schnittfeld von Land und Stadt. Werktstattbericht zur Solidaritätsarbeit mit bäuerlichen Bewegungen in Mali," *analyse & kritik (ak) – Zeitung für linke Debatte und Praxis,* vol. 604. Available at afrique-europe-interact.net/1353-0-Werkstattbericht-Office-du-Niger.html (Accessed 31 January 2019).

interface (ed.) (2005) *WiderstandsBewegungen. Antirassismus zwischen Alltag & Kritik*, Berlin/Hamburg, Assoziation A.

Jakob, C. (2016) *Die Bleibenden. Wie Flüchtlinge Deutschland seit 20 Jahren verändern*, Berlin, Ch.Links Verlag.

Mbolela, E. (2017) *Réfugié - Une odyssée africaine,* Paris, Libertaria.

transact! (ed.) (2014) *How is your liberation bound up with mine? Ideas about mixed organising-processes, the power of definition and critical whiteness,* Berlin/Bremen/Hanau/Wien, transact! Available at transact.noblogs.org/files/2014/02/transact6_en.pdf (Accessed 31 January 2019).

The Voice Refugee Forum (2009) *Unite Against the Continuation of Colonial Injustice in Germany. The Situation of Human Beings as Refugees and Migrants in Germany*. Available at afrique-europe-interact.net/241-0-voice-text.html?article_id=241&clang=1 (Accessed 31 January 2019).

Chapter 19

Participants at the screen print producing a bag with the slogan of the SOLIKON "We are one". (Image: CC BY-SA 2.0, Linda Dreisen, Solikon 2015 – Der Kongress)

Solidarity Economy: Paths to Transformation

Dagmar Embshoff, Clarita Müller-Plantenberg and Giuliana Giorgi

Clarita, Dagmar und Giuliana are all active in the German Forum Solidarische Ökonomie e. V. (Solidarity Economy Forum). Dagmar is a geographer, author, initiator of the Forum Solidarische Ökonomie, and co-founder of the network Solidarische Landwirtschaft (Solidarity Agriculture). Clarita is Professor Emeritus of Sociology at the University of Kassel. From 1981 to 2009, she was Head of Sociology in Developing Countries in the Department of Social Sciences. She has written several scientific books. Giuliana, political scientist and interpreter, is a member of the Forum Solidarische Ökonomie.

1. Working together as equals and creating an economy to meet people's needs – not to maximize profit

The core idea of solidarity economy is: cooperation instead of competition and meaning for people instead of profit.

In concrete terms, this means:

- Self-government, e.g. democratic decisions made by the community and common property/ownership;
- Internal and external cooperation;
- Focus on the common welfare;
- Inclusion of minorities, the disadvantaged, the unemployed, refugees and migrants;
- No discrimination because of sex, disability, religion, appearance, etc.;
- Transparency and education, process orientation;
- In ecology, the protection of ecosystems and biodiversity as the basis for people's existence in each respective region (maintenance and enhancement of the territory[1]);
- A concept of economy as a subsystem of ecology, meaning that the economy must fit into natural cycles and boundaries.

The aim and purpose of the economy is to satisfy people's needs. Healthy food, housing, mobility, healthcare, information and learning, culture and art, socializing, friendship, recognition, conviviality, contact with nature and recreation are needs that are common to all people.

In a housing-coop, lessor and lessee merge into one person, in a worker-coop, worker and boss become one and in pro-sumer projects, consumer and producer stop meeting each other at the market. Depending on the level at which the two main principles meaning (need-orientation) and cooperation (solidarity) are applied, Solidarity Economy can either contribute a tasty cake or switch the whole economy into a bakery of good life.

According to recent findings in neurobiology and many years of research in psychology and pedagogy, people are better suited to cooperation than to competition. Meta-studies show that cooperation is more efficient (and therefore more economic) than competition and "going at it alone." Above all, cooperation increases well-being (keyword "good life") and improves mental health. In the Global South, solidarity economy means, above all, a departure from all forms of neo-colonialism and exploitation that are carried out by old and new industrialized nations. Solidarity economy also means letting go of any form of cultural imperialism. In their search for resources, old colonial powers and new companies must stop displacing people from their ancestral territories – where they have lived in tune with nature for thousands of years – and depriving them of their livelihood.

We consider a vital part of solidarity economy to turn away from the food industry ruled by agricultural corporations, and to strengthen small-scale farming as the basis for food sovereignty. That is why city dwellers are now organizing themselves in groups and entering binding cooperation with organic farmers in the countryside. To some extent, they participate in decisions on the variety of crops grown and finance the harvest in advance. In English-speaking countries this is known as CSA (community supported/shared agriculture), in France AMAP, in Italy GAS, in Japan TEIKEI, and in Germany Solidarische Landwirtschaft.

The emergence of the solidarity economy in Latin America

In the 1980s, Luis Razeto (Chile) linked the concepts of economy and solidarity for the first time. The theoretical debate on solidarity economy, which is particularly lively in Latin America, derives from the practice of inclusion: on the one hand, unemployed or precarious workers incubate solidarity economy enterprises and workers take over insolvent enterprises. Thus, solidarity economy is primarily devoted to alternative forms of economic activity already in existence, which (especially in Brazil) are systematically supported through networking and the promotion of various social actors. As a rule, the practical development of solidarity economy enterprises stems from social movements.

Strategically, it is important to increase visibility for communities and economic enterprises based on solidarity, precisely because they are not in the mass media spotlight. The mapping of solidarity economy enterprises (SEEs) is therefore a meaningful next step after the inclusion of minorities, refugees, the unemployed, precarious workers and employees of insolvent companies. This is an important instrument in strengthening alternatives. This tool raises awareness of SEEs and people living alternative lifestyles and helps others to find them, encouraging the creation of new cooperative projects.

Euclides Mance, theorist on the solidarity economy and the philosophy of liberation in Latin America, emphasizes the importance of SEE mapping, including the flow of materials, so that, for example, one enterprise can supply another, or the waste produced by one company can be recycled by another and returned to the circuit.

Solidarity economy in Brazil

In Brazil, under Lula da Silva, the State Secretariat for Solidarity (SENAES, Secretaria Nacional de Economia Solidária) was established within the Ministry for Labor and Employment. It was legally created on 26 June 2003 on the initiative of President Lula, after a request by the former Solidarity Economy working group of the World Social Forum. Under the leadership of economist and sociologist Paul Singer, the SENAES worked with SEEs, which had organized themselves into regional fora within the individual states, and which together had created the Brazilian Solidarity Economy Forum (Fórum Brasileiro de Economia Solidária, FBES). Other supporters of the solidarity economy are also active in this forum, including church organizations, universities, trade unions, NGOs, municipalities, administrative districts, and federal states. All actors form independent, growing networks, while simultaneously forming part of the Grupo de Pesquisa em Economia Solidária (ECOSOL), a solidarity economy movement.

All the solidarity economy enterprises (SEEs) were repeatedly called upon by SENAES to discuss their priorities, and to send delegates to solidarity economy general conferences held in Brasilia, to share their needs and interests. During the first twelve years, three large general conferences were held, all of which were attended by more than 1200 delegates. At these meetings, joint planning processes were coordinated. In the same period, unemployment was virtually eliminated, and refugees from Haiti were increasingly integrated into this process of inclusion. When national policy shifted, and neoliberal adjustment measures were implemented in the form of interest rate hikes and austerity programs, unemployment began to grow once more.

Today, incubators (*incubadoras),* a special form of counselling centers, have been set up at more than 100 universities. People (often women) who want to join forces in small solidarity economy enterprises can contact these centers to ask for being accompanied in this process and to receive advice and support in their efforts to generate local income. The sharing of economic knowledge on a par with those who are in the incubating process which leads to the rising of awareness as citizens (following Paulo Freire's method) and also on gender issues and experiences inside the group, including joint decision-making. A mapping process throughout the country enables regional visits and learning processes within the movement. In this way, interested students and researchers can directly connect newly established SEEs with customers and suppliers from solidarity networks.

Those active in solidarity economy in the movement (FBES) as well as in the government (Paul Singer and his team in SENAES) were building up strong relations with SE activists who were building up and promoting SEEs in, for example Argentina, Colombia, Uruguay and Chile, as well as in their institutes and organizations.

France and Italy as European examples

In France, the social solidarity economy (SSE) has been a tradition since the end of the war. It is very active, and recognized by local authorities. The city of Lille promotes the SSE movement through, among other initiatives, two *maisons de l'économie solidaire* (solidarity economy houses), in which civic organizations run small offices promoting the common welfare. In July 2014, the French Parliament passed a law promoting the social solidarity economy. Among other things, the law improves access to project finance and supports forums encouraging the exchange of experiences. In addition, the law gives workers the right of cooperative acquisition of their company if the previous owners are not able to continue. In Italy, a law was promulgated in 1985 which promoted employee initiatives to take over insolvent companies in the form of cooperatives: the Marcora Act. In the current crisis, it also provides for the rescue of regional jobs, infrastructure and expertise. There are also now many Gruppi di Acquisto Solidale (GAS), solidarity purchasing groups, which enter into cooperative and purchase agreements with local organic farmers. Many organic farmers can survive solely due to their GAS customers. At the beginning, in the 1990s, this style of direct marketing was only widespread in north and central Italy, but over the last decade the first Sicilian smallholders visited Milan and learnt about the GAS groups at the Fa'la cosa giusta (do the right thing) fair, a trade fair supporting critical consumption and sustainable lifestyles. The smallholders then began to supply GAS groups in northern and central Italy with citrus fruits and other Mediterranean products such as almonds and olives, thus emancipating themselves from the predatory dominance of the Mafia-ruled large-scale commercialization. Landless farmer cooperatives are also active in the fight against the Mafia. They manage land that has been confiscated from Mafia bosses in accordance with organic guidelines.[2]

There are now hundreds of social cooperatives in Italy offering housing to refugees and supporting them in the integration process – also because the State leaves this to the municipalities.

We could name countless other examples. The solidarity economy is made up of inspiring stories, encouraging us to experiment and imitate. There is an "Intercontinental Network for the Promotion of Social Solidarity Economy," called RIPESS. One project of RIPESS-EU (Solidarity Economy Europe) is a survey on European initiatives of the Solidarity Economy, called "panorama;" another is a World Social Forum on Transformative Economies in Barcelona in 2019/2020. RIPESS is also an observer of the United Nations Inter-Agency Task Force on Social and Solidarity Economy (unsse.org), which started in 2013.

2. Solidarity economy includes many alternative economic practices and actors

Dealing with practical experience is at the core of this strategy. The theory of solidarity economy develops from what happens in real life; it learns from practice. Simultaneously, this practice benefits from the latest insights in the fields of theory and research. The mapping of the various existing initiatives and SEEs enables them to network with each other and work together: locally and regionally, but also across borders. They are gradually forming an alternative, decentralized, bottom-up system which can provide a livelihood for the growing number of people excluded from the current prevailing system.

Examples of solidarity economy initiatives include:

- Self-governed enterprises and progressive cooperatives, for example energy cooperatives, water cooperatives, social cooperatives run by people with disabilities, land purchase cooperatives, pub collectives, film and theatre collectives
- Housing projects, eco-villages, communes and other communities
- Fair trade, Community Supported Agriculture, community gardens including intercultural gardens, community land trusts
- Mutual assistance (mutualism); historically: health and accident insurance schemes organized by employees
- Self-organized financial instruments such as savings associations or credit unions; ethic cooperative banks; historically: cooperative banks, savings associations
- Food coops, member stores, producer-consumer communities and other forms of self-governed consumption or producer-consumption (consumption and co-production)
- Free knowledge, for example free software, encyclopedias, education, media and culture
- Self-governed free alternative schools and day-care centers, maternity centers, cultural centers, free radio stations and open channels etc.
- Open workshops (community workshops), repair cafes

As a representative of the social cooperative SOLCO in Mantova (Italy) once explained, the solidarity economy growth strategy is like a strawberry plant: when a strawberry plant is fully grown, it does not get any larger; instead it forms offshoots, new plants, which in turn form offshoots, until strawberry plants cover the whole hill. The initiatives do not wish to "grow bigger"; instead they multiply and spread their experience, knowledge, and methods. As a result, not all infrastructure is concentrated in the cities; instead jobs and services are distributed widely and can meet local needs in each respective region.

3. The solidarity economy and degrowth: common goals

By using the concept of the "solidarity economy" as a starting point here, we are building on initiatives in other parts of the world, raising awareness of them. This makes us all stronger, for example, when we make political demands for recognition, support and better conditions. The academic world encompasses a very broad range of activities on the solidarity economy, based on cooperation, self-administration, a focus on the common good, and links to nature. In the meantime, many other movements have also developed (transition towns, economy for the common good, degrowth, commons, sharing economy, collaborative economy, demonetization etc.). On the one hand, this diversity is a positive attribute that makes the host of alternatives more resilient: when one channel is hijacked by corporations (for example, car sharing), the whole movement is not simultaneously discredited. On the other hand, we should not overlook the fact that the variety of designations may ultimately be due to our current system, which is based on competition; every social innovation must emphasize its unique features to convince potential donors and the public.

For this reason, cooperation and coordination between the various movements is desirable, as they help to avoid "duplications" and increase the effectiveness of all efforts. Joint events, such as trade fairs and congresses on critical consumption, and joint campaigns have already taken place (e.g. Solikon 2015 in Berlin). At such events, one movement usually plays the role of "host." However, projects or campaigns jointly initiated by multiple movements working together are still lacking.

Solidarity economy and degrowth share a core idea, although they define it differently. Degrowth wants to renounce growth as the goal of the economy. Solidarity economy wants to enable inclusion through self-management, and to renounce the necessity to multiply capital (profit maximization), which in the mainstream media is glossed over as "growth."

The capitalist system has developed countless growth strategies: from colonial plundering, wars and the destruction of competitors, to built-in obsolescence and the creation of artificial "needs" through sophisticated advertising. Conversely, solidarity economy creates institutional frameworks, networks and value chains based on non-capitalist principles (cooperation instead of competition). Here, networks strengthen individual enterprises and initiatives and provide the possibility to learn and gain experience to create a culture of cooperation.

Solidarity economy also builds local distribution cycles, thus saving on transport energy, and addressing people's needs in harmony with nature. This necessarily involves the production of useful, long-lasting and repairable products. Much less scrap is generated, less rubbish is created, and fewer resources are wasted. This coincides with the goals of the degrowth movement.

Increased cooperation between solidarity economy and degrowth is desirable and would raise awareness of both.

4. Degrowth needs socially acceptable concepts and visions

The word "degrowth" is not drawing a vision – rather it describes what is not wanted: economic growth without meaning or reason. Degrowth criticizes the foundations of prevailing economic thought and its categories. It opposes the use of gross domestic product (GDP) and its growth as the measure of a society's "success," regardless of the social and environmental costs. Degrowth means: growth must stop. This means putting an end to waste, senseless infrastructure projects, dangerously uncontrollable technologies, arms exports, the ruthless exploitation of nature, and the destruction and poisoning of the environment. But we do not know how to do this; there's no strategy yet. Who can guarantee that this downsizing of society will be democratic and based upon the common welfare, that it will be social?

As degrowth is criticizing the whole system, it should provide an alternative design for society, especially alternative economic structures – or people won't listen or even become scared. Critique of the status quo and the development of alternatives belong together: a successful anti-nuclear or anti-coal movement cannot exist without a renewable energy's movement, strategies for converting destructive production in meaningful production, and the inclusion of the unemployed. The degrowth movement is on its way. Primarily it's sounding the alarm, and rightly so – the industrialized countries cannot go on like this. But what is a positive vision and strategy for all, including the Global South and even the European or North American regions which are left behind!? If they hear the degrowth bell from the left, they might also run to the right. So what we have to talk about is rather solidarity and self-help, economic safety, economic democracy, participation, equality and inclusion as well as the protection of natural resources in alliance with the culturally diverse protectors of ecosystems.

5. An entire toolbox for building solidarity-based perspectives

People sense that things cannot go on as they are, and a myriad of initiatives from around the world are calling for a different way of treating the planet and our fellow human beings. More and more people are taking responsibility, getting up from their sofas, turning off the TV, and getting involved in local affairs. Thousands of people have already begun working on the development of alternatives that are emerging all over the place.

Digital communication offers unprecedented opportunities for disseminating information and enabling participation. Appropriate internet-based tools can make a major contribution to helping alternative approaches break through.

Good practices in various countries and continents are demonstrating that alternative economic forms already exist, and that they are viable. We need to look in detail at these practices to sharpen our awareness of the path to another mode of production and consumption. University research centers dealing with degrowth, the solidarity economy, and other alternatives should seek contact with real-life practitioners; they should promote the establishment of solidarity economy enterprises (SEEs) and other alternatives, provide them with advice, and make new discoveries together. We can support existing alternative projects, and help them share their knowledge, create networking opportunities (for example, through common open source platforms, mapping, trade fairs), and inspire other people to tread new (or very old) paths. The goal is to weave a tapestry of solidarity, available at the local level all over the world, which offers the countless people "thrown onto the garbage dump" by the system, fleeing war and destruction, the chance of survival and a good living. But networking should become more than talking: A very important step are economic collaborations between SEE, like housing coops or democratic schools getting their food from CSAs, their energy from ecological energy cooperatives and using ethical banking. We have to build production chains between SEE e.g. from planting hemp to hemp clothing or insulant to build up a strong alternative.

In Germany, many refugee initiatives have emerged in recent times. They try to help refugees with accommodation, language acquisition and integration. Can this become a spontaneous movement for solidarity economy? It certainly corresponds to the movement's criteria, which are the acts of humanity: to regard others as equals, and to share with them so that everyone has enough, no matter the questionable standard of "homo economicus." Ultimately, the exact vehicle used to participate actively in the transformation doesn't matter – whether it's solidarity economy, degrowth, economy for the common good, commons, economy of contribution, collaborative economy, demonetarization, or simply empathy – if it's combined with self-help-structures.

Cooperation in practice is crucial – in community-supported agriculture, in residential projects, in refugee projects, in urban gardens, in urban commoning, in self-managed production enterprises, in political community work, but also in political education, in public relations, in books and films, on Internet platforms, and in the organization of congresses, trade fairs and other events. Various schools of thought provide further resources. Their common vision is already lighting up; those who look will find structures of cooperation. Synergies are being created. Recovering our connection to nature is on the agenda. We don't have just one key that might not fit everywhere: we have several to choose from, a whole toolbox. This is our chance.

Translation: Kate Bell

Endnotes

1 The "territory" refers to the ecosystem affected by the group of people living in it; the country with its geographic and climatic characteristics. A solidarity economy enhances awareness of the given territory as the common property of the people who live in it: it is their common home, unique and precious. Other territories belong to other people, and this must be respected. People must protect their own territory from privatization, speculation and contamination of all kinds.

2 Forno, 2011.

Links

Socioeco – Resource Website of Social and Solidarity Economy: socioeco.org/index_en.html

Workerscontrol – Archive of worker buyouts and takeover struggles: workerscontrol.net

Intercontinental / European Network for the Promotion of Social Solidarity Economy (RIPESS): ripess.org and ripess.eu

Solikon – Congress of the Solidarity Economy in Berlin and Brandenburg: solikon2015.org/en

Texts by Paul Singer on the experiences in Brazil: socioeco.org/bdf_auteur-71_fr.html

Literature

Bayer, K., Embshoff, D. (eds.) (2015) *Der Anfang ist gemacht (Band 1). Kultur der Kooperation. Die Gruppe,* Neu Ulm, AG SPAK.

Forno, F. (2011) *La spesa a pizzo zero,* Milano: Altreconomia. Available at degrowth.de/wp-content/uploads/2016/07/Fr-Forno.pdf (Accessed 23 January 2019).

Giegold, S., and Embshoff, D. (eds.) (2008) *Solidarische Ökonomie im globalisierten Kapitalismus,* Hamburg, VSA.

Migliaro, L. R. (2001) *Desarollo, transformacion y perfeccionamiento de la economia en el tiempo,* Santiago, Ediciones Universidad Bolivariana.

Müller-Plantenberg, C., and Gawora, D. (eds.) (2008) *Netze und Ketten Solidarischer Ökonomie,* Kassel, Kassel University Press.

Singer, P. (2001) "Solidarische Ökonomie in Brasilien heute: eine vorläufige Bilanz," *Jahrbuch Lateinamerika,* vol. 25, pp. 75-96.

Singer, P. (2006) "Eine Alternative zum Kapitalismus" (Interview), *Lateinamerika* Nachrichten, vol. 398. Available at lateinamerika-nachrichten.de/artikel/eine-alternative-zum-kapitalismus (Accessed 23 January 2019).

Singer, P. (2006) "Introdução à Economia Solidária." Available at paulsinger.com.br (Accessed 23 January 2019).

Verein zur Förderung der Solidarischen Ökonomie (eds.) (2011)

Schritte auf dem Weg zur Solidarischen Ökonomie, Kassel, Kassel University Press.

Voss, E. (2015) *Wegweiser Solidarische Ökonomie. Anders wirtschaften ist möglich!,* Neu Ulm, AG SPAK.

Utting, P. (ed.) (2015) *Social and Solidarity Economy: Beyond the Fringe?,* London, Zed Books.

Chapter 20

Bonn im Wandel plants, belonging to the action "Macht Bonn Essbar" (make Bonn edible) (Image: Gesa Maschkowski)

Transition Initiatives: How Communities start their own Transformation

Gesa Maschkowski, Stephanie Ristig-Bresser, Silvia Hable, Norbert Rost and Michael Schem

About the authors

This text is the result of a communication process. Over the course of writing it, not only the text and the content underwent changes, but also the authors themselves. Several people were involved in this transition process. Gesa is Transition Trainer, cofounder of Transition Town *Bonn im Wandel e.V.*, cofounder of the community-supported agriculture *SoLaWi Bonn* and working as scientivist. Her research and practice deals with social movements and Salutogenesis. Stephanie is a cultural studies practitioner, freelance journalist and lecturer and active in the Economy for the Common Good movement. Silvia is a journalist, community organizer, education consultant and mother, active with *Transition Town Witzenhausen* since 2011, and from 2014 to 2016 member of the board at *Transition Netzwerk e. V.*. Norbert is an IT business engineer, regional developer of the *City of the Future* project of the Saxon capital of Dresden and is active with *Dresden im Wandel*. Michael works in an industrial development department, has a doctorate in chemical engineering, and has been involved in *Transition Town Bielefeld* since 2009.

1. "Just getting on with it" – outdated paradigms, plan B, and the self-empowerment to change

Transition means shift, transformation, or even change. We want to preserve and nurture the earth as a living system, to treat each other with respect and to share the earth's resources justly and fairly with one another now, and with generations to come. These values have their origins in permaculture but they are also represented by the global climate justice movement. This kind of fair and respectful global community could also be called a post-growth society or a degrowth society.

The key question posed by people in transition initiatives around the world is: What will our neighborhoods, villages and cities look like in the future when they hardly need fossil resources anymore, when they have vibrant regional economic structures and when we live a good and meaningful life? What can we do now to start this process of transition? The answers and approaches are as diverse as the people involved. Since the establishment of the first transition town, Totnes, in 2005, a colorful portfolio of projects, ideas and approaches has emerged —a toolkit for transition. The international network has inspired, encouraged and given strength to many people.

Misconceptions of the growth-orientated and information society

We question two paradigms that are still present in our society:

1. If only there is enough economic growth, then even the underprivileged of the world will benefit;
2. If we simply educate people enough, then at some point their behavior will become "correct," i.e. environmentally friendly and sustainable.

However, both of these assumptions have proven false. First, capitalist economic practices are causing collateral damage to environmental and social systems – climate change and resource depletion, social inequality, indignity and the dehumanization of working conditions are the symptoms. Second, over the past forty years, efforts to raise awareness and to inform people on this subject have failed to bring about the desired lifestyle changes. Considering all the products that are produced for industrialized countries in other countries in the world, the former have since 1990 neither reduced their greenhouse gas emissions, nor their land and resource consumption. Information and educational campaigns may even have the opposite effect; they can lead to denial, to "climate fatigue" or even to eco-anxiety. As a result, many feel powerless and helpless in view of the overwhelming challenges. These kinds of feelings play a large role in determining whether societal transformation succeeds or not – why would you want to get involved if you think: How can I ever make a difference in regard to a problem so complex?

Plan B for the growth model or: What would be the future that we long for?

Campaigning has not led to the societal changes we desperately need. This was also recognized by the British permaculture teacher Rob Hopkins, who decided to focus on the power of positive vision. In 2005 he developed an energy and cultural transition plan together with his students from Kinsale College. The group worked on questions such as: What would our educational system be like if in 2021 we needed almost no fossil resources anymore? What about our transport, our health care, our food system? What measures do we need to take today to make this vision a reality? Hopkins and his students relied on the widespread involvement of citizens, the administration and politicians. After all, the Energy Descent Action Plan for Kinsale was adopted with broad support by politicians. Based on these experiences Hopkins co-founded the first Transition Town in Totnes, in South West England. The founders of the initiative started to document their ideas, methods and processes. They published them on their website and in books and they developed "Transition Trainings." The British *Transition Network* became a central contact point and networking center for initiatives in Great Britain and worldwide.

Now, there are several thousand transition initiatives in 50 countries, partially organized in 18 Hub Groups, mainly in Europe, South- and North America and Australia. The Brazilian Hub names seven, in Germany there are about 80, and in the US around 300 groups are active. They emerge in places where people dream of a positive future, where they have the courage to experiment and make mistakes. Research shows that transition initiatives thrive better in small cities than in larger ones. They grow well in a favorable context and in cooperation with other actors. As argued in one of the first international surveys: "Among the characteristics of successful TIs [Transition Initiatives] are: a large number of founders, a good representation of diversity in the broader community, the presence and size of a steering group, the organization in thematic subgroups, the official TN [Transition Network] recognition, the acquisition of a legal statutory form, specific training in transition and permaculture practice, resources (time and external funds)."[1]

Objectives of the transition movement

"We aim for a society that respects human rights of present and future generations, that is appreciative and peaceful," states the German Transition Charter. Further, it says

> We want to live in a frugal and environmentally-friendly way, to be less dependent on non-renewables and more resilient than today, that is to say more resistant and adaptable. The transition movement aims to inspire, encourage and support people to develop a positive vision of the future and to be active agents of this change. The solutions and ideas for implementing the vision are manifold.

In addition to objectives, the Transition Charter contains values and principles that form the basis of transition work. The charter aims to provide guidance and a minimum consensus on which transition activists can easily agree.[2]

The basic principle: self-empowerment to act

The transition approach can be understood as a pragmatic response to policy failure. In his second book Hopkins describes the problem in a nutshell: "If we wait for the governments, it'll be too little, too late; if we act as individuals, it'll be too little, but if we act as communities, it might just be enough, just in time."[3]

Thus, it is about self-empowerment in the spirit of Gandhi: "be the change that you wish to see in the world." The support and development of effective groups are at the heart of the transition work. Training and publications promote competence to effect change and aim to empower people to (re)gain more influence over their living environment. It is often this positive and pragmatic approach that attracts people to the idea: "It's so refreshing to see how the weight of the world is broken down into small, achievable steps," wrote a visitor at the premiere of the film *In Transition 2.0* in Bonn. In many transition projects, in gardens, community-supported agriculture, repair cafés or regional currencies, it's about the joy of a structural and social change, which you are shaping yourself. The transition idea is also able to inspire transition processes in regions, for example, within the scope of the REconomy project (see below).

2. Diversity: The people involved and their topics

The first German transition town was created in 2009 in the district of Friedrichshain-Kreuzberg in Berlin, followed by Bielefeld. Since 2010 there have been annual conferences at changing locations. The growth of initiatives was significantly supported by Transition Trainings. Also, a transition network was established, which encourages interaction between the initiatives in Germany and initiates common projects, such as trainings, fundraising support, coaching and network meetings to specific topics.

The people involved in transition initiatives are very heterogeneous. A survey of visitors at the third German Transition Town Conference in 2012 showed that all ages and largely all income groups were represented. The education level, however, was above average.[4] We therefore assume that the founders often come from the middle class. Nonetheless, the setting approach (i.e. working in a neighborhood) enables the initiatives to reach other population groups, for example, through repair cafes, community gardens or with the project Transition Streets (sustainable neighborhoods). Often, young families are active in transition groups. This in itself leads to a multi-generational approach that is perceived as enriching.

As in other groups, time is the limiting factor for transition initiatives, as most people are volunteers. Even if many activists would like to be less dependent on money in the future, it is virtually impossible to build the necessary infrastructure with volunteer work only. There are some groups that provide permanent jobs; some initiatives experienced that this can lead to the establishment of unwanted hierarchies or reduce people's motivation to get involved on a voluntary basis.

Topics and tools of transition initiatives

Something quite unique about the transition movement is that there is no elaborate blueprint. The projects and methods come from many movements and fields of research. The transition initiatives did not invent the World Café or the gift economy, deep ecology or repair cafés. They experiment with them and develop them further. The activities on the ground closely match the skills of the people involved, and they are shaped by the motivations and needs of the people on site. Practical projects include:

- Projects for improving food sovereignty such as community gardens, community-supported agriculture, food cooperatives or edible city initiatives;
- Share and repair initiatives such as share and give-away shops, repair cafés, bicycle workshops, upcycling projects or bartering clubs;
- Projects referring to alternative mobility and sustainable urban development such as cargo bicycle projects, a car-free "good-life day," transition city tours or transition city maps;
- Cohousing communities and alternative construction methods such as Earthships, straw-bale or clay construction;
- Projects with renewable energy, such as solar cookers, pyrolysis stoves or "biomeilers" (compost heating);
- Educational projects and programs on sustainability such as reskilling, workshops or "transition days";
- Community-based projects such as the operation of culture and neighborhood centers, support and exchange of experience on health issues and care activities, as well

as neighborhood assistance;
- Projects on the culture of change, for example, transition storytelling, transition theatre, and groups that look at deep ecology, inner change, or the psychology of change.

Beyond the many local practical projects, there are other transition projects and formats with trans-regional relevancy. The transition network complies and distributes manuals and films, which pass on proven tips and tricks, methods and examples from the whole world. Next to this DIY approach, there are international acknowledged transition trainings and coaching programs for people who want to start transition initiatives or are already active in this field. The Transition Trainer group also meets at the international level, to learn from each other and to continuously develop Trainings according to the local needs.

Beyond the regional, there is support through the international Transition Hubs Group. The hubs schemes aim at various levels of scale to catalyze and support Transition. They have created an online working platform based on an agreed upon handbook about self-governance. Moreover, they meet for exchange and development of joint strategies. The British Transition Network has been supporting the rise of the international Hubs group for years. Meanwhile, it is an active member of this international circle. National (and regional) Hubs are a distinctive layer in the Transition Movement, connected by regular international gatherings, communications, international working groups and a very strong shared sense of purpose. A National Hub can be particularly useful for relating to bodies outside the Transition network: governments, national organizations, journalists or social movements. And at the local level there are the core teams of local initiatives.

One trans-regional project is "Transition in Municipalities." This project is designed to provide tools and education both for grassroots activists as well as for official municipality workers to get transition topics on the official agenda. This approach is inspired by the increasing evidence that either bottom up or top-down approaches alone cannot achieve sustained behavioral change.

In some places, there are already fruitful relationships between transition initiatives and municipal bodies. Those involved in initiatives contribute their know-how in urban development processes, for example, as facilitators, as members of parliaments, as consultants (Climate Advisory Board in Bonn) or in vision or strategy processes as is the case with the Dresden "City of the Future Project."

Furthermore, there are other trans-regional projects that aim at specific elements of the transition idea. The "Transitionese Project" is the Transition Network's linguistic project, aiming to support the international development of the Transition movement as a diverse learning network. Then there is the "Inner Transition" project. Inner Transition is about creating healthy cultures at all levels of scale – personal culture, group culture and the culture within communities, movements, the world and ecosystems more generally. Directed at education is the project "Schools in transition." Its aim is to set up pathways for transition-based education within the official school system.

Another trans-regional project is the Transition Research Network, a platform providing support, information, material and opportunities to connect researchers and practitioners. It is aiming for research that is mutually beneficial for both Transition initiatives (part of the Transition movement) and academic researchers. Experiences from Universities that are in a Transition process are collected in the Booklet "How to do Transition in your University." In Germany, there are some Universities running Transition Seminars and Trainings e.g. Münster, Tübingen, Hannover or Bochum. Among the materials which are provided by the Transition Network, there are several practical guides on how to Transition. The "Essential Guide to

Doing Transition" contains a collection of the most important learnings and tools from the first 10 years of the movement. Among others it contains the so called "Health Check" for Groups, which helps local groups all over the world to identify weaknesses and strengths within their community. This essential guide has been translated into 16 languages.

The Transition street project was replicated in several countries. It comprises a self-guided learning program for neighbors who collectively want to change their lifestyle in various areas, for example, to cut energy use. It has been proven to significantly reduce carbon emissions, to strengthen the neighborhood and enhance health indicators of the people involved.

REconomy is a concept that includes various approaches to restructuring the economy. It provides strategies and tools on how to run local entrepreneurs' forums, how to develop community-supported enterprises or how to analyze the economic potential of a relocalized economy. Best practice examples include the "Local Economic Blueprint" for the region of Totnes or the analysis of food resilience in Bristol (Who Feeds Bristol).

3. Degrowth: a goal – Transition: a path

Before we discuss the relationship between degrowth and the transition town movement, we have to talk about two assumptions shaping this question: first, that the transition movement and the degrowth movement comprise two more or less discernible and definable groups, and second, that they can be distinguished from each other. We do not agree with either assumption. We understand degrowth as an appeal to put an end to an unsustainable economic system and to work on alternatives. In our opinion "green growth" in industrialized countries is not a solution anymore. Key issues in the transition movement are how this social change can be supported, what conditions are needed to make this happen, and what new economic forms are appropriate and vital. This is a good reason for those active in the transition movement to also engage in degrowth events and debates. Perhaps degrowth can be understood as one of the many goals of a post-growth society, and transition as one of several approaches to experiment with social change.

More and more people are now trying to rethink and reshape society. In this regard degrowth activists have used their presence and their activities to create platforms and opportunities for meetings and conferences reaching a broad audience. This is in our view a good starting point to leave the "you" and "us" mentality behind and form a community of transformation movements. We therefore want to thank and acknowledge the organizers of degrowth events for launching a debate on transformation that has inspired and mobilized many people.

Networking as an opportunity for the future of degrowth and transition towns

The exchange of experience between both the initiatives and the movements is often too brief due to capacity constraints. Degrowth conferences and transition network meetings are good opportunities to facilitate this exchange. Another important step was the establishment of the European grassroots network *Ecolise* in 2014. This process was supported by the British Transition Network, the international ecovillage movement, the permaculture movement and many other organizations. It seeks to enable an exchange of experience, education, research and lobbying beyond the individual movements. A possible future of these movements could lie in creating synergies between existing networks.

4. Transition movement proposals: Growth in the right places

Conceptually, the transition movement goes beyond degrowth

or sufficiency perspectives. We ask not only how we can consume less – we also ask what kind of economic system will satisfy the needs of all people in the long term rather than satisfying the needs of a few people in the short term. One inherent question in this discussion is, to what extent our current economic system fulfils basic needs such as meaningful work, creativity, leisure, freedom, affection and participation?

Growth of skills and quality (of life)

In our view the term "degrowth" does not make it clear enough that we in many areas still need growth to achieve "The Great Transformation." This applies to both skills and qualities: We need growth in courage, confidence and organizational capability, in participation, empathy, solidarity and sense of community. We need more and better self-organization and decision-making skills. It is all about adding more meaning and more sustainability to life and work. And not least: The climate justice and post-growth movements need more people, time and resources to prove successful in the long run. This is another issue that needs to be debated in society. How and when do we gain skills and resources for a large-scale societal transformation?

Weaknesses: The social and psychological requirements for change

In many degrowth and transition debates there is not enough consideration of cultural and psychological dimensions of change. Many events and debates continue to rely on a cognitive and hierarchical education model, where degrowth and transition experts explain to "lay people" how the world works and what they need to do. After the latter have listened to this and perhaps put in a word or two, they go home and nothing happens. Forty years of environmental education, but also health and transition studies show that this education concept does not hit home effectively. The great transformation is a process of social learning.[5] This process requires empowerment and not indoctrination; it calls for empathy and enquiry. For example: What do people need in order to feel that the great transformation is meaningful and feasible? The transition movement draws here, at least in theory, from the experience of environmental and health psychology.[6] Finding which social and psychological conditions facilitate change and what methods and formats develop transformative power would be of great value —not only for the degrowth debate.

5. Growing together - Inspiration and cooperation

In the long run we see many opportunities to strengthen each other, and we would like to see collaboration taking place. Here we let the individual authors have their say:

Gesa: Self-empowerment for a sustainable life is created and lived by people in the settings of their everyday life; where they learn, work, play, and love. Transition initiatives are part of a network of active movements that are present on the ground and pursue real change through their projects and activities. Their strength lies in an extensive array of approaches and many encouraging practical examples. The humanistic, person-centered approach of the transition movement is of great significance for me. It enables change to come about through experience in a relationship. The potential of different movements working on the ground can lie in kick-starting transformation projects together and using diverse routes to get there.

Stephanie: If we want to achieve the great transformation, this is only possible in collaboration with many initiatives. It needs to be based on trust and respect, underpinned by the fundamental position that we all make a valuable contribution to this change and sometimes one, sometimes another movement will take the initiative. Between the movements we need respectful communication and behavior that is based on mutual trust, with which we already live the good life that we envision, and shake off the old and firmly established thinking of "higher, further, faster,""who's number one?" and "who's the winner?" This is a great task and transition tools can certainly contribute to its successful fulfilment. Fields of experimentation can be large, global issues such as the TTIP. Here we are all on the same page and thereby perceived as one voice. This way our proposals are "leaked" into society. This means that subsequently we can draw greater attention with other activities and projects.

Silvia: We have already managed to create utopias that encourage people. They show that change (on a smaller scale) is possible. These experiences are transferable and repeatable and therefore of great social relevance. Even though the transition movement works mainly with concrete projects such as gardens, repair work, neighborhood assistance and the like, it is not only the "what," but in particular the "that" (something happens) that encourages and inspires people to (re)assume responsibility and the power to act in all areas of life and particularly in their own life! This rids us of a diffuse feeling of hopelessness that is based on fear and is pushing people into the arms of conspiracy theorists or the new right wing, which play with the unfulfilled longings for structure and order.

Norbert: The core issue is how we can work across different milieus. How do we also reach out to all those who we normally do not reach? If we succeed in building bridges and initiating transmission processes, we will also manage the same at a Meta level, i.e. between the different "emancipatory" movements.

Michael: Friends of the Earth Germany coined the motto: "Fewer, better, more beautiful." We must change our world by freeing ourselves from our obsession with consumption and starting a simpler life. To reach a large audience it is important not to preach what people have to renounce to, but to emphasize the advantages. Here degrowth is a great inspiration, which we would like to combine with the transition slogan: "Just getting on with it." Transition aims to develop and test those examples in practice, which open our eyes to another world in which all people live more self-sufficiently and enjoy life.

Endnotes

1 Feola and Nunes, 2013, p. 1.
2 The Transition Charter was adopted with broad approval at the network meeting in 2015 and comments are currently being submitted. See transition-initiativen.org/unsere-philosophie-transition-charta (Accessed 5 February 2019).
3 Hopkins, 2011, p. 17.
4 Maschkowski and Wanner, 2014.
5 Manzini, 2009.
6 Hopkins, 2008.

Links

British Transition Network website: transitionnetwork.org
In Transition 2.0 - documentary film: intransitionmovie.com.archived.website/index.html
German transition initiatives' website: transition-initiativen.de
REcomony: http://reconomy.org
Examples for REcomony: https://reconomycentre.org/home/economic-blueprint and http://bristolfoodpolicycouncil.org/who-feeds-bristol
Transition Health Check in 16 languages: transitioninitiative.org

Literature

Feola, G. and Nunes, R. J. (2013) Failure and Success of Transition Initiatives: A Study of the International Replication of the Transition Movement (Research Note 4). Reading, Walker Institute for Climate System Research. Available at core.ac.uk/download/pdf/42147521.pdf (Accessed 5 February 2019).

Hopkins, R. (2008) *The Transition Handbook: From Oil Dependency to Local Resilience*. Vermont, UIT Cambridge Ltd., 2008.

Hopkins, R. (2011) *The Transition Companion.* Totnes, Green

Books.

Hopkins, R. and Astruc, L. (2018). *The Transition Starts Here, Now and Together*. Paris, Actes Sud.

Hopkins, R. (2015) *21 Stories of Transition*. Totnes, Transition Network.

Manzini, E (2009) "A Social Learning Process – Promising Cases, Teachers, Students and Designers," in: Jégou, F., Thoresen, V., Manzini, E. (eds.), *LOLA – Looking for Likely Alternatives*, Hamar/Elverum, Hedmark University College, pp. 42-43. Available at issuu.com/acunar/docs/lola_brochure (Accessed 5 February 2019).

Maschkowski, G. and Wanner, M. (2014) "Die Transition-Town-Bewegung – Empowerment für die große Transformation?" *pnd online*, vol. 2, pp. 60-71. Available at planung-neu-denken.de/content/view/297/41 (Accessed 5 February 2019).

Chapter 21

Collective bargaining in the public service sector: Mounting a large-sized poster "Wir sind die Guten" (roughly 'We are the good ones') at the facade of the ver.di federal administration in Berlin. 25.02.2014 (Image: Jungeblodt/ver.di)

Trade Unions: Who can afford to degrow?

Jana Flemming and Norbert Reuter

Jana is a doctoral candidate at the Department for Sociology at the University of Jena, Germany. Her doctoral project examines employee and trade union perspectives on socio-ecological ways of life from a cultural sociological standpoint. Norbert is head of the Department *for* Collective Bargaining Policy on the national executive board of the United Services Union (Vereinte Dienstleistungsgewerkschaft, ver.di) in Berlin. He is also senior lecturer in Economics at RWTH Aachen University.[1]

1. A link to the past – socio-ecological transformation as part of trade union interest representation?

By international comparison, German trade unions are very strongly institutionalized and have exceptionally high membership levels. With 2.3 million and 2.0 million members respectively, the Industrial Union of Metalworkers (IG Metall) and the United Services Union (ver.di) have some of the largest memberships among independent trade unions globally. Therefore, compared with other countries the German trade unions are in general in a relatively good position to propose and develop solutions for the society at large.

Nevertheless, the German trade unions, representing mainly employees, are frequently accused of tending to make extensive concessions to companies, particularly in times of economic crises, in order to secure their members' jobs and income. As such, they de facto assume the role of "co-operative crisis management," which, as Klaus Dörre states, can have fatal consequences: "Despite, or possibly because of their incontestable successes in managing the crisis, the German unions are also in danger of becoming mere pressure group agencies." According to Dörre, such trade union policy is primarily about the wages and jobs of (core) employees in the individual sectors. This leads to the representation of particular employee interests, which may also be in opposition to general societal interests such as ecological sustainability.[2]

Contrary to the assumption that unions dedicate themselves solely to securing income and jobs, unions have dealt with many socially important issues in the past. Since the beginning of the 1970s

> the concerns of the anti-nuclear, international development, environmental and conservation movements, of advanced feminist thought and activism, environmental critique of technology, the new alternative and cooperative economy, as

> well as various emancipation movements of social, ethnic and sexual minorities [...] have also been reflected in discussions at trade union conferences; these issues were prioritized by the trade union press and educational initiatives.[3]

In light of the multiple crises at present, these debates are also beginning to reappear in the current discussions and decisions in the trade unions. IG Metall, for example, has called for a "fundamental change of course. Our aims are qualitative growth and sustainable transformation of industrial production in order to create opportunities for future generations to have a 'good life'".[4] Ver.di has similar priorities:

> In order to rally a majority behind ecological transformation and implement it, a concept is needed which both contributes to quality of life for the majority of people and promotes social and employment objectives. This requires an alternative economic policy, which is focused on qualitative, selective, socio-ecologically governed GDP growth. Therefore, the goal is a socio-ecological transformation.[5]

2. Entrenched differences, ignored similarities

The conflict between jobs and the environment

There are still virulent disputes between trade unions on the one hand and environmental movements on the other. Both sides frequently criticize each other. Environmental movements accuse unions of refusing to include environmental issues in their policy as a matter of course. In part, there is indignation and incomprehension about "the" trade unions which, for example, continue to promote environmentally damaging lignite mining in order to secure jobs. Against the backdrop of the wider environmental crisis and the associated criticism of economic growth, trade unions find it difficult for their involvement in a socio-ecological transformation of the economy to be accepted. Many of those who are critical of economic growth on environmental grounds consider trade unions to be both uncritical and powerful proponents of economic growth. Conversely, trade unions sometimes accuse the environmental movement and those involved in the degrowth movement of not taking any, or only little, account of the interests of employees or maintaining jobs in their political demands.[6]

These reciprocal accusations often overlook the fact that there is an objective conflict between environmental, economic and social demands, which can be described as a "magic triangle." "Magic" because achieving one objective generally goes hand in hand with damaging another. It is almost impossible to meet all objectives equally. A solution will thus always have to be compromising in nature. Extracting fossil fuels, for example, both creates jobs and income in Germany and in many other countries, and simultaneously drives a process that is damaging to the environment. Globally, there are numerous examples of trade unions that are fighting alongside companies to maintain industries that are damaging to the environment, but these trade unions are also fighting to maintain the jobs and livelihoods of many people. This phenomenon is also described as the "jobs versus environment dilemma."[7] On the other hand, there are numerous examples of the environmental and degrowth movement broadly ignoring the negative social and employment impacts of their demands. One such example would be demanding the phasing out of industries that are damaging to the environment.[8]

Oppositions to the de- or post-growth perspective can also be observed in the historical development of trade unions: for example, key improvements in working conditions for the working population were once achieved in coal and steel production. Today, trade unions are trying to prove their competence in modern environmentally friendly sectors such as the wind energy sector, and advocate for works councils and collective agreements. According to Dörre, a socio-ecological perspective for society as a whole would have to go beyond this and take the comprehensive transformation of production and way of life into account.[9] It would also revitalize the trade union discussion on what constitutes a good life, considering socio-ecological factors.

3. Seeking solutions: A socio-ecological way of life as a shared reference point

The search for solutions to the socio-ecological crisis frequently involves aiming to introduce policy measures to curb growth. These range from tax incentives to production bans. A further important dimension involves the (re-)shaping of our current way of life, based on the uninhibited exploitation of nature and fossil fuels, in particular. From the degrowth perspective, changing one's way of life is of central importance. The so-called "*Wirtschaftswunder*" ("economic miracle") in Germany in the 1960s and 1970s fueled the creation of new consumption standards and value patterns. In the past, of course, employees also profited from the wealth generated by economic growth. But this hegemonic way of life in the Global North depends on environmental destruction and the exploitation of workers in the Global South via global value chains.

The term "way of life" raises the question of what it now means to have a good life and how this can be approached as a socio-political phenomenon. For this, one needs a new understanding of wealth. In the de- and post-growth-movement, for example, how we organize our time plays an important role. The intention is to counteract somewhat the accelerated temporal structures of modernity[9] by developing societal forms of collaboration, which both give more space to the quality of human life in terms of leisure and free time, and promote more environmentally appropriate ways of life. Quality of life should no longer be assessed in purely monetary terms, that is, based on one's bank balance or level of consumption. In trade union circles too, positions in which wealth is no longer solely measured in terms of income are increasingly common. However, the struggle for wage justice also makes environmental sense, as in this way, for example, consumption patterns can be diverted more towards quality and "being," and less towards having.

These are not new issues. German trade unions considered the subject of the good life and the environmental consequences of the production of goods and services early on. As early as 1972, IG Metall held an international conference with the title "Aufgabe Zukunft: Verbesserung der Lebensqualität" ("Task for the Future: Improving Quality of Life"), which was documented in ten conference volumes.[11] However, these early humane and environmental approaches to far-reaching social policy and transformation were pushed into the background by the political and economic developments of the ensuing decades. In particular, economic crisis situations have repeatedly pushed the importance of maintaining jobs and income for a longer period of time to the forefront.

Social situations determine one's perception of the good life

So far, responding to the environmental crisis has primarily remained a matter for relatively well-off or educated circles. The degrowth perspective is also popular in these circles. As a result of this, an understanding of the situation of other social groups is often lost. For many, the prefix "eco-" remains more an insult and "de- and post-growth" an esoteric debate that has little to do with everyday life. In a society, which is based on paid work and oriented towards social advancement, people generally only adopt conscious, socio-ecological ways of life if they have decided to do this voluntarily and on the basis of a relatively secure economic situation. Those lower on the social and wealth ladder want to climb further up first. Generally, only people who have reached a certain level of wealth are willing and able to consider and implement fundamental changes in behavior, which can also include doing without.

A trade union perspective can help ensure that socio-ecological issues do not remain the concern of only the relatively wealthy and educated, but instead promote engagement at every level of society. This affects, for example, energy production and supply, a policy area in which the conflict between the economy and the environment is particularly evident. As long as employees have no alternative employment prospects, the focus of the trade unions must be on maintaining jobs. This means protection of the environment and global climate justice issues are reduced to a secondary issue. Conversely, those motivated by environmental concerns tend to ignore employment concerns. They vehemently demand an immediate withdrawal from coal mining, while the futures of those employed in and in relation to these industries are, at best, treated as a side issue. In case of doubt, the problem tends to be suppressed and tolerated as "collateral damage" for resolving the environmental matter.

Constructive discussions about wage labor in the face of the socio-ecological crisis are needed. Firstly, this is of strategic relevance. Because, after all, trade unions are a vital, influential ally on the path towards socio-ecological transformation. Secondly, however, this is also about the important interests that unions represent: as long as people are not in possession of assets, they are dependent on their income from work. This banal truth and its consequences are often ignored by those motivated by environmental concerns, as well as by critics of capitalism. They are, to some extent, blind to social issues.

It can generally be assumed that actors involved in the debate know the stated positions. However, it can be observed that trade unions, critics of capitalism and environmentalists frequently only focus on specific elements. They frequently pursue their own particular political strategies and targets, often do not take each other seriously, and feel misunderstood by one another. This leads them to pursue primarily social *or* environmental interests. A necessary balance of interests does not occur as a result.

4. Reshaping production and one's way of life: Just transitions for all!

An emancipatory perspective in the discourse on environmental issues and a good life for all must be based on the analysis that environmental issues often go hand in hand with social issues, and that conversely, social issues always have environmental components. This is seen, for example, in the discourse on lignite strip mining in Germany: The mining and burning of lignite is not only a threat to the livelihoods of people in the Global South. For many people, mining means that the region that they feel connected to is being destroyed, and yet are dependent on these polluting industries at the same time. If lignite is no longer mined, it is not only the miners who become unemployed; there is also the risk of a domino effect resulting in the economic decline of entire regions. In this conflict situation, trade unions are sometimes heavily criticized for their employment concerns. However, successes in the battle for sustainable energy supply remain limited without trade union participation, that is, they are restricted to the environment policy area with the risk of significant social "collateral damage." A solution-oriented approach ought to advocate structural transformation that takes social *and* environmental factors into account.

The key task for unions and people from the environmental and de- and post-growth movement should be to actively work towards reducing the conflict between environmental and workers' movements. This would mean, for example, involving employees who are dependent on mining or other production methods that are damaging to the environment in strategies for socio-ecological transformation as part of a comprehensive policy concept. Experiences in other areas of the world show that labor policy struggles can be in harmony with environmental aims.

Trade unions have played an important role in the development of environmental policies in industrial countries around the world in the past century. Health and safety issues in the workplace have often resulted in alliances with community-based movements.[12] Among other places, there are examples in the USA of how environmental and social issues can be linked. There, trade union and environmental actors are collaborating within the "Just Transition" framework. When scaling down polluting or carbon-intensive industries, both environmental interests and worker demands are taken into consideration. The social inequality that makes its mark in areas with industries that are damaging the environment is also part of the political discussions: Who lives close to industries that are damaging to health and who can afford to live in the countryside? It is not just workers who are affected by industries that damage the environment but also the – primarily poorer – people who live in the regions in question.

Politicians and trade unions must aim to create good employment opportunities while also ensuring that jobs are designed so as not to create (lasting) environmental damage. Without doubt, this does not apply to many jobs today. It is not only that workers (e.g. in the services industry) suffer from enormous work pressure and increasing working hours: there are also many jobs, particularly in mining or the nuclear industry, which are an extreme burden to the environment. The solution cannot be to ignore the needs of the workers and simply close the works. Instead, fair transitions must be created, which promote alternative jobs and income sources. What these transitions look like and what they should lead to must be discussed by all affected with the involvement of politicians. Generally, the removal or restructuring of damaging, unsustainable jobs should not be seen as an individual problem for those employed there, but as a challenge to be solved with the participation of society at large. To this end, society as a whole must take responsibility if works are closed for good environmental reasons, for example, and people become unemployed as a result.[13]

The de- or post-growth perspective can encourage trade union representatives to reconsider their understanding of interest representation: Do trade unions see themselves as working for far-reaching socio-ecological transformation? If they do, this would involve alliances with social movements. As such, the focus on both trade union policy and socio-ecological transformation policy should not just be on particular companies and associated industries. Employee living conditions must also be included, taking into account such questions as: What should be done about the fine dust particles produced by lignite strip mining, which affect the health of employees and local residents? Is it in the workers' interests when entire towns, and thus entire social networks, disappear? The transformation of production and one's way of life involves environmental protection and the maintenance of the quality of life in the social sphere, as well as good, health-related and environmental working conditions.

One tool for at least reducing both environmental, and social and economic problems is the organization of working time. Here, trade union traditions are aligned with the de- and post-growth perspective. The call for more free time, which individuals may freely choose to use for leisure or for caring for family and friends, is a prominent demand both from those who fall under the banner of the de- or post-growth movement and (again) increasingly from trade unions. It is getting clearer that a fixation on formal salaried work is insufficient. New working time models are currently being discussed by trade unions and politicians.[14] It is increasingly clear that in order to implement changes in the economy, and to secure and increase wealth in a broader sense, more time resources are needed – especially by those who actually produce the economic output. This affects the activities of the services and industry sector, as well as care work. Here, discussions on a societal level are needed to establish what, how, how many and where we want to produce and consume, in light of the socio-ecological crisis *and* with regard to enjoying a good life against a background of growing abundance. In the meanwhile, in more and more collective agreements in Germany employees have the choice between a reduction in working time and an increasing of incomes. The fact that experience shows that the majority of employees choose the reduction in working time, is a hopeful sign.

Another means of driving forward socio-ecological transformation is strengthening the principle of co-determination within companies and developing it further towards an economic democracy. In this way, socially and environmentally sound approaches to production could not only be raised and discussed with those affected, but direct practical consequences could also be drawn. Hans-Jürgen Urban, a board member at IG Metall, considers setting the course for fundamental economic change to be a key element of social transformation. According to Urban, this primarily includes making production, consumption and distribution more environmentally friendly; secondly, it involves a new system of distribution of income, assets and social opportunities; and thirdly, it involves the democratization of business decisions and structures.[15] These points can be seen as an agenda for the debate between unions and the de- or post-growth movement.

Trade unions traditionally have a rich experience and expertise when it comes to the implementation of political demands. In the de- and post-growth movement, the focus is on the development and expansion of alternative structures, with less focus on adequate, specific strategies for implementation and overcoming resistance. If, to begin with, it were possible to find crossovers in current demands, successive comprehensive strategies for the specific implementation of socio-ecological transformation could be developed on this basis.

5. Joint perspective from unions and social movements – overcoming social imbalances and establishing socio-ecological production and a socio-ecological way of life

Without trade unions as a socio-political player, socio-ecological transformation is not deliverable. Equally, how this ecological transformation should occur in concrete terms remains a subject of debate. Trade unions are thus frequently confronted with the dilemma that ecological transformation risks occurring at the expense of workers. Reducing this tension and involving workers in the socio-ecological transformation will be a core challenge. An economy that holds on to capitalist driven growth will not only continue to damage the environment but also lead to heightened social inequality.

People are increasingly aware of the global and socio-ecological upheavals caused by the growth paradigm. However, the strategies engendered by this awareness are eclectic and contradictory in daily actions, especially when they have been developed on an individual basis. The expression "way of life" opens up prospects for collective and democratic action as part of a socio-ecological transformation. Exactly what an appropriate life should look like remains a subject of collective debate. These debates and, above all, the issue of how trade unions and the workers represented by them try to overcome the inequalities associated with the current capitalist way of life, can be a decisive key to developing interfaces and joint actions with the de- and post-growth movement. For trade unions, cooperation with civil society actors is called for, however:[16] "Occasionally [...] an input from outside is required in order for social change to become effective in unions as well; in other cases [. . .] union policy itself contributes to change in political relations."[17]

Through productive collaboration between de- and post-growth perspectives on the one hand and union positions on the other, a broad alliance for socio-ecological transformation can develop. The question remains whether the necessary transformation will occur "by design or by disaster" to use a prominent phrase from the de- and post-growth movement. Forging a societal alliance between unions and the de- and post-growth movement would be a welcome attempt to achieve the inevitable change "by design."

Translation: Anonymous

Endnotes

1 We would like to thank Daniel Förste for inspiring the title.
2 Dörre, 2011, p. 278f.
3 Wiesenthal, 2014, p. 402.
4 Lemb, 2015, p. 12.
5 Ver.di, 2011, p. 2.
6 Reuter, 2014, p. 555.
7 Räthzel and Uzzell, 2011.
8 Felli, 2014.
9 Dörre, 2015.
10 Rosa, 2005.
11 IG Metall, 1972; Wiesenthal, 2014.
12 Felli, 2014.
13 The chairman of the union IG Bergbau, Chemie, Energie (IGBCE – Industrial Union for Mining, Chemistry and Energy), Michael Vassiliadis, has, for example, proposed a private fund, financed with profits, to secure the socially responsible withdrawal from lignite mining long-term. The fund should also finance the regeneration of mining areas.
14 The German party Bündnis 90/Die Grünen, for example, is currently discussing a new working time model as part of its programme "Politik für mehr Zeit – Damit Erwerbsarbeit besser in unser Leben passt" ("Policy for more time – so

that paid work fits life better"). An SPD project group has published a dialogue paper entitled "Neue Zeit – Arbeits- und Lebensmodelle im Wandel" ("New Time – Changing Working and Life Models"). ver.di has proposed a new working hours model, which combines reduced working hours for full-time employees with extended working hours for part-time employees via additional paid "Verfügungstage" ("availability days").

15 Urban, 2014.

16 Lemb, 2015, p. 18.

17 Wiesenthal, 2014, p. 396f.

Literature

Dörre, K. (2011) "Funktionswandel der Gewerkschaften. Von der intermediären zur fraktalen Organisationsmacht," in: Haipeter, T., Dörre, K. (ed.), *Gewerkschaftliche Modernisierung,* Wiesbaden, Springer VS, pp. 268-301.

Dörre, K. (2015) "'Wir für mehr' — Ausgangspunkt für eine tranformative Industripolitik?," in: Lemb, W. (ed.) *Welche Industrie wollen wir?*, Frankfurt am Main: Campus, pp. 233-252.

Felli, R. (2014) "An Alternative Socio-Ecological Strategy? International Trade Unions Engagement with Climate Change," *Review of International Political Economy*, vol. 21, pp. 372-398.

IG Metall (ed.) (1972) *Aufgabe Zukunft: Qualität des Lebens. Beiträge zur vierten internationalen Arbeitstagung der Industriegewerkschaft Metall für die BRD, 11. bis 14. April 1972 in Oberhausen*, Frankfurt am Main, Europäische Verlagsanstalt.

Lemb, W. (2015) "Ein nachhaltiges Wirtschaftsmodell der Zukunft braucht, Gute Industriepolitik,'" in: Lemb, W. (ed.) *Welche Industrie wollen wir?*, Frankfurt am Main, Campus, pp. 7-22.

Räthzel, N., and Uzzell, D. (2011) "Trade Unions and Climate

Change: The Jobs versus Environment Dilemma," *Global Environmental Change,* vol. 21, no. 4, pp. 1215-1223.

Reuter, N. (2014) "Die Degrowth-Bewegung und die Gewerkschaften," *WSI Mitteilungen,* vol. 7, pp. 555-559.

Rosa, H. (2013) *Social Acceleration: A New Theory of Modernity,* New York, Columbia University Press

Urban, H.-J. (2014) "Stillstand in Merkelland: Wo bleibt die Mosaik-Linke," *Blätter für deutsche und internationale Politik,* vol. 59, pp. 73-82.

Ver.di (2011) "Sozial-ökologischer Umbau statt pauschaler Wachstumskritik. Kontroversen um das Wachstum," *Wirtschaftspolitische Informationen,* vol. 2.

Wiesenthal, H. (2014)" Gewerkschaften in Politik und Gesellschaft: Niedergang und Wiederkehr des Modells Deutschland,'" in: Schroeder, W. (ed.) *Handbuch Gewerkschaften in Deutschland,* Wiesbaden, Springer VS, pp. 395-421.

Chapter 22

A summer day in the community garden Annalinde in Leipzig, Germany. (Image: Inga Kerber)

Urban Gardening: Searching New Relationships Between Nature and Culture

Christa Müller

Christa has a PhD in sociology and is the director of the Munich-based research foundation anstiftung. During the 1990s, she carried out research on peasant movements and modernization processes in Spain, Latin America and Westphalia. The gardening project Internationale Gärten Göttingen sparked her scientific interest in the urban gardening movement in Germany, which anstiftung has both supported and studied from the beginning. Her work is based on the action research approach, where the subject-object relationship is constantly questioned and used as a basis for reflection.

The present text mainly focuses on the new urban gardening

movement in Germany, and was written without directly consulting those involved. However, it does take into account the multiplicity of voices within the movement. Christa sees her role as that of an observer and does not speak on behalf of anybody else.

1. Non-commercial spaces for all

The main idea or field of action of the urban gardening movement is the creation of non-commercial, green spaces for all. The activists, of their own initiative, turn abandoned lots, parking garage roofs and other neglected spaces into welcoming green environments. Using old crates, Euro-pallets and industrial tarp, they build – often with widespread help from the neighborhood – mobile community gardens in the middle of the city. They keep chickens and bees, produce honey, grow and harvest crops, cook, produce seeds, build clay ovens and cargo bikes, transform ship containers into workshops and garden bars, teach themselves artisanal techniques and bring people of all social and cultural backgrounds in contact with nature.

Although many urban gardening projects see their work as political, not everyone involved necessarily sees gardening as an articulation of political will. I personally agree with Hannah Arendt in that the interaction between different people in a public space (and this includes the urban community gardens that identify as "open") is per se a form of political action. Some, however, simply want to be in touch with nature, meet people, or have a place to rest and look at the greenery; others want to help shape a concrete space or just work with their hands; and yet others invest their energy in these projects to stop the privatization of public space, recover public space as a common good and make the city greener.[1]

Vegetable growing is an especially important part of their work. It enables an exchange beyond specific social groups and cultures and also serves to question, subvert and change the system of industrial food production and its market chains. This concern with how food is grown, which environments and types of care it needs and how it can be processed is then combined with socio-political questions: Who owns the ground? Whose ideas of participation and wealth should it serve? And – a decisive question – where should the food and the resources for mass consumption come from in the future? The urban gardening movement thus deals with the issues surrounding a sustainable transformation of society, and it does so in a remarkably non-ideological way, approaching its topics not from theory, but through direct practice and experimentation in situ. In this way, urban gardening is not a glorification of rural life, but a quest for a different city.

I see this movement as representing a new type of urban garden, which does *not* seek to be a place of refuge from the big, loud city, like the traditional allotment gardens so typical of the modern industrial era. Instead, the protagonists of these new gardens seek to establish a relationship with the city and the neighborhood around them and make their own contribution to sustainable urban development.[2] That is why the historical precursor to the urban community garden is not the allotment garden, which – especially in Germany – clearly fits into the tradition of an industrial and social colonization of nature (neatly trimmed hedges, widespread use of pesticides, etc.). This new type of community garden breaks away from these techniques of domination. As a matter of fact, its existence is dependent on its dense urban environment, the public space in relation with which it places itself and that it seeks to renegotiate.

The first example of this new type of community garden was created in Göttingen in the mid-1990s as a consequence of the Yugoslav Wars; by Bosnian women in migration centers who missed the gardens they had used to feed their large families at home. The primary goal in this case was to (also) use community gardening as a way of dealing with certain social issues, such as trying out a resource-oriented approach and creating a space where they could feel at home.[3] In general terms, the subsistence-based approach of gardens empowers those involved and allows them to meet others as equals. Unlike many other integration projects, the gardens represent in many ways a corridor (not to be confused with a one-way street) between the country of origin and the receiving country, as well as between a biographical past and a present. Community gardens are an ideal space for intercultural exchange, as the fact of working and being active together makes it possible to express, interpret and value both the differences and the similarities between those involved. Gardeners from different countries of origin come together, contribute their knowledge and skills and produce a surplus that they can give away. This economy of reciprocity, which can only exist if you have something to give in the first place, leads to the creation of fruitful ties with other societal subsystems.

Since the mid-2000s, the community gardening approach has continued its unique development. In large cities there have been examples of guerrilla gardening actions, as well as of neighborhood gardens in densely populated city areas, such as the Rosa Rose community garden created in Berlin-Friedrichshain in 2004. The main goal of the founders of this garden was to occupy and take control of abandoned land – in a neighborhood lacking in green space – in order to use it themselves and make it available to the less privileged members of the community for common activities. When the land was sold to an investor and developed, the garden had to go. The subsequent move took place in the form of a demonstration/parade that provides insight into the performative forms of political expression of urban gardening. Today, a pink memorial plaque in the ground in the street Kinzigstraße commemorates the Rosa Rose garden.

2009 saw the launch of the Prinzessinnengarten, a project based on the principle of nomadic gardening in mobile containers. With its paradoxical concept, the garden – which occupies a 6000 m² abandoned lot at Moritzplatz in Berlin-Kreuzberg – received widespread media attention. The fascination it continues to inspire is due, in no small part, to its "aesthetics of the unfinished," created by the reuse and upcycling of discarded and scavenged objects. Here, objects that (according to the industrial logic of production, consumption and waste) are considered used up and worthless, are given a new value without using any money or industrial energy in the process.

Increasingly, gardens are beginning to appear in museums and theatres as well. They are open, creative spaces that complement (and qualify) the existing, highly regulated spaces they inhabit. The principles of DIY (do-it-yourself) and DIT (do-it-together) are used to break down the barriers between high culture, institutions and the daily life of city dwellers. The same applies in different ways to community gardens in refugee accommodations, company gardens, or open student gardens at universities, among others.

2. Urban gardens: open to different social backgrounds and generations

The more than 650 urban community gardens in Germany[4] are among the few places in the country – or in any other country – where people from different social backgrounds and generations are active together. The initiators of these projects are often young, well-educated, ecologically-minded and well-connected. Thanks to the Internet, they have learned to look for practical solutions and, unlike the previous generations of the post-war decades, they have grown up in democratic settings. Their families, their schools and Web 2.0 have taught them that everything is possible, that the future isn't written, and that it's up to them to make a difference. Their life experience has shown them the power and effectiveness of their actions, so they naturally want to have a say in how their city is designed. The sharing of knowledge on the Internet and the resulting experience of effectiveness thus migrates into analogue space and, once there, challenges the established institutions.

These actors are aware of the disappearance of public space, and they seek to expand predesigned and pre-planned city spaces with their architecture and activities. Through their social practices they make demands for democratic urban planning in keeping with our times: the creation of room for interaction between urban nature and people, for encounters and productive uses of space, with an emphasis on opening up instead of closing down. These are the messages that the city gardeners send out to the urban planners, and they don't limit themselves to words, but speak through their "installations" as well. The garden itself is the message; it is the realization of a concrete utopia. You could say it is an example of the "normative power of the factual," because a tangible, publicly accessible "fact" is created – and although it may not be officially sanctioned, the political status quo cannot ignore it and is disturbed by it.

In Western societies, many of those born after 1980 are critical of authorities and hierarchies. They demand transparency, direct participation and freedom of movement. However, they do not do this only for themselves. The reclaiming of public space for commons and subsistence-based practices goes hand in hand with a consistent practice of openness. Access is free: you don't have to pay an entrance fee or consume anything; and the diverse structural approaches help to attract a wide range of people. Thanks to their use of space, urban community gardens are also attractive for those already familiar with urban agriculture and temporary/informal land occupations in the tradition of "hands-on urbanism";[5] a tradition that includes the Gastarbeiter in the 1960s and 1970s, who grew vegetables informally on abandoned land in German cities, or the self-made constructions and "casitas" in the New York City Community Gardens, often built by immigrants with Latin American roots (Mees, 2017). For people from poorer parts of the world, garden projects are not only attractive because they give access to agricultural products. They also allow them to shape, together with others, a space that is open and that receives attention from the world around it. In other contexts this access is often denied to them because they cannot overcome the (invisible) access barriers. Michael J. Sandel, for example, uses the term "skyboxification" to describe how it is becoming more and more rare for people from different social backgrounds to encounter each other in public spaces, something that the American philosopher sees as a fundamental problem for democracy.[6] For this reason, urban gardens should not only be seen as expressions of an urban ecological or activist movement, but as an innovative contribution to reorganizing coexistence in a society that seems increasingly bent on dividing people.

For individual projects to become a movement, they have to come together and form networks. Examples of local and interregional networks of community gardens can be found around the world: e.g. the British Federation of City Farms and Community Gardens (FCFCG), the Austrian network Gartenpolylog, the French network Jardins Partagés or the New York City program Green Thumb. In addition, urban gardens often host farmers' markets in order to make visible their ties to regional agriculture networks. At an international level, the urban gardening movement is also well-connected with other movements such as the counter-globalization movement, the peasant movement, the Landless People's Movement, the right to the city movement, the free seeds and food sovereignty movement and, of course, the degrowth movement.

Many of these projects see themselves as open learning and teaching spaces that host academies, webinars and practical courses on topics as diverse as herbal medicine, clay construction, or the building of small biogas reactors. Several also have hands-on libraries, where old glass shelves or shopping carts are used as containers for printed knowledge covering a range of topics, from agriculture to politics and everything in between.

Another of the movement's remarkable features is its approach to the resources crisis, which includes using informal construction techniques and upcycling locally-sourced, second-hand objects. The solution is not to renounce, but to reinterpret and reuse, to find another context where objects can find new applications. The goal is not simply to save resources, but to discover a new way of dealing with objects in order to achieve a good life with a lower level of material consumption. Thus, already existing materials are seen as a source of multiple possibilities for creative reinvention. In urban community gardens you will find ingenious lamp structures made from mustard buckets, shopping carts used as plant containers, self-built outdoor kitchens, shipping containers transformed into garden restaurants, or old pallets used for growing vegetables such as beans, lettuce and corn. Ultimately, the message is that there are always enough materials, all you have to do is see the potential in objects that are freely available and in surplus in the city. The members of this movement do not see the sense in increasingly complicated products – they believe in finding and using what is already available, and slowly but surely rebuilding the world around them.

3. Urban gardening puts degrowth into practice

Degrowth and urban gardening are not two separate phenomena. They are different expressions of new currents seeking social and civilizational change. All over, experimental spaces are being created where, in contrast with mainstream contexts, new forms of thought and action are sought after. We thus see a continuously growing diversity of small, flexible, ad hoc movements and actions that can be temporary or a part of local networks, or neither of the above. They approach space as a stage and through the creativity of their actions change the spaces they use. In this context, one of the greatest sources of potential is the continuously changing diversity of actors involved. Individual activities such as gardening, building, repairing or demonstrating are embedded in a multi-dimensional structure that is bigger than any individual project. The practices of DIY and DIT in urban gardening are an expression of a radical-practical testing out of new ways of living beyond the dominant industrial growth paradigm, which continues to define – both culturally and economically – our Western societies in crisis. All of these activities, on their own but also in their totality and interconnectedness, are an expression of a civilizational turning point that is approaching. They are all seeking, in the context of speculative realism – leaving constructivism behind and once again placing a greater emphasis on reality – to find new ways forward in the present. They believe that everything must be questioned and, above all, that there is nothing that cannot be changed.[7] The result is the creation of new political concepts and styles. Today, politics are less about theories, speeches, demands and utopian statements, and more about the creation of new spaces and the transformative action that takes place in them: through gardening, cooking, food saving, repairing, rebuilding, reusing, breaking down barriers and taking action. This new style of political action consists in repairing the world, i.e. of achieving practical transformation.[8] The main form of reacting to "that which should be different" is no longer to criticize it, but to diagnose the problem, provide possible solutions, and put them into practice together with as many people as possible. Ultimately, it is about assuming responsibility and taking action.

One criticism often directed at urban gardening is that it cannot be used to feed an entire city. Regardless of whether or not that has actually been proven, it is (at least for the time being) not the point. The significance of the gardening movement lies in its appreciation of small-scale agriculture and self-sufficiency, combined with the implementation of a logic that is not based on exploiting but on providing. Like degrowth, urban gardening is a platform for putting into practice the realization that the issue of food is a fundamental social question that remains unsolved; and that we should no longer leave the provision of basic needs to the industry or the global market. Urban gardens and many other projects belonging to the urban food movement offer practical ideas for a sustainable and ethically motivated practice of production and consumption. Together, all those involved highlight the importance of regional food supply networks, e.g. through mobile cooking events, vegan and vegetarian lifestyles, and an emphasis on regional and seasonal cooking. Their goal is to establish meaningful ties in all directions, in order to personally contribute to creating a plural economy in their region and a solidarity-based and ecological economy at a global level. For this to be achieved, reflection, political debates and above all a differentiation of practices (e.g. towards open-source ecology) are necessary.

One step in this direction was the common drafting and publishing of the Urban Gardening Manifesto, in which the urban gardens movement identified itself as part of the commons movement. The manifesto, which was translated by gardeners from around the world into languages such as English, Spanish or Arabic, emphasizes how important it is for a democratic urban society to have freely accessible public space where there is no pressure to consume. Ultimately, it makes clear that urban gardening is more than just an individual search for a nice place to escape from the city. As the manifesto shows, it is a collective movement that is drawing attention to itself thanks to its new ideas for shaping the future of cities.

4. Open to all classes, cultures and forms of nature

In my opinion, there are two things that could be useful for the discussions, perspectives and practices of degrowth. On the one hand, there should be a deeper reflection on the constitution of modern society, with its (gender-connoted) structure of separation between subsistence and commodities, paid and unpaid work, nature and culture, etc.

On the other hand, it is impossible to overstate the importance of a practice that allows those who are perceived as "others" to find their own place, turning DIY places into open spaces and creating ideal conditions for involving city inhabitants from different social and educational backgrounds in the transformative processes taking place. Especially now, in light of current migratory movements, spaces that are inclusive instead of exclusive are a fundamental resource. Modern urban societies currently face the challenge of facilitating the arrival of uprooted individuals and helping them start a new life. (Intercultural) community gardens have already led to a wealth of experience and ideas in this regard, without resorting to dominant culture fantasies or folkloric simplifications.

5. The vision: a civilizational turning point

In my view, the most important illusion that must be overcome is the dualistic separation of nature and culture. Over the last five hundred years, this separation has been used to justify the colonization of nature and human communities (which for the purposes of their exploitation were declared to be a part of nature). Today we recognize that nature is a complex system of interactions, e.g. as represented in Bruno Latour's Nature/Culture concept, with which the French sociologist tries to express both the cultural determination of nature and the fact that human beings are themselves embedded in nature. Already in the 1990s, Latour developed perspectives that seek to facilitate the sociological study of the fragile, diverse networks that exist in this living cosmos of human and non-human beings.

When the urban practice of community gardening is viewed through this lens, it becomes a visual irritant that contradicts the supposed separation of city and countryside. The result is an ecological sensitivity that finds its expression in its relationship to both things and to plants and animals. I would like to illustrate this briefly using the example of a handbook published in 2014 on the subject of learning in urban gardens.[9] By applying some visual hermeneutics, the self-made, screen-printed cover of the handbook by Berlin-based garden activists can be seen as its own universe, with corn plants overgrowing a mass of skyscrapers, tomatoes sprouting from rooftops, and a giant grasshopper calmly overlooking its urban biotope. Inside the book we are presented with the image of a watering can with bird's legs and a human being with the body of an onion. Just as in Bruno Latour's "Parliament of Things," here plants and animals are not resources, but themselves actors – and they have a right to their own place in the city environment.

Such a broad view of nature and society can be found in the experiments of these new urban interventionists. In their parallel worlds of reused pallets, shrubs, chickens and bees, people can learn from each other in cohabitation with plants, animals and things. In this hustle and bustle of activity a free space is created that seeks to renegotiate the relationship between society and nature. And the gardeners discover that the things that nourish them often come from other sources than themselves.

Translation: Santiago Killing-Stringer

Endnotes

1 Müller, 2011.
2 Ibid.
3 Müller, 2002.
4 Here you can find a map for the German network: anstiftung.de/urbane-gaerten/gaerten-im-ueberblick (Accessed 31 January 2019). Almost all national or urban networks have maps where you can find the gardens, e.g. the New Yorker Garden Map at: greenthumb.nycgovparks.org/gardensearch.php (Accessed 31 January 2019).
5 Krasny, 2014.

6 Sandel, 2012.
7 Baier et al., 2013.
8 Baier et al., 2016.
9 Halder et al., 2014.

Links

Information on urban gardens (including a map of urban community gardens): anstiftung.de/urbane-gaerten

Urban Gardening Manifesto: urbangardeningmanifest.de

Translation of the manifesto into English, French, Spanish, Arabic, Turkish and Polish: urbangardeningmanifest.de/mitmachen

The Neighborhood Academy of the Prinzessinnengarten (Berlin): nachbarschaftsakademie.net

Another world is plantable (texts und films by Ella von der Haide on community gardens around the world): eine-andere-welt-ist-pflanzbar.de

Literature

Baier, A.. Müller, C., and Werner, K. (2013) *Stadt der Commonisten. Neue urbane Räume des Do it yourself*, Bielefeld, transcript.

Baier, A., Hansing, T., Müller, C., and Werner, K. (2016) *Die Welt reparieren. Open Source und Selbermachen als postkapitalistische Praxis*, Bielefeld, transcript.

Halder, S., et al. (eds.) (2014) *Wissen wuchern lassen. Ein Handbuch zum Lernen in urbanen Gärten*, Neu-Ulm, AG Spak.

Krasny, E. (ed.) (2014) *The Right to Green: Hands-On Urbanism 1850-2012*, Wien, Turia+Kant.

Mees, C. (2017) *Participatory Design and Self-building in Shared Urban Open Spaces. Community Gardens and Casitas in New York City*, Basel, Springer.

Müller, C. (ed.) (2011) *Urban Gardening. Über die Rückkehr der Gärten in die Stadt*, München, oekom.

Müller, C. (2002) *Wurzeln schlagen in der Fremde. Die Internationalen*

Gärten und ihre Bedeutung für Integrationsprozesse, München, oekom.

Sandel, M. J. (2012) *What Money Can't Buy: The Moral Limits of Markets*, New York, Farrar, Straus and Giroux.

Degrowth in movement(s) – Endmatter

The project *Degrowth in movement(s)* is available online: degrowth.info/en/dim.

Besides some of the texts of this book, you can find pictures, videos and podcasts as well as more texts in German and Spanish.

The Degrowth web portal on degrowth.info/en provides information around degrowth. For example, news on current projects and information about the international Conferences on Degrowth for Ecological Sustainability and Social Equity. The web portal is further home to the degrowth media library with audio, video and text materials, an international blog, as well as a calendar of events.

CULTURE, SOCIETY & POLITICS

Contemporary culture has eliminated the concept and public figure of the intellectual. A cretinous anti-intellectualism presides, cheer-led by hacks in the pay of multinational corporations who reassure their bored readers that there is no need to rouse themselves from their stupor. Zer0 Books knows that another kind of discourse – intellectual without being academic, popular without being populist – is not only possible: it is already flourishing. Zer0 is convinced that in the unthinking, blandly consensual culture in which we live, critical and engaged theoretical reflection is more important than ever before.
If you have enjoyed this book, why not tell other readers by posting a review on your preferred book site.
Recent bestsellers from Zero Books are:

In the Dust of This Planet
Horror of Philosophy vol. 1
Eugene Thacker
In the first of a series of three books on the Horror of Philosophy, *In the Dust of This Planet* offers the genre of horror as a way of thinking about the unthinkable.
Paperback: 978-1-84694-676-9 ebook: 978-1-78099-010-1

Capitalist Realism
Is there no alternative?
Mark Fisher
An analysis of the ways in which capitalism has presented itself as the only realistic political-economic system.
Paperback: 978-1-84694-317-1 ebook: 978-1-78099-734-6

Rebel Rebel

Chris O'Leary

David Bowie: every single song. Everything you want to know, everything you didn't know.

Paperback: 978-1-78099-244-0 ebook: 978-1-78099-713-1

Cartographies of the Absolute

Alberto Toscano, Jeff Kinkle

An aesthetics of the economy for the twenty-first century.

Paperback: 978-1-78099-275-4 ebook: 978-1-78279-973-3

Poor but Sexy

Culture Clashes in Europe East and West

Agata Pyzik

How the East stayed East and the West stayed West.

Paperback: 978-1-78099-394-2 ebook: 978-1-78099-395-9

Malign Velocities

Accelerationism and Capitalism

Benjamin Noys

Long listed for the Bread and Roses Prize 2015, *Malign Velocities* argues against the need for speed, tracking acceleration as the symptom of the ongoing crises of capitalism.

Paperback: 978-1-78279-300-7 ebook: 978-1-78279-299-4

Meat Market

Female Flesh under Capitalism

Laurie Penny

A feminist dissection of women's bodies as the fleshy fulcrum of capitalist cannibalism, whereby women are both consumers and consumed.

Paperback: 978-1-84694-521-2 ebook: 978-1-84694-782-7

Romeo and Juliet in Palestine
Teaching Under Occupation
Tom Sperlinger
Life in the West Bank, the nature of pedagogy and the role of a university under occupation.
Paperback: 978-1-78279-637-4 ebook: 978-1-78279-636-7

Sweetening the Pill
or How We Got Hooked on Hormonal Birth Control
Holly Grigg-Spall
Has contraception liberated or oppressed women? *Sweetening the Pill* breaks the silence on the dark side of hormonal contraception.
Paperback: 978-1-78099-607-3 ebook: 978-1-78099-608-0

Why Are We The Good Guys?
Reclaiming your Mind from the Delusions of Propaganda
David Cromwell
A provocative challenge to the standard ideology that Western power is a benevolent force in the world.
Paperback: 978-1-78099-365-2 ebook: 978-1-78099-366-9

Readers of ebooks can buy or view any of these bestsellers by clicking on the live link in the title. Most titles are published in paperback and as an ebook. Paperbacks are available in traditional bookshops. Both print and ebook formats are available online.
Find more titles and sign up to our readers' newsletter at http://www.johnhuntpublishing.com/culture-and-politics
Follow us on Facebook at https://www.facebook.com/ZeroBooks
and Twitter at https://twitter.com/Zer0Books